Longman Group Limited,
Longman House, Burnt Mill,
Harlow, Essex CM20 2JE, England
and Associated Companies throughout the world.

*Published in the United States of America
by Longman Publishing, New York*

First published 1995

ISBN 0 582 051134 CSD
ISBN 0 582 051126 PPR

British Library Cataloguing-in-Publication Data

A catalogue record for this book is
available from the British Library

Library of Congress Cataloging-in-Publication Data
Clough, Arthur Hugh, 1819–1861
   [Poems.   Selections]
   Clough—selected poems / edited by Joseph Phelan.
    p. cm. — (Longman annotated texts)
   Includes bibliographical references and index.
   ISBN 0-582-05113-4 (cased). — ISBN 0-582-05112-6 (paper)
   I. Phelan, Joseph, 1963- . II. Title. III. Series.
  PR4456.P48 1995
  821'.8—dc20
                       94-20379
                       CIP

Set by 8FF in 10/11pt Ehrhardt Roman
Produced by Longman Singapore Publishers (Pte) Ltd.
Printed in Singapore

Clough
Selected Poems

Longman Annotated Texts

General Editors:

Charlotte Brewer, Hertford College, Oxford
H.R. Woudhuysen, University College London
Daniel Karlin, University College London

Published Titles:

Michael Mason, *Lyrical Ballads*
Alexandra Barratt, *Women's Writing in Middle English*
Tim Armstrong, *Thomas Hardy: Selected Poems*
René Weis, *King Lear: A Parallel Text Edition*
James Sambrook, *William Cowper: Selected Poems*

Clough
Selected Poems

Edited by
J.P. Phelan

Longman
London and New York

Contents

Acknowledgements

I am grateful to the Bodleian Library for permission to publish material from the following manuscripts in its possession: MS Eng. poet. d. 122 folios 20–24 (*Seven Sonnets*); MS Eng. poet. d. 124–5 and d. 133 (The 'Venice' Notebook) folios 4–12 (*Adam and Eve*); MS Eng. poet. d. 127 (The 'Lamech' Notebook) folios 1–7 (*The Song of Lamech*), folios 28–35 (*Sa Majesté Très Chrétienne*), and folios 37–44 (*Jacob's Wives*); MS Eng. poet. d. 128 (The 'Smith' Notebook) folio 9 (*Alteram Partem*), folios 14–15 (*Hymnos ahymnos*), folios 16–18 (*Jacob*), and folio 20 (*In Stratis Viarum I*); MS Eng. poet. d. 129 folio 15 ('In controversial foul impureness'); folio 28 (*Epi-Strauss-ium*); folios 56–8 (*Resignation – to Faustus*); folios 104–113 (*Easter Day* and *Easter Day II*); MS Eng. poet. d. 130 (the 'A' manuscript of *Amours de Voyage*), folios 4, 11, 12, 18, 24, 25, 33–6, 42, 45, 47, 61, 63 and 64; MS Eng. poet. d. 131 (the 'A' manuscript of *Amours de Voyage*), folios 11, 16, 17, 23, 25–6; MS Eng. poet. d. 133 folios 34 and 69–70; MS Eng. poet. d. 134–6 (the First and Second Revisions of *Dipsychus and The Spirit*); MS Eng. poet. d. 138 folios 1–2 (*In Stratis Viarum II*); MS Eng. Lett. e. 77 folio 123; and MS Eng. Lett. d. 176 folios 88, 96, 110, 111. I am also grateful to Balliol College Oxford for permission to quote from the 'Roma' Notebook (Balliol MS 441 (a)), which includes *Adam and Eve* scenes 2, 3, 4, 5, 9, 13.77–95 and *Uranus*; and the Houghton Library at Harvard for permission to quote from Harvard bMS Eng 1036 (2) (*Bethesda – A Sequel*, *The Latest Decalogue*, 'It fortifies my soul to know', *In Stratis Viarum: III* and *IV* and the changes to *Amours de Voyage* suggested by Clough in a letter of March-April 1859 to C.E. Norton) and Harvard bMS Am 1088 No. 1366.

Danny Karlin's assistance in the preparation of this volume has been invaluable. I would also like to thank the Governing Body of Christ Church Oxford for the research funding which enabled me to complete this project, and John Woolford and the Department of English Language and Literature at King's College London for advice and support. My indebtedness to previous editors of Clough, especially Patrick Scott and F.L. Mulhauser, should be apparent throughout.

We are indebted to the following for permission to reproduce copyright material:

Bodleian Library, Oxford; Miss Katherine Duff and the Master & Fellows of Balliol College, Oxford; Houghton Library, Harvard University.

List of Abbreviations

The following abbreviations are used throughout the text and notes to poems:

AM   *Atlantic Monthly.*
Corr.   Mulhauser, F. (ed.), *The Correspondence of Arthur Hugh Clough*, 2 vols, OUP, 1957.
PR   Mrs Clough (ed.), *Prose Remains of Arthur Hugh Clough*, Macmillan, 1888.

The following dates (italicised) are given in the notes to Shorter Poems:

1862: *Poems by Arthur Hugh Clough* (Macmillan, 1862). A nearly identical American edition was published in the same year: C.E. Norton ed., *The Poems of Arthur Hugh Clough* (Boston: Ticknor and Fields, 1862). This date therefore signifies that the poem in question first appeared in these two editions.
1863: *Poems by Arthur Hugh Clough* (Macmillan, 1863).
1865: *Letters and Remains of Arthur Hugh Clough* (Spottiswoode and Co., 1865).
1869: Mrs Clough ed., *The Poems and Prose Remains of Arthur Hugh Clough*, 2 vols, (Macmillan, 1869).
1951: H.F. Lowry, A.L.P. Norrington and F.L. Mulhauser eds., *The Poems of Arthur Hugh Clough* (OUP, 1951).

Chronology

1819	1 Jan.: C. born in Liverpool, the second son of James Butler Clough, a cotton merchant, and Anne Perfect.
1822–3	Moves with family to Charleston, S. Carolina.
1828	Oct.: Returns to England to attend school, first at Chester, then (1829) at Rugby.
1836	Nov.: Wins Balliol Scholarship.
1837	Oct.: Goes up to Balliol College Oxford.
1841	June: Fails to obtain the expected first-class degree in Schools.
1842	March: Elected Fellow of Oriel.
	June: Death of Dr Arnold, Head Master of Rugby.
1844	Oct.: Death of C.'s father.
1847	Nov.: Beginning of acquaintance with Ralph Waldo Emerson.
	Dec: Begins negotiations with Edward Hawkins, Provost of Oriel, about resigning his post.
1848	Feb.: Outbreak of revolution in France.
	May-June: Visits Paris with Emerson to see the progress of the revolution at first hand.
	July: Sends *Adam and Eve* to Matthew Arnold for comment.
	Oct.: Resigns his Fellowship.
	Nov.: Publication of *The Bothie of Toper-na-Fuosich*, C.'s 'Long-vacation Pastoral'.
1849	Jan.: Publication of *Ambarvalia*, including poems by C. and Thomas Burbidge.
	April-Aug.: Visits Italy; is present during the entire period of the siege and occupation of the Roman Republic by French forces under General Oudinot.
	Oct.: Takes up post as Principal of University Hall, a quasi-collegiate institution attached to the University of London.
	Nov.: Sends first draft of *Amours de Voyage* to J.C. Shairp for comment.

Introduction

Clough thought about calling the opening poem in this selection *The
Questioning Spirit*; and the title is, I think, an appropriate one for his
poetry as a whole. His natural port, to paraphrase Dr Johnson on
Shakespeare, is neither tragic nor comic, but interrogative. The reader
of his poetry encounters a flurry of questions, arguments, expostula-
tions and replies. Clough conducts arguments within poems –
Dipsychus and The Spirit is simply an extended argument between the
two characters named in the title – between poems, and with other
poets. He seems incapable of setting down a definite statement of any
position without immediately feeling the need to dissent from or quali-
fy it. This fact helps to explain the large number of 'paired' poems in
his work: 'The human spirits' finds its answer in *Bethesda: A Sequel*, as
Peschiera does in *Alteram Partem*. Clough's poetry, it might be said, is
always looking for the 'alteram partem', the other side of the question.

This argumentativeness means that reading Clough for his opinions
is a singularly unproductive exercise; to adopt one of his favourite
metaphors, we continually find that he fights on both sides in the great
night-battle of contemporary opinion.[1] One example will serve to make
the general point. In his book *God and Two Poets*, which deals with
Clough and Hopkins, Anthony Kenny cites *Epi-Strauss-ium* as evidence that 'Clough welcomed contemporary higher criticism, and
professed that it was no threat to the essence of Christianity' (Kenny
1988: 77). By 'contemporary higher criticism' Kenny means the movement which promoted the reading of the Bible according to the canons
of interpretation applied to other historical documents. This move-

---

1. This figure occurs in *The Bothie of Toper-na-Fuosich*, the 'Long-vacation
Pastoral' which Clough wrote and published towards the end of 1848
(IX.73–100). *The Bothie*, which is not included in the present selection, has
been seen as Clough's most 'committed' poem, a paean to the radicalism of
1848; but the hero's use of the 'night-battle' metaphor points to the fact that
even this poem is not free from Clough's characteristic uncertainties.

ment was seen as deeply impious by many people in the nineteenth century, especially after the appearance of David Friedrich Strauss's *Life of Jesus* in 1835, a book which purported to show that the gospel narratives, the very foundation-stones of the Christian religion, were almost entirely devoid of historical content. In his poem, which alludes to Strauss in the title, Clough compares the four evangelists to the stained-glass windows traditionally placed in the eastern wing of cathedrals. In the morning of faith these brightly coloured representations were necessary to support belief; but now, the poem suggests, in the evening of the world, the sun of truth can stream unimpeded through the plainly glassed western windows: 'The Place of Worship the meantime with light/ Is, if less richly, more sincerely bright,/ And in blue skies the Orb is manifest to sight' (13–15). Far from destroying Christianity, the poet implies, Strauss's discoveries have helped to free the religion from its once necessary but now outdated dependence on primitive modes of thought. Kenny would, then, appear to be right. But *Epi-Strauss-ium* is simply the first of a number of poems dealing with the Higher Criticism. It is 'answered', in typically Cloughian style, by *Easter Day. Naples, 1849*, a poem which sees Strauss's findings as a disaster for Christianity. In an analysis clearly indebted to the Straussian 'mythological' method of biblical criticism, Clough meticulously dismembers the gospel accounts of the resurrection, concluding each section with the refrain 'Christ is not risen!' He sees himself and his contemporaries as 'men deceived' by a fable: 'Of all the creatures under heaven's wide cope/ We are most hopeless who had once most hope,/ We are most wretched that had most believed' (73–5). It seems difficult, to say the least, to read this poem as making the point that the Higher Criticism is 'no threat' to Christianity. This is not, however, the end of the story. Clough tacked another poem on to the end of *Easter Day* – later entitled *Easter Day II* – which simply contradicts without refuting the propositions in its partner-poem; then, later still, included *Easter Day* in *Dipsychus and The Spirit* as the starting-point for Dipsychus's inquiry into the sustainability of Christian virtues without Christian dogma. Both these poems can, I think, be seen as partially successful attempts to neutralise *Easter Day*'s stark and uncompromising statement of unbelief. Taking the sequence as a whole, then, we have a full range of responses to the Higher Criticism, from the blithe welcome of *Epi-Strauss-ium*, through the despair of *Easter Day*, to the fascinated and appalled anxiety of *Dipsychus and The Spirit*. This illustrates, I think, the difficulty, and possibly the futility, of trying to pin Clough down to a single opinion on this question.

It seems worth making this point because so much of the (comparatively meagre) critical attention Clough has received has concentrated on trying to establish the opinions behind his poetry. I shall, in this introduction, have comparatively little to say about Clough's opinions on specific subjects. The interesting thing about Clough's poetry is not the conclusions he arrives at, but the extreme scrupulousness he exhibits in trying to arrive at them. He has, as the hero of *Dipsychus and The Spirit* puts it, a fear of 'adding up too soon' (2.4.42), of short-circuiting the search for truth by settling for some easy or attractive solution. In the words of R.H. Hutton, one of Clough's earliest and best critics: '[He] realised, as few ever realised before, the enormous difficulty of finding truth . . . [the] stronger the desire, he teaches, the greater is the danger of illegitimately satisfying that desire by persuading ourselves that what we *wish* to believe, is true' (Bagehot 1895: i, xxxvi). What Claude, the hero of *Amours de Voyage*, calls 'the ruinous force of the will' has the capacity to interfere with and distort our perception of the truth. The only way to avoid this pitfall is to exercise a constant and unstinting vigilance over one's beliefs, a kind of Cartesian scepticism which eliminates all beliefs not absolutely verified by personal experience.[2] Clough's attempts to exercise this vigilance over his own beliefs result in the kind of poetic sequence seen in the last paragraph. But his most interesting poetry comes about when he takes this sceptical attitude to its logical conclusion and calls the questioning spirit itself into question. The heroes of both *Amours de Voyage* and *Dipsychus and The Spirit* attempt to exercise a Cloughian vigilance over their beliefs and actions, and in so doing highlight both the attractions and the limitations of this approach to life. Its principal attractions are its innocence and integrity; it keeps the individual in a kind of prelapsarian state – what Clough calls 'the garden of the infinite choices' – which reduces the possibility of the 'fall' into false beliefs and actions. Its limitations, on the other hand, are its solipsism and asceticism; it is, the poet suggests, the product of an immature and self-reinforcing fear of life which systematically over-represents the wickedness of the world. Both poems, that is to say, manifest a powerful ambivalence about the validity of the sceptical attitude. *Dipsychus and The Spirit* is, however, noticeably more decided in its antipathy to the questioning spirit than *Amours de Voyage*; and it is, I shall argue, no coincidence that this poem, which brings Clough's argument with himself to an end, also brings to an end the poetically significant portion of his life.

2. This point is also made by Wendell V. Harris: ' "Scepticism is the chastity of the mind" says Santayana, and Clough seems to have been one who would take this statement in an almost literal sense. Premature decisions and unconscious compromises are dangerous . . . because . . . they clutter, sully, and finally destroy the temple of the mind in which Clough hopes some day a revelation will occur' (Harris 1970: 55).

'An hieroglyphical abruptness of expression': Clough's shorter poems

It might, I think, be said with only a small amount of aphoristic licence that all Clough's poetry aspires to the condition of narrative. His shorter poems always seem somewhat cramped, as if he is trying to compress too much matter into too small a space. One of the reviewers of *Ambarvalia*, the collection of lyrics which Clough published in conjunction with his friend Thomas Burbidge in January 1849, commented on the poet's 'hieroglyphical abruptness of expression', and the expression seems justified when trying to follow the twists and turns of the argument in a poem like 'The human spirits' or *Qui laborat, orat*. This 'careless roughness of form', to quote another early reviewer, is not, of course, simply the result of incompetence or bad judgement; it is the product of a deliberate rhetoric of sincerity, an attempt, in accordance with contemporary poetic theory, to make the poems look like spontaneous utterances, 'the wild sad outpourings of an Aeolian harp, or the broken murmurings of a brook over rough places' (Thorpe 1972: 80). Nevertheless, the *Ambarvalia* lyrics often look like dismembered parts of a larger work or argument, *disjecta membra poetae* in the words of the reviewer in *Fraser's* (Thorpe 1972: 89); themes and ideas adumbrated in one poem recur in another, but in a way which leaves no opportunity for cumulative exploration or development of them. Instead of being able to build on what has gone before the poet has to start again with each new lyric. 'The human spirits' and 'Duty – that's to say complying' both deal with the question of duty, and arrive at seemingly opposite conclusions, but no relation between the two positions is implied, as it could be (and indeed is) in *Amours* and *Dipsychus*.

Clough's best and most enduring work, then, takes the form of narrative; and the analysis of his narrative poetry will, accordingly, be the main task of this introduction. It is, nevertheless, worth pausing to consider Clough's shorter poems, not least for the insight they provide into the longer and more substantial works. Clough's shorter poems divide naturally into two categories; there are the *Ambarvalia* lyrics – the present selection includes ten of the thirty-one poems in Clough's section of the volume – and the other, miscellaneous poems. The former date from the ten or so years before 1849, while the latter were mostly, though not exclusively, written after that date. One of the most interesting of the *Ambarvalia* lyrics is 'Why should I say I see the things I see not?', a poem whose title announces a typically Cloughian militancy with regard to truth. This poem succeeds in making a virtue of the restrictions of the lyric form. It is based upon a comparison between social convention and the elegant formalities of the dance, a comparison which becomes one of the recurring metaphors or *idées fixes* of Clough's poetry. The poet's struggles with the demands of convention are set out in verse which mimics the awkwardness of the reluctant dancer both in its rapid and unexpected fluctuations in line length and in its oscillation between elevated and demotic diction. Another interesting experiment is *Natura naturans*, in which the poet celebrates the natural energy of sexuality as he experiences it during a chance encounter in a railway carriage. The poem attempts to convey the poet's rapture at his sudden and overwhelming feeling of oneness with the universe through the use of extravagant alliteration. This indulgence of rapture is, however, balanced by a reminder that the depersonalising and quasi-automatic mechanisms of sexual desire fall far short of 'the mystic name of Love'; a distinction which, as we shall see, assumes crucial importance in the narrative poetry. The collection's religious poems, *Qui laborat, orat* and *When Israel came out of Egypt*, highlight one of the most treacherous pitfalls on the road to truth, namely the human mind's tendency towards idolatry. Walter Bagehot, another early supporter and acute critic of Clough, described him as one of those who 'will not *make their image*' (Bagehot 1895: ii, 262); will not, that is to say, accept the expedient of a necessarily imperfect approximation to the truth. These poems exemplify Clough's reluctance to 'make his image'. In *Qui laborat, orat* the poet defends his reluctance to pray on the grounds that prayer necessarily implies some conception of the being to whom it is addressed; the believer constructs an image of the deity, however minimal, while praying, and this runs counter to the poet's feeling that it is 'profanely bold' to make any such image, even '[in] thought's abstractest forms'. This severe asceticism is, however, tempered by the hope that '[the] beatific supersensual sight' might occasionally descend 'unsummoned' as a reward for the poet's diligent and uncomplaining toil. In *When Israel came out of Egypt* Clough compares his spiritually perplexed generation to the Israelites wandering in the desert after their release from Egyptian servitude. (The local polemical context of this poem is discussed in the Headnote; see below, p. 36.) Clough exhorts his contemporaries not to repeat the errors of the Israelites, who reverted to idolatry in the temporary absence of Moses on Mount Sinai, but to 'wait it out' for an authoritative and genuine revelation of the divine. The suspicion of the human mind's tendency to hypostatise and venerate its own creations expressed in these poems is, as we shall see, applicable beyond the religious sphere; Claude in *Amours* sees a kind of practical idolatry at work in the field of human relations, and determines to avoid it.

Mrs Clough, the poet's principal editor throughout the nineteenth century, divided her husband's shorter poems into a number of different categories. According to this arrangement, the current selection from Clough's other (non-*Ambarvalia*) poems includes nine 'Poems on

Religious and Biblical Subjects' (plus *Adam and Eve*), four 'Poems on
Life and Duty', and six 'Miscellaneous Poems'. This analysis gives, I
think, a fair indication of the bias of my selection. In choosing thirty
poems from Clough's hundred and thirty or so shorter pieces some bias
is inevitable, indeed necessary, and mine has been towards those poems
which illuminate or complement the ethical and religious dilemmas
examined in the narrative poems. This has, it should be said, entailed a
certain loss of representativeness. Clough did not just write intense
poetry of moral and intellectual struggle; he also wrote things like *July's
Farewell*, which begins: 'Yet once again, ye banks and bowery nooks,/
And once again, ye dells and flowing brooks' - and so on. The sacrifice
of representativeness to quality is, however, wholly justifiable. Clough
is at his best when grappling with serious and complex issues; it is,
indeed, only at such moments that he is worthy of the kind of sustained
attention which this edition presupposes. It would, therefore, be point-
less, even counter-productive, to exclude *The Song of Lamech* (for
example) solely in order to dilute the collection and distract the
reader's attention with pieces which do not invite or repay scrutiny.
The editor's task is to clear away obstacles to the recognition of
Clough's distinctive achievement, not multiply them. It is worth men-
tioning, in passing, that the Clough who emerges from this process is,
on the whole, the Clough with whom nineteenth-century readers
would have been familiar; of the shorter poems reprinted here only
one, *Sa Majesté Très Chrétienne*, did not appear in any of the nineteenth-century editions in one form or another. Mrs Clough and her
co-editors have come in for a good deal of modern criticism for bowd-
lerising *Dipsychus and The Spirit*, and such criticism is, no doubt,
justified.[3] A lot of her editing, however, had no such designs on the
reader; she omitted things which struck her as trivial, or unfinished, or
both, and tried to present the best of her late husband's work to the
public. Modern editors have, quite rightly, retrieved and printed the
fragments, juvenilia and notebook jottings which Mrs Clough omitted,
but for the most part they have, I think, merely emphasised the cor-
rectness of her initial judgements in the choice of material for
publication.

It would be impossible to attempt anything like a thorough survey of
the shorter poems here; I can do little more than point out some of
their more notable features. The three poems based on passages from
the Book of Genesis – *The Song of Lamech*, *Jacob's Wives* and *Jacob* –
draw on contemporary historiographical techniques. In his *Prolegomena
to Homer* (1795) F.A. Wolf put forward the idea that the Homeric epics
were late redactions of a collection of popular ballads commemorating
the Trojan war. This idea was taken up and applied to early Roman

3. See, for example, the Introduction to McCue (1991).

history by the German historian Niebuhr, leading Macaulay, in his 1842 *Lays of Ancient Rome*, to attempt the reconstruction of the lost 'lays' or ballads underlying the fabulous early history of Rome.[4] In *The Song of Lamech* Clough tries to suggest what one of the 'lays' behind the early chapters of Genesis might have looked like. John Keble, the Tractarian poet and scholar, was of the opinion that the Song of Lamech was 'the most ancient of all songs that remain to us' (Keble 1912: i, 59), and it is clear from Clough's treatment of it that he regards it as the source of the myth of Cain and Abel. *Jacob's Wives* is (in the critical jargon of the time) less 'objective' than *The Song of Lamech*; although the trappings of oral narrative are retained, the principal focus is not so much on historical reconstruction as on the elaboration of the symbolic contrast between Rachel, emblem of romantic love and illusion, and Leah, who stands for the prosaic reality of marriage. *Jacob*, finally, makes no pretence at being a 'lay'; like *Sa Majesté Très Chrétienne* it is clearly indebted to the dramatic monologue form developed by Browning and Tennyson over the previous decade, and depicts a character racked by feelings of belatedness and disappointment with his lot in life. All three poems are characterised by a restrained, even austere diction which attempts to convey both the pastoral simplicity and the grandeur of the Patriarchal era.

Other noteworthy poems include *The Latest Decalogue*, a witty and satirical rewriting of the Ten Commandments, and *Hymnos ahymnos*, another expression of the poet's habitual fear of idolatry. The former is printed here in two versions: the familiar much-anthologised version; and the later revision sent by Clough to his American editor C.E. Norton. This revision is not an improvement on the earlier version in all respects, but it does include the magnificent lines 'Adultery it is not fit,/ Or safe, for women, to commit' – a memorable summary of Victorian sexual hypocrisy. *Hymnos ahymnos* – 'A hymn, yet not a hymn' – is, like *Qui laborat, orat*, an apology for the poet's inability to pray; yet it goes even further than the earlier poem in its iconoclastic asceticism. The poem opens with an address to the deity – 'O thou, whose image in the shrine/ Of human spirits dwells divine' – but never gets round to the substance of its imprecation; subordinate clauses open out within one another, and are only arrested by a more urgent reformulation, at the start of the second stanza, of the original exclamation. This syntactic incompleteness mirrors the poet's inability to construct an adequate image of the divinity. Every attempt to represent the divine image in the medium of language gives too much scope to the 'wilful fancy' to substitute for it a shape of its own devising. The

4. The 'lays' began to appear during the 1830s; Clough read them, and reviewed one of them, 'The Battle of Ivry' (not, incidentally, a poem on a Roman subject), for *The Rugby Magazine* while still a schoolboy; see Trawick (1964).

poem's 'imperfect utterance' must, therefore, be cancelled as soon as it begins to be written: 'I will not frame one thought of what/ Thou may-est either be or not' (19–20). This poem, more than any other, highlights the rigour – one might even say the fanaticism – of Clough's determination to search for the truth.

'The garden of the infinite choices': the structure of Clough's narrative poetry

The ability to enjoy narrative poetry is not, on the whole, one which comes easily to the modern reader. Most of us would agree with Walter Bagehot that poetry should be 'memorable and emphatic, intense, and *soon over*' (Bagehot 1895: ii, 341). Those acres of verse stretching for page after page weary us in advance with the thought of sustaining the high level of concentration and attention appropriate to poetry for an inordinate and almost painful length of time. It might, therefore, be appropriate at this stage to say something about the general demands which Clough's narrative poetry makes on the reader before moving on to more specific matters. Clough's narrative poetry solicits different levels of attention at different moments. To take an example from *Amours de Voyage*: Georgina Trevellyn's

> At last, dearest Louisa, I take up my pen to address you.
> Here we are, you see, with the seven-and-seventy boxes,
> Courier, Papa and Mamma, the children, and Mary and Susan:
> Here we all are at Rome, and delighted of course with St. Peter's. (I.51–4)

is of a very different order from Claude's

> [Juxtaposition] is great, – but, you tell me, affinity greater.
> Ah, my friend, there are many affinities, greater and lesser,
> Stronger and weaker; and each, by the favour of juxtaposition
> Potent, efficient, in force, – for a time.' (III.151–4)

Georgina's statement has nothing of the declamatory tone and esoteric vocabulary of Claude's; it is, moreover, embedded in the circumstances of its production, while Claude's utterance aspires to a more general significance. The principal skill required for the reading of Clough's narrative poetry is not, then, perseverance but agility, the ability to switch rapidly between very different levels and registers. At times the language approaches the baldness and directness of prose statement, and demands the kind of attention we would give to a novel; at others it approaches the intensity of the lyric, and demands that we weigh the significance of each word.

The two narrative poems included in this selection, *Amours de Voyage* and *Dipsychus and The Spirit*, are very different on the surface;

one is a comedy of manners, the other a Faustian dialogue. There is, however, a consistent symbolic structure at work in both poems. This symbolic structure is best approached by way of the 'Lecture on the Development of English Literature from Chaucer to Wordsworth' which Clough gave during his time as Professor of English at University College, London. In this lecture Clough attempts to see English literature as a record of the development of the English character, and to this end sets up an analogy between the life-history of the individual (ontogeny) and that of the people or race (phylogeny). Chaucer, accordingly, stands for the 'boyhood' of the English people and Shakespeare for its 'early manhood', the time of 'thought, contemplation, doubt':

> Free and serene in youth, newly emancipated from teachers and directors, unfettered any longer by precept or injunction of others, unbound as yet by any self-imposed restriction, or even any formed determination – in the richness of a reflectiveness which even now is all but a malady, in the fulness of an almost premature maturity of thought – in a distant preconception or presentiment wandering undecided in the garden of the infinite choices; free as yet to select, loving much rather as yet to forbear; with a tranquil wistfulness, with a far-sighted consciousness, looking down those unnumbered, diverging, far-reaching avenues of future actuality, each one of which, but, if any *one*, then not any other, he may follow – such I venture to picture to myself the second poet of the English series – the second and the greatest – the creator of Othello and of Falstaff, of Hotspur and of Hamlet.   (*PR* 337–8)

This portrait of Shakespeare is clearly indebted to Teufelsdrockh's account of early manhood in Carlyle's *Sartor Resartus*: 'our young soul is all budding with Capabilities, and we see not yet which is the true one' (Bk II, ch. iv). This state cannot last, however; by the time we arrive at Milton, we find that one irrevocable path of 'future actuality' has been chosen:

> Not uncompromised, not uncommitted any longer, self-committed, strongly, deliberately, seriously, irreversibly committed; walking as in the sight of God, as in the profound, almost rigid conviction that this one, and no other of all those many paths is, or can be, for the just and upright spirit possible, self-predestined as it were, of his own will and foreknowledge, to a single moral and religious aim – such, I think, are we to imagine the writer of 'Paradise Lost' and of 'Samson Agonistes', the third of the English poets. To what purpose these myriad phenomena, entering and traversing the field of that mighty object-glass of the speculative intellect? Is it life to observe? Is it a man's service to know? As if it was a thing possible for us to forbear to act; as though there were not in God's world, amidst ten thousand wrongs, one right, amidst the false choices that offend Him, the one that is His will. (*PR* 338)

Within the terms of Clough's analogy we might expect Milton to represent maturity; but this is not the case. '[The] proper manhood of the

English nation', according to Clough, is achieved in 'the generation which rejected Milton', the generation of the Restoration and the Glorious Revolution. Milton's Puritanism placed upon the neck of the nation 'the yoke of an iron system of morals, proved by experience not coextensive with facts, not true to the necessary exigencies and experiences of life' (*PR* 341); only when this yoke had been removed could the English mind devote itself to the thorough and clearsighted appraisal of the world around it which denotes full maturity.

Milton's somewhat anomalous position in Clough's otherwise tidy developmental schema results from the confluence of two contradictory narratives. For if, on the one hand, Clough sees in English literature the story of the English people's achievement of maturity, on the other he sees in it the record of a disastrous and irreversible Fall. Shakespeare, it will be remembered, is pictured 'wandering undecided in the garden of the infinite choices' and this prelapsarian state is one which English poetry afterwards strives to recover in vain. The first instinct of the post-Miltonic poets, the poets of England's maturity, is to return to this 'garden of the infinite choices', but they find the way barred:

> Fain to return to that larger range from which for a while we had remained self-excluded, but incapable any longer of sustaining ourselves upon the unsupported elevation of speculative vision; eager again to see what in Shakespeare we had viewed, to feel ourselves again within the circle of those infinitely various relations, but too far engaged in actual things to be competent now of seeing merely, of feeling only; eager, were it possible – which it no longer is – to find satisfaction to adult impulses in the gratification of those old boyish instincts, dispositions, tempers, tendencies, left behind so far away as Chaucer; resolute, however, in any case, come what would or might, to face and confront, to acknowledge and accept the facts of that living palpable world which cannot for any long time be disowned or evaded, with the vision of the universe departed, with innocence and the untroubled conscience forfeited, behold us here at the close of the seventeenth century, embarking, in whose name we know not, and profess to ourselves that we care not, upon the seas of actual and positive existence.   (*PR* 341)

The maturity of the Augustan age is, then, a reluctant maturity, as much an exile as a fulfilment; the narrative of growth is crossed and thwarted by the contradictory narrative of the Fall. Milton, superfluous as far as the first narrative is concerned, is crucial to the second. His early works manifest 'a little of that poetic hesitance, that meditative reluctance to take a part' which characterise Shakespeare; but, urged on by the exigencies of the time, he leaves such things behind and becomes the poet of fixed and unshakeable purpose. Milton, that is to say, enacts in his person the Fall which forms the subject of his great epic poem, introducing into the national character notions of moral earnestness which preclude the possibility of a return to the 'tranquil wistfulness' of prelapsarian innocence.

The symbolic vocabulary elaborated in this lecture can be seen at work in *Adam and Eve*, the fragmentary biblical drama which Clough wrote just before embarking on *Amours* and *Dipsychus*. The poem is, indeed, a direct and literal embodiment of this symbolic vocabulary, dealing as it does with the story of the Fall itself. It begins on the morning after the event. Adam's account of the experiences of the previous day – 'One, two, and three, and four; – the Appetite,/ The enjoyment, the aftervoid, the thinking of it' (1.3–4) – could refer to the story of the apple; but the calculated ambiguity of the language seems designed to play on the traditional identification of sex as the true cause of the Fall. Eve laments the guilt of the expelled couple, but Adam tries to see their sudden and drastic change of state in a more positive light:

That which we were, we could no more remain
Than in the moist provocative vernal mould
A seed its suckers close, and rest a seed.
We were to grow. Necessity on us lay
This way or that to move; necessity too
Not to be over-careful this or that
So only move we should. (1.13–19)

As in the 'Lecture on the Development of English Literature', the contradictory paradigms of growth and the Fall are superimposed upon one another. Adam is not sure whether to view his expulsion from the garden as a catastrophe, or as the first stage in a natural and inevitable process which will eventually yield some compensation for the loss suffered.

The journey from 'the garden of the infinite choices' to 'the seas of actual and positive existence' also underpins the narratives of both *Amours de Voyage* and *Dipsychus and The Spirit*. The heroes of these two poems are forced to attempt this journey and are, like Adam, unsure whether they should regard it as a disastrous and irreversible Fall or as the first stage in the process of growth towards maturity. Claude, the hero of *Amours*, bears a striking resemblance to Clough's portrait of Shakespeare; he is an explicitly Hamlet-esque figure, the very embodiment of 'the questioning spirit' whose 'meditative reluctance to take a part', initially a source of delight, becomes increasingly burdensome to him. He longs for some escape from the garden of the infinite choices which will avoid the trauma of the Fall, and (unsuccessfully) seeks it in the prospect of falling in love with Mary Trevellyn. Dipsychus, on the other hand, is (in Clough's terms) a much more Wordsworthian than Shakespearian figure. His decision to remain in the garden of the infinite choices is motivated by a residual Puritanism which makes him envisage contact with the world as pollution of the soul. Like Adam, both Claude and Dipsychus associate sex with the Fall, and indeed see it as the paradigmatic instance of the descent into

experience. The analysis which follows will, I hope, illustrate the rigour
and consistency with which this symbolic schema is followed out
beneath the clutter of surface detail and argument in the two poems.

Amours de Voyage

It is difficult to know where to start in discussing a poem as bewilder-
ingly heterogeneous as *Amours de Voyage*. It is an anti-romance which
looks ironically at the romantic *topoi* of love, chivalry and war; a travel-
ogue; a comedy of manners; a satirical portrait of the modern
intellectual; a series of oblique meditations on the nature of love and
belief; and a quasi-journalistic account of a real historical event, the
French siege and capture of Mazzini's Roman Republic in 1849. And
this list is by no means complete. Perhaps the best place to begin is
with the plot. One of the most striking things about *Amours* in comparison with other 'verse-novels' of the period – Elizabeth Barrett
Browning's *Aurora Leigh*, for example – is the comparative untidiness
of its plot. Claude, the poem's hero, arrives in Rome, muses on the
monuments in letters to his friend Eustace, meets an English family by
the name of Trevellyn, forms a tentative attachment to Mary
Trevellyn, fails to accompany her and her family to Florence thanks to
some inopportune remarks concerning his 'intentions' towards her,
thinks better of it when he discovers that Mary knew nothing about the
remarks, arrives in Florence only to find the Trevellyns gone, sets off
on a fruitless chase around Italy in search of her, fails to find her, gives
up, and returns to Rome a sadder and (possibly) a wiser man. There is
very little here that could be described as action, and this in spite of the
ample opportunities for melodrama provided by the siege of Rome in
the background. The flimsiness of the poem's plot, and especially its
eschewal of the expected happy ending, caused a certain amount of dis-
quiet among the poem's first readers; Emerson, Clough's friend and
supporter, wrote decrying the 'balking end or no end' of the poem, and
lambasted Clough for having '[wasted] such power on a broken dream'.
'It is true' he continues 'a few persons compassionately tell me, that the
piece is all right, and that they like this veracity of much preparation to
no result. But I hold tis bad enough in life, and inadmissible in poetry'
(*Corr.* ii, 548). What Emerson sees as critical special pleading motivated
by 'compassion' is, however, likely to strike the modern reader as a
plausible reason for the poem's failure to conform to any of the
expected narrative patterns. If we take seriously the editorialising voice
of the 'Envoi', which describes the poem as 'flitting around from brain
unto brain of/ Feeble and restless youths born to inglorious days'
(V.221–2), then the deliberate bathos of 'much preparation to no result'
looks like the only possible outcome. Only by frustrating the reader's

expectations of clear comic or tragic outlines can Clough give some feeling of the confusion and muddle which he finds at the heart of contemporary life. To have furnished Claude with a clear dramatic imperative – a role to fulfil – would have been false to that Hamletesque feeling of alienation from all possible social roles which he expresses with such vehemence in the poem.

The epistolary form of the poem means that character is revealed not so much by what the characters do as by what they say. In this respect the poem resembles the dramatic monologue; and it is, I think, reasonable to suggest that Clough's poem depends, at least in part, on the technical achievement of Browning and Tennyson in exploiting this new form of poetry. *Amours* differs from what might be called the 'univocal' dramatic monologue, however, by making what the characters say (or rather write) about one another part of an interlocking series. Our impression of Claude's character comes not only from what he has to say, but also from what Mary and Georgina have to say about him and about the events on which he comments. For example: Claude spends a good deal of time in the first Canto emphasising his cultural superiority to the middle-class Trevellyns and worrying about 'the horrible pleasure of pleasing inferior people' (I.214), but it is clear from Georgina's first letter that she is far from overwhelmed: 'Who can a Mr. Claude be whom George [her fiancé] has taken to be with?/ Very stupid, I think, but George says so *very* clever' (I.63–4). The clash of perceptions here works both ways, highlighting Claude's pretentiousness and self-importance but also saying something about Georgina's provincial narrowness, and in particular her very middle-class mistrust of 'cleverness'. Moreover, Claude's letters also form their own sequence, allowing him to comment on and reinterpret his earlier beliefs and attitudes. The insertion of the letters (or individual monologues) into these sequences results in what William Empson calls 'double irony', the unstable coexistence of two antithetical judgements or attitudes about the characters in the poem;[5] and it is through this 'double irony' that Clough articulates his ambivalence about the progress, or lack of progress, of Claude, the poem's 'unfortunate fool of a hero'.[6]

Claude begins the poem as an inhabitant of 'the garden of the infinite choices': 'Here in the Garden I walk, can freely concede to the Maker/ That the works of his hands are all very good' (I.146–7). Clough's description of Shakespeare, the archetypal inhabitant of the garden, seems, indeed, to fit Claude almost exactly; he is in Rome, 'newly emancipated from teachers and directors', and in particular from

5. See the chapter entitled 'Double Plots' in *Some Versions of Pastoral* (1935; rpt. Chatto and Windus, 1986).

6. Clough describes Claude thus in a letter to his friend J.C. Shairp (see Thorpe 1972: 123).

Eustace, who we might, from the tone of Claude's letters, imagine to
stand in the relation of teacher to him:

> It is a blessing, no doubt, to be rid, at least for a time, of
> All one's friends and relations, – yourself (forgive me!) included, –
> All the *assujettissement* of having been what one has been,
> What one thinks one is, or thinks that other suppose one   (I.28–31)

He is, moreover, 'unbound' either by 'self-imposed restriction' or by
'formed determination'; he has no definite project, no plan of action to
follow. Finally, the richness of his 'interior life' is apparent from the
soaring speculations on the history and culture of Rome which occupy
the first canto. Claude questions everything he comes across: the
appropriation of pagan cultural and religious artifacts by the Roman
Catholic church; the true nature of the relation between Ancient and
Modern in the city; and the nature of his incipient relationship with the
Trevellyn family. This last subject rapidly becomes the focus of his
attention, as the desire for a 'help-meet' for 'poor critical coxcomb
Adam' (I.150) leads him to consider abandoning the pleasures of this
state of innocence and undertaking the perilous descent into experience. It is within this metaphorical context that the extraordinary
'caving' metaphor at the end of the first canto should be seen. It articulates Claude's desire for a provisional and reversible descent which can
be aborted should the premises upon which it was undertaken prove to
have been mistaken:

> Lo, with the rope on my loins I descend through the fissure; I sink, yet
> Inly secure in the strength of invisible arms up above me;   ·
> Still, wheresoever I swing, wherever to shore, or to shelf, or
> Floor of cavern untrodden, shell-sprinkled, enchanting, I know I
> Yet shall one time feel the strong cord tighten about me, –
> Feel it, relentless, upbear me from spots I would rest in . . .
>   [I shall]
> Feel underneath me again the great massy strengths of abstraction,
> Look yet abroad from the height o'er the sea whose salt wave I have
>   tasted.   (I.242 . . . 252)

Claude wants, that is to say, to taste the 'salt wave' of experience – 'the
seas of actual and positive existence' – while at the same time retaining
the possibility of returning to the heights should his mission prove
abortive. This provisional Fall into experience is, moreover, meta-
phorically associated with sex; the figure of 'descending through the
fissure' needs no elucidation to the post-Freudian reader. This Fall is,
however, as Claude will find out, a perilous enterprise; a taste of the salt
wave, no matter how brief or provisional, changes the character of the
garden of the infinite choices for ever, and turns what had seemed a
paradise into a prison.

It is, I think, significant that Claude considers the possibility of undertaking the Fall into experience before he is sure which of the Trevellyn sisters he likes; at this stage it is still 'Susan or Mary Trevellyn'. His interest in them, and in the possibility of romance, derives largely from simple 'juxtaposition' rather than from any intrinsic compatibility. This term – juxtaposition – and its counterpart 'affinity' play a considerable role in the moral argument which Claude constructs around his tentative courtship, and therefore deserve closer scrutiny. Both terms derive from contemporary chemical theory. Elements which manifest a natural tendency to unite with one another are described as having an 'elective affinity'; juxtaposition, on the other hand, is the enemy of affinity because it leads to the formation of a permanent bond between weakly compatible elements which would otherwise have formed attachments to different partners. The metaphorical potential of this theoretical distinction was first realised by Goethe; in his novel *Elective Affinities* (1809), he explicitly compares marriage to 'juxtaposition' – the rendering permanent of a bond between weakly-compatible elements – and examines the effect on this union of the introduction of a third party with whom one of the married partners has a genuine 'elective affinity'. Some reflections on these terms and their significance appear in Clough's *Roma* Notebook: 'The wrong doctrine of habits is *philika poiountes philoi gignometha* / By doing acts *like* those of love, we shall come to love. / Given the higher affinity these circumstances of lower kind of juxtaposition are only temporary – if I do not allow myself in affinity to them – when I shall presently be rid of them, I shall be all right for the higher' (*Roma* Notebook, f44v). The Aristotelian notion of habituation to the good is, Clough suggests, inappropriate when dealing with love; the correct strategy here is rigorous suppression of all 'inferior vital effluxes' of emotion until such time as the higher affinity manifests itself. These rather abstruse theoretical considerations help to explain Claude's conduct during the second Canto; that is to say, after he begins to feel attracted to Mary Trevellyn. Aware that precipitate action on his part might lead to the cementing of a relationship based on mere juxtaposition he remains resolutely inactive, scrutinising his relationship with Mary for warning signs of 'something factitious, / Some malpractice of heart and illegitimate process' (II.273–4). If their feelings for one another are genuine, they will, he suggests, grow naturally and spontaneously into commitment without any conscious 'knowledge [or] effort' on the part of the lovers. Will and duty, that is to say, are the enemies of genuine affinity; like 'the beatific supersensual sight' promised to the devout in *Qui laborat, orat*, human love must be a free gift of unmerited grace. Returning to the governing metaphor, Claude implores the heavenly powers not to expel him from 'the garden of the infinite choices' on a false pretext: 'Drive me not out, ye ill angels with fiery swords, from my Eden, / Waiting, and watching, and looking! Let love be its own inspiration!'

(II.277–8). Given the chemical analogy, Claude can almost be seen as a scientist conducting an experiment on himself; having placed the elements together, he is waiting for unmistakable signs of a positive reaction before continuing.

Unfortunately for Claude, the results of the test are negative; both he and Mary attest to the existence of a force of 'repulsion' between them (II.299, 329–30; III.28–30). The term is precisely chosen: repulsion is the force which exists between atoms of the same element. The suggestion – one reinforced by Claude and Mary's use of the same terms – is that they are too similar to be genuinely compatible. This finding links up with Claude's worries about the erosion of masculinity in the modern world; women, he suggests, prefer 'the audacious, the wilful, the vehement hero' (II.292), but the conditions of modern life and the depredations of culture leave men in the mid-nineteenth century few opportunities for the exercise of Byronic heroism, thereby diminishing the difference between the sexes and reducing the possibility of genuine romantic love. The apparent failure of this experiment leads Claude to consider a quick retreat to 'the vision of things in general' (II.310), in line with the proposal articulated in the 'caving' metaphor cited earlier. This possibility is, however, scuppered by the advent of a revelation which completely changes Claude's understanding of his relationship with Mary, and leads him to reappraise the validity of the 'abstractions' upon which he had previously relied. This revelation comes in the form of George Vernon's 'hints' about Claude's intentions towards Mary, hints which lead him to suspect that what had seemed to him a delicate and spontaneous growth was in fact nothing more than a 'permitted flirtation', a part of the elaborate bourgeois courtship ritual. In the wake of this 'discovery' – which is not, incidentally, revealed to the reader until letter xii of the third canto – Claude fails to accompany the Trevellyns to Rome, and instead embarks on a thorough re-examination of the beliefs which have so far guided his conduct.

This iconoclastic sequence of letters is the pivotal moment of the poem. Claude begins by examining the figure of growth. He had wanted to be 'growing, where [he] was growing' (II.268) in his relationship with Mary, to pass inexorably over from inclination to engagement, or innocence to experience, without having to undergo the trauma of the Fall. He now, however, suggests that this idea of growth is inapplicable to the human situation. Our self-conscious ability to 'compare, and reflect, and examine one thing with another' represents a 'painful victorious knowledge' which estranges us from the rest of organic nature without allowing us to escape involvement in the natural cycle of birth, maturity, decay and death (III.44, 53). We are, Claude suggests, echoing Byron in his more embittered moments, rootless creatures, the 'offspring uncared-for' (III.52) of Nature forced to drift forever in a hostile and alien element. In letter iv the motifs of growth and the Fall are brought together again, as in *Adam and Eve*; but Claude suggests that knowledge, far from being the forbidden fruit which secures our painful but ultimately victorious exit from the garden, is simply a 'needless, unfruitful' blossom on the Tree of Life (III.84). The word 'unfruitful' is significant here; Claude's premature recognition of the futility of any knowledge he might gain on leaving the garden pre-empts the possibility of the blossom of knowledge ripening into the fruit of temptation. His 'Eden' of '[waiting], and watching, and looking' has, in short, been turned into a prison by the absence of any imperative to action, and the result is disenchantment with 'the garden of the infinite choices'. The 'richness of reflectiveness' now reveals itself as a 'malady': '*HANG* this thinking, at last!' Claude exclaims; 'what good is it? oh, and what evil!' (III.207) In the sixth and seventh letters Claude reflects upon the distinction between affinity and juxtaposition, and comes to the conclusion that the former differs from the latter in degree, not in kind; what the world takes for affinity is simply juxtaposition rendered permanent by 'the law of the land and the ruinous force of the will' (III.155). Men, Claude suggests, in what is likely to strike the modern reader as one of his more obscure arguments, only accept the 'illusion' of eternal marriage in the expectation of achieving a more perfect consummation after death; marriage is 'an *ad-interim* solace and pleasure' which will eventually yield to 'a perfect and absolute something,/ Which I then for myself shall behold, and not another' (III.143–5). This turn towards the consolations of religion as a possible source of recompense for the frustration of earthly hopes is, as we shall see, repeated later in the poem.

By the end of the third canto, Claude's 'provisional fall' has resulted in failure on the one hand and disenchantment with 'the garden of the infinite choices' on the other. He has lost the illusions which made the garden appear such a delightful place, but has been unable to discover any imperative to action, any motive for positive 'engagement' (to use the poem's own pun) with the world. This is, in essence, the situation in which he remains until the end of the poem. When he discovers that Vernon's hints were not authorised by Mary he makes renewed efforts to find her, but this time with considerably lower expectations of the kind of happiness which might be waiting for him at the end of his search. Where earlier he had wanted love to be 'its own inspiration', and had mistrusted obligation as the enemy of love, he now looks forward to 'the marriage-morn' and all its conventional trappings, and derides himself for 'fiddle-faddling' when opportunity presented itself (IV.iii). Even this lower level of happiness is now denied him, however; his search for Mary ends in failure. Claude responds to this second disappointment in two ways. He resolves to forget Mary; his memory of her is fading – he cannot recall her features with any certainty (V.157)

– and to continue the search for her would be to run the risk of chasing after an image conjured up by his own imagination: 'Is she not changing, herself? – the old image would only delude me' (V.47; see also 31–3 and 157). The first draft of the poem makes the submerged metaphor of idolatry here much clearer; Claude tells himself that he '[must] not set up an idol, to live and die in its presence'. Claude is here replicating his creator's reluctance to 'make his image'; he is, if we might take the pun seriously for a moment, on guard against succumbing to the temptations of Mariolatry. Claude's second response to his failure to find Mary is more explicitly religious in its implications; he resolves to 'aspire evermore to the Absolute only' (V.49). The 'Absolute', like the 'things in general' towards which Claude turns at the end of the second canto and the 'Actual Abstract' of the third, is one of the poem's code-phrases for God; and Claude, here as before, responds to the frustration of his hopes for earthly happiness by seeking religious consolation. The vagueness of his terminology is, on one level, the product of Clough's nervousness about addressing religious questions in a serio-comic narrative; but on another it highlights the very nebulousness of Claude's religious convictions, the fact that his concept of the deity is a mere void without specific content. It is not, then, surprising to find that the aspiration towards 'the Absolute' collapses almost as soon as it is articulated: 'Utterly vain is, alas, this attempt at the Absolute, – wholly!' (V.63). The 'religious assurance' which Claude thought he had attained (see III.125–9) now seems 'factitious'. Instead of aspiring towards some nebulous and unknowable concept of deity, Claude decides to turn his attention to the world around him: 'I will look straight out, see things, not try to evade them' (V.100). This new-found commitment to reality is sealed by the rewriting of Paul's first Epistle to the Corinthians: 'Ere our death-day,/ Faith, I think, does pass, and Love; but Knowledge abideth' (V.197–8). Faith and Love, the two goals which have proved elusive during the poem, are set aside in favour of Knowledge – the accurate perception of reality as it is. This knowledge is, however, sterile, since, as we have seen, it cannot issue in or precipitate purposeful action; and Claude is doomed to remain the perennial tourist, hovering, like his '[cormorants], ducks and gulls' (III.96), above the seas of actual and positive existence.

The significance which we attach to Claude's progress depends, as I have already suggested, on the way in which we choose to interpret the poem's inherently unstable sequences of letters.[7] If we approach the

---

7. The two approaches are exemplified, respectively, by Michael Timko in his 1963 *Innocent Victorian: The Satiric Poetry of Arthur Hugh Clough* (Ohio: Ohio UP), and by John Goode's essay '*Amours de Voyage*: The Aqueous Poem' in I. Armstrong (ed.), *The Major Victorian Poets: Reconsiderations* (Routledge & Kegan Paul, 1969).

poem as a satire – giving weight, that is to say, to the testimony of the other voices in the poem, and to Claude's apparent *volte-face* in the fifth canto – we emerge with a narrative which portrays Claude's gradual if grudging adjustment to reality as it is. By the end of the poem he recognises that his ideals were little more than immature fantasies generated by inexperience and timidity, and resolves to abandon them. This, remembering the underlying symbolic structure, is to see the journey from the garden of the infinite choices towards the seas of actual and positive existence as a chronicle of maturity, or at least of the first faltering steps towards maturity. If, on the other hand, we adopt Claude's earlier point of view, then the loss of the infinite potential of the prelapsarian state, and the recognition of the 'fallen' state of the world, assume genuinely tragic proportions. His change of mind towards the end of the poem is not an admission of error, but a reluctant acquiescence in the inevitable. His radical and idealistic aspirations for a world in which the relations between the sexes might be governed by genuine inclination rather than social pressure are not shown to be wrong, but simply thwarted by the practical hegemony of the English middle classes and their values.[8] The poem's ability to support these competing readings highlights Clough's profound ambivalence about the journey upon which Claude has embarked. As in the 'Lecture on the Development of English Literature', he has built two different ways of viewing the events in question into the poem; and *Amours* is, in this respect, the consummate poetic embodiment of Clough's life-long argument with himself.

Before leaving *Amours*, I would like to step back a little from what has been a detailed and fairly intense thematic analysis. *Amours* does address serious questions and invite sustained scrutiny, but exclusive concentration on these aspects can obscure some of its other qualities, and especially its lighter and more comic aspects. Much of the poem's delicate social comedy comes from the mutual misunderstandings between Claude and the Trevellyns. The aftermath of the Oxford Movement (see below, p. 36) had seen a fairly large number of conversions to Roman Catholicism among young Oxford graduates; the Trevellyns are, therefore, slightly suspicious of Claude, and he plays on their suspicions. Thus, when he speaks of a 'daily service' he attends at the Pantheon Mrs Trevellyn suspects that he 'may be turning a Papist' (I.259–60). Georgina breathlessly informs her correspondent 'Louisa'

8. This hegemony is emphasised by the defeat of the Roman Republic in the background of the poem, a defeat which extinguishes one of the last sparks of the revolutionary conflagration of 1848 and confirms the apostasy of France. On Clough's interest in and connection with the revolutionary movements of 1848-9 see esp. John Goode, '1848 and the Strange Disease of Modern Love' in John Lucas (ed.), *Literature and Politics in The Nineteenth Century* (Methuen, 1971).

of this news, adding: 'This [i.e. the Pantheon] was a temple, you know, and now is a Catholic church; and/ Though it is said that Mazzini has sold it for Protestant service,/ Yet I suppose the change can hardly as yet be effected.' (I.262–4) Georgina has to remind (or inform) her friend that the Pantheon was a Pagan temple; and she compounds the impression of provinciality by believing a patently false item of anti-Mazzinian propaganda in the English press. Similarly economical delineations of character and attitude can be found throughout the poem, and it is such moments as these which make one think of Henry James and E.M. Forster when reading *Amours*. It is a verse-novel, and due emphasis needs to be given to both halves of this term. *Amours* is, in fact, a remarkably suggestive poem in its anticipations of future developments in both genres. Claude can, as has often been pointed out, be seen as a precursor of Eliot's Prufrock in his existential angst and Hamlet-esque indecisiveness; while the poem as a whole seems to anticipate what might be called the 'symbolist' novels of the late James and Forster, as well as the 'stream of consciousness' techniques of Joyce and Woolf. This is probably not – indeed almost certainly not – a question of direct 'influence', which makes it all the more interesting. Clough's ability to anticipate some of the characteristic techniques and concerns of the later modernist movement in *Amours* stems, I think, from his willingness to take what he and others saw as typically 'modern' states of mind – *ennui*, solipsism, alienation – to polemical extremes as part of a bold thought-experiment designed to test out their fitness and appropriateness as responses to life.

Dipsychus and The Spirit

Dipsychus – the name means 'double-minded', and its provenance is discussed in the Headnote to the poem – is, I think, best seen as a more explicit, simplified, and even schematic examination of the problems discussed in *Amours*. The questions of love, sex, action and religious belief are surveyed once again; but where the earlier poem encoded them in cryptic language and embedded them within a narrative full of novelistic detail and social comedy, *Dipsychus* reduces these problems to their bare outlines, almost in the manner of a medieval morality play. The poem is very loosely based on Goethe's *Faust* – in the first long draft of the poem the characters are called 'Mephisto' and 'Faustulus' – and consists entirely of a dialogue between a tempter, The Spirit, and the hapless and naive hero of the piece, Dipsychus. There is, however, a typically Cloughian bathos about the comparison which the poem's form invites; for The Spirit's temptations are not those of power, wealth or godlike knowledge, but those of everyday life. He tries to persuade the idealistic and other-worldly Dipsychus to abandon his scruples about sex, marriage, employment and religious worship, and to adopt the casual hypocrisy of his fellow men (and I use the word 'men' advisedly). Dipsychus, on the other hand, tries a variety of stratagems to resist this apparently inevitable Fall – for the poem is, of course, a full-length version of what Clough's Adam calls 'the mighty mythus of the Fall' (1.80), with The Spirit playing the role of the Serpent – but by the end of the poem seems to have run out of excuses, and acquiesces in his fate.

The poem begins in the Piazza San Marco in Venice on the day of the Assumption, with Dipsychus reciting part of Clough's *Easter Day* ode to himself. This poem is, as we have already seen, a solemn lament for the traditional Christian beliefs destroyed by the mythological approach to the New Testament, and Dipsychus's recitation of it at this point is clearly intended to signify his profound and unsettling doubts about the Christian revelation. These doubts are reinforced by the behaviour of the crowd in Venice, which ignores the solemn feast of the Assumption and devotes itself to sensual pleasures, albeit of a very mild form: 'Ah heaven! too true at Venice/ Christ is not risen either' (1.1.75–6). This opening to the poem means that Dipsychus cannot fall back on the certainties of the Christian religion to justify his ascetic and high-minded reluctance to participate in everyday life during his subsequent temptations. The difficulties which this leads to are apparent in the next scene, when Dipsychus attempts to resist the attractions of a Venetian prostitute. This scene takes place in the symbolic setting of the Public Gardens at Venice – almost a cruel parody of the garden of the infinite choices – and the nature of the temptation which Dipsychus faces serves to emphasise once again the function of sex within Clough's symbolic economy as the paradigmatic instance of the fall from innocence to experience. Dipsychus, indeed, makes sure that we do not miss the allusion by referring to the prostitute's (real or imagined) advances in the following terms: '[The] toad that whispered in Eve's ear/ Whispered no dream so dangerous as this' (1.2.31–2). Dipsychus tries to resist this temptation with a variety of arguments, citing the cases of 'fallen' women – a phrase which, incidentally, illustrates the depth of the identification between sex and the Fall in the Victorian psyche – and reminding himself of the sanctity of marriage and the family; but his most interesting response is one which invokes the protecting and purifying spirit of nature:

> Ah me, me
> Clear stars above, thou roseate westward sky
> Take up my being into yours: assume
> My sense to know you only: fill my brain
> In your essential purity. (2.50–4).

This attempt to find moral guidance in 'nature and the language of the sense' is, of course, reminiscent of Wordsworth, especially of *Tintern Abbey*, and begins a dialogue with the idea of Wordsworthianism as a moral code to live by which persists throughout the poem. Throughout this episode, the ramifications of which also occupy scenes 1.3 and 1.4, The Spirit provides a running commentary on Dipsychus's pious effusions, correctly identifying the symbolic nexus which induces his paralysing fear of sex:

> [It's] mainly your temptation
> To think the thing a revelation
> A mystic mouthful that will give
> Knowledge and death – none know and live.   (1.3.41–4)

From the other side of the great divide, he tries to persuade Dipsychus that sex is simply a natural appetite – 'as innocent a thing/ As picking strawberries in spring' (1.3.33–4) – which cannot be effectively suppressed and ought, therefore, to be indulged. Having failed with the prostitute The Spirit moves seamlessly on to marriage, seeing this as a less efficient but more respectable way of procuring his end. This easy transition from prostitution to marriage – 'if you really hate the street, my friend,/ Why, one must try the drawing room, one fancies' (1.4.10–11) – undermines Dipsychus's attempt to invoke the sanctity of marriage as a safeguard against prostitution. For The Spirit marriage, like prostitution, is a pecuniary and social arrangement rather than a union of souls, and Dipsychus's attempts to pretend otherwise are mere 'sentimentality'.

Dipsychus next attempts to set forth the attractions of the purely specular relation to life which he currently enjoys in the garden of the infinite choices. This attitude is represented by a gondola ride, which allows him access to the life of the city without obliging him to participate in it. It is, I think, because this scene attempts to depict the general state in which Dipsychus exists instead of advancing the argument that Clough (and subsequent editors) have found it so difficult to place.[9] The Spirit uses two arguments in the attempt to shake Dipsychus's complacency. The first is to remind Dipsychus that the luxury and ease of the spectator are obtained at the expense of those who have to work; this is the point of The Spirit's rattling song, 'How pleasant it is to have money' (1.5.126–91). The Spirit's second and perhaps more important argument is to stress the unreality of this way of life compared to the benefits of involvement and experience. The Spirit calls Dipsychus's raptures '[these] airy blisses, skiey joys/ Of vague romantic girls and boys' and compares them to the meal of warm water offered by Shakespeare's Timon to his fair-weather friends (1.5.236–45). He continues the dialogue with Wordsworthianism by urging his *alter ego* to '[quote] us a little Wordsworth', and suggesting some lines from *Tintern Abbey* as appropriate:

---

9. For the justification of my positioning of this scene as 1.5 see Headnote to *Dipsychus and The Spirit*, below, p. 150.

Those lines which are so true, they say:
'A something far more deeply' eh
'Interfused' what is it, they tell us?
Which and the sunset are bedfellows? (1.5.258–61)

This quotation establishes a link between the Wordsworthian mood of reverie and Dipsychus's 'meditative reluctance to take a part', a link which, as we shall see, points to one important aspect of the poem's overall significance.

Dipsychus's next two temptations constitute an implicit dialogue with that other great Romantic precursor, Byron. He is insulted by a Croat soldier of the occupying Austrian army, and has to decide how to respond. The Spirit is irate and demands that Dipsychus exact retribution in the form of a challenge to a duel. Being a man of the world he does not expect any actual violence: ' 'twon't come to fighting/ Only some verbal small requiting;/ Or give your card – we'll do't by writing' (1.6.14–16). Dipsychus, however, refuses to have anything to do with the idea of the duel, preferring instead to refer the matter to the 'awful judgement-seat of truth' which he and his antagonist will face in the life to come (1.6.36). Dipsychus's suspicions about the ethics of personal honour and chivalry echo those voiced by Claude in *Amours* (II.iv); he can see the point of fighting for a noble cause, but not for merely personal trifles, and least of all for the nebulous and bogus ideas of honour and chivalry. The last scene of the first part seems to examine the possibility of redemption through the life of the senses. It is set, with calculated bathos, at the Lido, 'the ground which Byron used to ride on/ And do I don't know what beside on' (1.7.3–4); Dipsychus's sensualism, however, manifests itself in nothing more debauched than an invigorating bathe. He plunges into the sea to 'taste again the old joy/ I gloried in so, when a boy' (1.7.210–11) and attempts to experience some kind of sensual communion with nature: '[Come] come; great waters, roll!/ Accept me, take me, body and soul!' (1.7.220–1) This scene is, incidentally, a useful warning against any mechanical interpretation of Clough's symbolism; the water into which Dipsychus plunges here seems to have more to do with ideas of baptismal regeneration than with 'the seas of actual and positive existence'. The Spirit is predictably cynical about this latest substitute for religious belief:

[You] – with this one bathe no doubt
Have solved all questions out and out.
'Tis Easter Day, and on the Lido
Lo, Christ the Lord is risen indeed, O! (1.7.232–5)

The Spirit's observation closes the first part of the poem by reminding us of the original problem – the loss of the discipline of Christian faith – and of Dipsychus's failure to find an acceptable substitute for it in his vague notions of redemption through nature.

The second part of the poem can be dealt with more briefly. Dipsychus decides to confront his tempter directly, asking his terms for a bargain. The Spirit's demands do not seem particularly harsh; they amount to no more than participation in everyday life. He insists that Dipsychus should attend church – '[no] infidelity, that's flat' (2.2.64) – marry, and follow a respectable profession such as the law. These suggestions prompt Dipsychus to conduct a general review of his options. The scene in which he does so (2.3) can be regarded as a summary of the thematic preoccupations of Clough's poetry. Dipsychus surveys religion, love, and action, and finds each beset with insurmountable difficulties. God has disappeared from the modern world; love is 'so so rare/ So doubtful, so exceptional' that it is '[a] thing not possibly to be conceived/ An item in the reckonings of the wise' (2.3.33–7); and heroic action is no longer an option in a mechanised and co-operative world. Dipsychus had hoped that 'instinct' might reveal the correct and authentic course of action to him, but he now realises that the mechanical age has entered the soul; the 'full stream' of instinct has been '[sluiced] out . . . into canals/ And [lost] all force in ducts' (2.3.107–8). There is, then, no longer any reason to stand apart from society. Dipsychus, however, makes a few more desperate attempts to stave off the inevitable Fall, including, significantly, a return to Wordsworth. He is on the point of submitting when he remembers certain moments in which he has felt centred and at home in the universe:

> There have been times, not many but enough
> To quiet all repinings of the heart . . .
> O happy hours
> O compensation ample for long days
> Of what impatient tongues call wretchedness.   (2.4.1 . . .19)

This is, of course, an allusion to the Wordsworthian notion of 'spots of time' –

> that blessed mood,
> In which the burthen of the mystery,
> In which the heavy and the weary weight
> Of all this unintelligible world,
> Is lightened   (*Tintern Abbey*, 37–41)

The Spirit, however, quickly undercuts this 'blessed mood' by suggesting that it might be nothing more than the product of 'happier-tempered coffee' (2.4.133). Other attempts at escape prove equally futile. By the end of the poem Dipsychus is forced into the realisation that there is no alternative; the 'Eve' for whom he has been waiting in the garden of the infinite choices turns out to be 'th'hard naked World', and it is this which he must learn to live with (2.6.77–8).

Dipsychus and The Spirit seems, then, to oblige us to read it in what I called the 'satirical' sense when discussing *Amours*; we are strongly encouraged to see it as the abandonment of what The Spirit calls 'a dreamy unhealthy sleep' (2.5.110) and the achievement, or potential achievement, of maturity. This reading is, moreover, reinforced by the 'Epilogue' which Clough attached to the poem. This takes the form of a discussion between the poet and a brisk, no-nonsense 'Uncle' who finds the poem 'unmeaning, vague, and involved', and criticises the amount of space given to 'the devil'. This latter accusation prompts the poet to defend himself in the following terms:

> '[Perhaps] he wasn't a devil after all. That's the beauty of the poem; nobody can say. You see, dear sir, the thing which it is attempted to represent is the conflict between the tender Conscience and the World – now the over-tender conscience will of course exaggerate the wickedness of the world, and the Spirit in my poem may be merely the hypothesis or subjective imagination, formed –' (See below, p. 225).

At this point the poet is interrupted, and the conversation diverges into an analysis of the aetiology of this 'over-tender conscience'; but his remarks are suggestive. He argues that The Spirit might be merely the 'hypothesis or subjective imagination' of the wickedness of the world formed by Dipsychus's 'over-tender conscience' rather than an accurate representation of the world. This would help to explain the otherwise slightly baffling decision to name the poet's worldly and materialistic character The Spirit, and seems consistent with the general tendency of the poem to see Dipsychus's complaints against society as an expression of his own temperamental weakness. Isobel Armstrong has recently suggested (in her book *Victorian Poetry*) that the point of this argument is to highlight the interdependence of the two supposedly antithetical attitudes in the poem, making clear the way in which The Spirit's materialism and sensualism feed off and are reinforced by the kind of dreamy and aetiolated Romanticism indulged in by Dipsychus. This is an interesting argument, but one which is, I think, rather too subtle for the poem it claims to describe. Clough wants us to reach comparatively clear-cut judgements about the value and legitimacy of Dipsychus's stance, and adds this 'editorial' voice to ensure that we do so. *Dipsychus* represents, that is to say, the end of the productive stage of Clough's argument with himself, a truce in which the faction of clearsightedness and maturity gains a decisive – but, as we shall see, poetically damaging – advantage over its rival.

'Righteous abhorrence of illusion': Clough and the legacy of Romanticism

The 'Envoi' to *Amours de Voyage* claims that the poem was written 'When from Janiculan heights thundered the cannon of France'; that is to say, during the French siege and capture of the Roman Republic in 1849. There may well be a certain amount of poetic licence in this statement, but we can certainly say that the first draft of the poem was completed by November 1849 when Clough circulated it among some of his friends for comments. The poem did not, however, appear in print until the beginning of 1858, and then only in the American magazine *Atlantic Monthly*. It was unknown to the British poetry-reading public at the time of Clough's death in 1861; and most reviewers of his posthumously-issued *Poems* assumed that it was a previously unpublished work. *Dipsychus and The Spirit*, similarly, began life during Clough's visit to Venice in 1850, but did not appear in print until four years after the poet's death. There seems, then, to have been a reluctance to publish both poems on Clough's part; and this reluctance forms part of a more general turn away from poetry during the last decade of his life. The years 1848–51 had seen an astonishingly sustained burst of poetic creativity – *Adam and Eve*, *The Bothie of Toper-na-Fuosich*, *Amours de Voyage*, *Easter Day* and *Dipsychus and The Spirit* all have their roots in this period – but after this point there was an unmistakable decline in both the quality and the quantity of Clough's poetic output. His poetic activity during the 1850s was largely confined to reworking his old pieces, and he diversified into other areas of literary activity such as journalism and translation. A number of 'external' reasons for this turn away from poetry have been advanced, such as Clough's engagement and marriage; but the underlying reasons for it are, I think, to be sought in the poems themselves, and especially in *Amours* and *Dipsychus*. Clough came, I think, to the conclusion that the kind of poetry he was writing was complicit with the 'immature' tendencies criticised in these two poems, and resolved to adopt a more helpful and constructive mode of expression.

In order to understand how Clough arrived at this conclusion, it is first necessary to look again at the 'Lecture on the Development of English Literature'. This, it will be remembered, is based on an analogy between the stages in the growth of English literature and the stages in the life-cycle of an individual. There is, however, a very obvious problem with this analogy. Clough places the achievement of maturity in the Restoration and Augustan eras; this makes it hard to account for the very obvious differences between the poetry of the early eighteenth century and that of the mid-nineteenth. Clough solves this problem by following his analogy out to its logical conclusion. The organic life-cycle does not, of course, terminate with maturity; ripeness is the precursor to decay, death and rebirth. The mature society of the eighteenth century stands for a brief period before falling into decay, dying and being replaced by a new and youthful form. It is clear from Clough's other writings that he sees such a process at work in the transformation of Augustanism into Romanticism. One of the distinguishing features of the era of Dryden was, he argues, its turn away from theology; Dryden himself helped to divest English of its 'cumbrous theological vesture' (*PR* 327) and make it a language fit for courtiers as well as clerics. Towards the middle of the eighteenth century, however, there was a resurgence of 'enthusiasm' or religious feeling which eventually permeated all levels of society, attaining its 'literary patriciate' in the work of William Cowper (*PR* 350). Clough suggests that this 'enthusiasm' did for the increasingly moribund Augustan settlement what the barbarians did for Rome, destroying the corrupt ancient civilisation and sowing the seeds of a new one; and that the fruit of this new harvest was Romanticism.

Within this second and briefer recapitulation of the literary life-cycle, Wordsworth represents a partial return to the garden of the infinite choices. This much is clear from the 'Lecture on Wordsworth' which Clough wrote during the early 1850s. 'I cannot help thinking', he writes, 'that there is in Wordsworth's poems something of a spirit of withdrawal and seclusion from, and even evasion of, the actual world' (*PR* 318). This 'evasion' of the world is not, however, in Wordsworth's case, a result of the excessive plenitude and imaginative richness of the world of thought, as it was in Shakespeare's, but a result of his imaginative poverty. He is a product of the postlapsarian, post-Miltonic world, and his 'moral and almost religious selectiveness' and 'nice picking and choosing' indicate his 'spiritual descent from the Puritans' (*PR* 316). It is this 'religious selectiveness', this Puritanical disgust with reality, which motivates his 'mawkish' reluctance to look the world squarely in the face:

> [Instead] of looking directly at an object, and considering it as a thing in itself, and allowing it to operate upon him as a fact in itself, he takes the sentiment produced by it in his own mind as the thing, as the important and really real fact. The real thing ceases to be real; the world no longer exists; all that exists is the feeling, somehow generated in the poet's sensibility.   (*PR* 315)

This portrait of Wordsworth sheds a good deal of light on the numerous allusions to the poet in *Dipsychus and The Spirit*. These allusions are, as we have seen, designed to establish links between the hero's enervated and introspective stance and the Wordsworthian mood of reverie. It is now possible to recognise these allusions as part of a more general attempt to project all the least attractive aspects of the Wordsworthian inheritance onto Dipsychus. His withdrawal from reality is, like Wordsworth's, motivated by a kind of residual Puritanism; and he too exhibits the 'mawkish' reluctance to look reality squarely in the face:

> Why will you fool yourself?
> Why will you walk about thus with your eyes shut?
> Treating for facts the self made hues that float
> On tight pressed pupils, which you know are not facts.

> To use the undistorted light of the sun
> Is not a crime; to look straight out upon
> The big plain things that stare one in the face
> Does not contaminate; to see pollutes not
> What one must feel if one won't see; what is,
> And will be too, however we blink, and must
> One way or other make itself observed.   (2.5.123–33)

The poem's ultimate repudiation of Dipsychus's stance can, then, be construed as a repudiation of Wordsworthianism. There is, similarly, an implicit dialogue with Romanticism at work in *Amours*. Unlike Dipsychus, who traces his descent through the Puritan line of Wordsworth and Milton, Claude is a representative of the neo-Shakespearian school of Romanticism, and his direct poetical ancestors are Hamlet and John Keats. For him the garden of the infinite choices is not a monastery, but a place of endless imaginative delight and experiment. This version of Romanticism is, however, just as solipsistic and self-absorbed as its Wordsworthian counterpart; hence Claude's tendency to allude to Keats at moments of renunciation and withdrawal from the world. His denial of the possibility of genuine happiness in marriage, for example, is preceded by what looks like an allusion to Keats's recently published letters, and in particular to his opinion that 'the mighty abstract Idea of Beauty in all things, I have, stifles the more divided and minute domestic happiness' (see below, III.108–12 and note). Like Dipsychus, moreover, Claude finds it difficult to acknowledge the reality of the world around him, a tendency exemplified in the letters of reportage (II.v and vii) which remain focused on Claude's own opinions, doubts and conjectures rather than on the 'really real' facts he observes. It is, then, possible to see Claude's final resolution to 'look straight out, see things, not try to evade them' as an implicit rejection of Romantic solipsism.

Within the terms of his own analogy, Clough would, then, appear to be recommending in these poems a return to the maturity of the eighteenth century after the solipsistic excesses of Romanticism; and this is precisely what he advocates in his critical writings after *Dipsychus and The Spirit*. The article on 'Recent English Poetry', published in the *North American Review* for July 1853, is probably Clough's best-known critical work, in part because some of the recent poetry in question is Matthew Arnold's 1852 volume *Empedocles on Etna, and Other Poems*. In this review Clough criticises Arnold for his refusal to 'look straight out' at the things before him:

> Not by turning and twisting his eyes, in the hope of seeing things as Homer, Sophocles, Virgil, or Milton saw them; but by seeing them, by accepting them as he sees them, and faithfully depicting accordingly, will he attain the object he desires.   (*PR* 368)

This kind of poetry ministers to what Clough calls the 'over-educated weakness of purpose' besetting contemporary Europe. Instead of indulging itself in this way, poetry ought to deal with 'the obvious rather than the rare facts of human nature', those 'actual, palpable things with which our every-day life is concerned' (*PR* 357). In his article Clough contrasts Arnold's evasiveness with the work of Alexander Smith, a 'Glasgow mechanic', whose poems 'have something substantive and lifelike, immediate and first-hand, about them' (*PR* 358). Smith, that is to say, at least recognises the need to look at the world as it is. His laudable determination to 'keep his eye steady upon the thing before him' (*PR* 377) is, however, vitiated by a lack of acquaintance with those poets who could help him most in this endeavour. Clough suspects him of being a disciple of Keats who has read nothing between Milton and Burns – that is to say, from the period of English poetry's maturity – and recommends, in all seriousness, that he write out passages from Goldsmith to cure himself of the habit of over-indulgence in metaphor.

This recommendation of a return to maturity and clearsightedness creates problems for Clough himself, however; for the two poems in which he recommends it are themselves products of the very attitude they end up renouncing. *Amours* is an introspective and solipsistic critique of introspection and solipsism. The epistolary form of the poem imprisons us within the minds of the participants and denies us access to an objectively described reality in a way which seems to militate against the conclusion reached at the end of the poem; we cannot 'look straight out, see things, not try to evade them' even if we want to, because our version of reality is always refracted through the more or less dense medium of the individual consciousness. *Dipsychus* is, if anything, even more solipsistic. *Amours* at least occasionally frees us from Claude's overheated consciousness by allowing us to see things through the eyes of Mary and Georgina; in *Dipsychus* there is no resting-place from the dialogue of the mind with itself.

That last phrase is, of course, taken from Matthew Arnold's 1853 *Preface*, the document in which he – rather grandly and self-importantly – announced his reasons for not reprinting *Empedocles on Etna*. Arnold, it will be remembered, suppresses his poem because its accurate delineation of the doubts and discouragements of the modern situation is not the 'one thing needful' for the present age. There are, I think, similar reasons behind Clough's reluctance to publish *Amours* and *Dipsychus*, and indeed behind the more general turn away from poetry – or at least the kind of poetry he had previously written – which characterises the last decade of his life. Having come to the conclusion that what the modern age required was a return to the 'maturity' and objectivity of the Augustan era, he could not publish poems which prolonged 'the dialogue of the mind with itself' – or, in Cloughian rather than Arnoldian terms, 'the questioning spirit' – even if they eventually recommended the suppression of this spirit. His task was to inculcate the 'austere love of truth' and 'righteous abhorrence of illusion' characteristic of the greatest eighteenth-century writers, and the publication of poems like *Amours* and *Dipsychus* could only hinder this task. These considerations also help, I think, to lend coherence to Clough's apparently diverse literary activities during this decade. He devoted a substantial amount of labour to a revision of Dryden's translation of Plutarch. This might seem simply the kind of thing which an out-of-work classical scholar would turn his hand to; but it also represents an attempt on Clough's part to imbue himself and his generation with something of Dryden's virtue. In his lecture on 'Dryden and His Times' Clough credits the Restoration poet with the renovation of the language; having inherited a language which had been rendered unfit for most practical purposes by its 'cumbrous theological vesture', Dryden purged it and reformed it along classical, secular lines. Modern English, Clough suggests, is in need of a similar service after the 'enthusiastic' and neo-religious interlude of Romanticism. It is not, I would suggest, too far-fetched to think that he himself supposed he was performing it, or at least performing part of it, by revising Dryden for the readers of the nineteenth century. Indeed, he might almost seem to have been taking the advice he gave to Alexander Smith, and copying out extracts from the best prose writer in English as a kind of penance for his Romantic debauches.

Poems from *Ambarvalia*

Publication: London: Chapman and Hall, 1849.

Text and MSS: The text used here is that of 1849, the only one published during C.'s lifetime. Three copies of C.'s portion of the volume with suggested emendations in his own hand survive: Poems (A), a proof-copy; Poems (B); and Poems (Norton), a copy given to C.E. Norton in 1852. A and B are in the Bodleian Library in Oxford; Norton is in the Yale University Library. Variants and suggested titles from these copies given below are identified accordingly.

Biographical and literary notes: This volume consists of poems by C. and his friend Thomas Burbidge. C. had known Burbidge since his Rugby days, and their friendship extended to poetic collaboration at an early stage; C. seems to have contributed at least one poem to Burbidge's 1838 collection, and regularly submitted his poetic efforts to his friend for comment during the following decade. The idea of joint publication appears, however, to have come about as the result of external circumstances. While he was British chaplain at Trieste during the 1840s Burbidge charged C. with the task of finding an English publisher for his poems. In November 1844 he hinted at the possibility of joint publication, and C.'s response was enthusiastic: 'As for a joint folly – I should like it greatly – had I poemata enough or money!' (*Corr.* i, 160). (It was normal at the time for poetry to be published at the author's rather than the publisher's risk.) The project seems to have lain fallow for a couple of years until December 1847, when C. wrote to an unnamed publisher that he and Burbidge were considering bringing their poems out 'in a series of cheap numbers' in imitation of Browning's *Bells and Pomegranates*, and suggested the title 'Myths and Monologues' for them (*Corr.* i, 190). When *Ambarvalia* appeared just over a year later, however, it came out in the traditional single volume, with C.'s contribution clearly separated from Burbidge's.

The title eventually adopted refers to an Ancient Roman ceremony of ritual purification in which animals were led around the bounds of the city; a clue to its significance may be found in the following cancelled lines from 'Why should I say I see the things I see not?':

Age on age succeeding fast
From a far heroic past
They went their rounds
And beat the bounds
Of old Imperial Rome
The Ambarvalian brothers Nine with hymns and sacred song
That immemorial line along
Of that august and holy home.
Even so Poets now
With more than priestly vow
Made separate from their birth
Walk the great world and mete the measures of the Earth.

                                              (Mulhauser 1974: 579)

C.'s contribution represents, in his own words, 'the casualties of at least ten years' (*Corr.* i, 240), and includes material written as early as 1840. His failure to give titles to most of his poems must have been extremely unusual at the time, as it attracted (generally unfavourable) comment from almost all of the volume's reviewers (see Introduction, p. 4). It might have been this criticism which prompted him to abandon the experiment; the various titles which he later suggested for his 'unnamed bits' (Thorpe 1972: 75) are given in the notes below.

> The human spirits saw I on a day,
> Sitting and looking each a different way;
> And hardly tasking, subtly questioning,
> Another spirit went around the ring
> To each and each: and as he ceased his say,   5
> Each after each, I heard them singly sing,
> Some querulously high, some softly, sadly low,
> We know not, – what avails to know?
> We know not, – wherefore need we know?
> This answer gave they still unto his suing,   10
> We know not, let us do as we are doing.
>
> Dost thou not know that these things only seem? –
> I know not, let me dream my dream.
> Are dust and ashes fit to make a treasure? –
> I know not, let me take my pleasure.   15

1. 'The human spirits'] A couple of possible titles were suggested by C.: 'Through a glass darkly' (I Corinthians 13:12) (*A*) and 'The Questioning Spirit' (in a letter to C.E. Norton dated 28 December 1858; see *Corr.* ii, 560–2). C. originally wrote 'Seven human spirits' but changed the line on Matthew Arnold's advice: 'The 7 Spirits Poem does well what it attempts to do I think. Tho: I still ask why 7[?] This is the worst of the allegorical – it instantly involves you in the unnecessary – and the unnecessary is necessarily unpoetical' (Lowry 1932 12: 60). The poem alludes to the description of the pool of Bethesda in John 5:3–4; see *Bethesda: A Sequel*, below, p. 247.

What shall avail the knowledge thou hast sought? –
I know not, let me think my thought.
What is the end of strife? –
I know not, let me live my life.
How many days or e'er thou mean'st to move? –   20
I know not, let me love my love.
Were not things old once new? –
I know not, let me do as others do.
And when the rest were over past,
I know not, I will do my duty, said the last.   25

Thy duty do? rejoined the voice,
Ah do it, do it, and rejoice;
But shalt thou then, when all is done,
Enjoy a love, embrace a beauty
Like these, that may be seen and won   30
In life, whose course will then be run;
Or wilt thou be where there is none?
I know not, I will do my duty.

And taking up the word around, above, below,
Some querulously high, some softly, sadly low,   35
We know not, sang they all, nor ever need we know!
We know not, sang they, what avails to know?
Whereat the questioning spirit, some short space,
Though unabashed, stood quiet in his place.
But as the echoing chorus died away   40
And to their dreams the rest returned apace,
By the one spirit I saw him kneeling low,
And in a silvery whisper heard him say:
Truly, thou knowst not, and thou needst not know;
Hope only, hope thou, and believe alway;   45
I also know not, and I need not know,
Only with questionings pass I to and fro,
Perplexing these that sleep, and in their folly
Imbreeding doubt and sceptic melancholy;
Till that their dreams deserting, they with me,   50
Come all to this true ignorance and thee.

44-51] The questioner's words are addressed to the spirit who promised to do
his duty, implying that he alone has the Socratic virtue of 'true ignorance' (see
the discussion of the poem in Kenny 1988: ch. 3).

As, at a railway junction, men
Who came together, taking then
One the train up, one down, again

Meet never! Ah, much more as they
Who take one street's two sides, and say   5
Hard parting words, but walk one way:

Though moving other mates between,
While carts and coaches intervene,
Each to the other goes unseen,

Yet seldom, surely, shall there lack   10
Knowledge they walk not back to back,
But with an unity of track,

Where common dangers each attend,
And common hopes their guidance lend
To light them to the self-same end.   15

Whether he then shall cross to thee,
Or thou go thither, or it be
Some midway point, ye yet shall see

Each other, yet again shall meet.
Ah, joy! when with the closing street,   20
Forgivingly at last ye greet!

---

1. 'As, at a railway junction, men'] First published under the title 'Differ to
Agree' in *The Balance* (13 February 1846); C. also suggested 'Sic Itur' as a possible title (from Virgil, *Aeneid*, IX, 641: 'sic itur ad astra' – 'This is the way
that leads to the stars') (*A*). The poem is typical of C.'s determination to use
imagery drawn from modern life; compare the simile of the railway tunnel in
Amours V.ix. Here the image is rather forced, and C. in fact abandons it for a
more adequate one after the first stanza.

Qui laborat, orat

O only Source of all our light and life,
    Whom as our truth, our strength, we see and feel,
But whom the hours of mortal moral strife
    Alone aright reveal!

Mine inmost soul, before Thee inly brought,   5
    Thy presence owns ineffable, divine;
Chastised each rebel self-encentered thought,
    My will adoreth Thine.

With eye down-dropt, if then this earthly mind
    Speechless abide, or speechless e'en depart;   10
Nor seek to see – for what of earthly kind,
    Can see Thee as Thou art? –

If sure-assured 'tis but profanely bold
    In thought's abstractest forms to seem to see,
It dare not dare the dread communion hold   15
    In ways unworthy Thee,

O not unowned, Thou shalt unnamed forgive,
    In worldly walks the prayerless heart prepare;
And if in work its life it seem to live,
    Shalt make that work be prayer.   20

Nor times shall lack, when while the work it plies,

Title Qui laborat, orat] 'Who works, prays.' The poem was composed after a discussion with Tom Arnold concerning the dangers of excessively fervent prayer: see Arnold's 'Arthur Hugh Clough: A Sketch' in *The Nineteenth Century*, Vol XLIII (1898). The motto of Rugby School was *Orando Laborando*. The motto of the Benedictine monks, *Laborare est Orare*, occurs in Carlyle's (1899) *Past and Present* Vol. X p. 200: 'Admirable was that of the old Monks, "*Laborare est Orare*, Work is Worship".' The poem was admired by Tennyson (see *Corr.* ii, 412).
15-16] Anthony Kenny suggests that these lines should read 'It dare not dare thee dread communion hold/ In ways unworthy Thee' in order to stress the fact that the soul, aware of its own imperfections, does not dare ask God to descend and hold communion with it (see Kenny 1988: 62–3). The current reading makes perfectly good sense, however; 'the dread communion' is the communion with God (and also, by implication, the communion service itself), and the reiteration of 'dare not dare', far from being redundant, emphasises the extreme hesitancy which the pious soul must feel before any attempt at direct contact with God. In addition, 'Thee' would have been spelt with a capital letter, as throughout the rest of the poem; so any confusion with 'the' would be extremely unlikely.
21-4] The poem does not assert that communion between God and man is impossible, but that the human desire for such communion destroys the possibility of it; it must descend 'unsummoned'. This notion is consistent with the Protestant idea that divine grace is an unmerited free gift from God.

Unsummoned powers the blinding film shall part,
And scarce by happy tears made dim, the eyes
    In recognition start.

As wills Thy will, or give or e'en forbear   25
    The beatific supersensual sight,
So, with Thy blessing blest, that humbler prayer
    Approach Thee morn and night.

When Israel came out of Egypt

Lo, here is God, and there is God!
    Believe it not, O man;
In such vain sort to this and that
    The ancient heathen ran:
Though old Religion shake her head,   5
    And say in bitter grief,

25. wills Thy will] One of a number of such constructions in the poem; e.g. 'sure-assured', 'dare not dare'. Here the effect is to stress the submission of the human to the divine will.

Title. When Israel came out of Egypt] C. later suggested 'The New Sinai' as an alternative title (*Corr.* ii, 562). Stanzas 8 and 9 are crossed out in *B*. The poem takes its title from Psalm 114:1–2: 'When Israel came out of Egypt: and the house of Jacob from among the strange people,/ Judah was his sanctuary: and Israel his dominion' (Prayer Book version). The poem itself is based on Exodus 32:1–4: 'And when the people saw that Moses delayed to come down out of the mount, the people gathered themselves together unto Aaron, and said unto him, Up, make us gods, which shall go before us; for *as for* this Moses, the man that brought us up out of the land of Egypt, we wot not what is become of him./ And Aaron said unto them, Break off the golden earrings, which *are* in the ears of your wives . . . and bring *them* unto me./ . . . And he received *them* at their hand, and fashioned it with a graving tool, after he had made it a golden calf: and they said, These *be* thy gods, O Israel, which brought thee up out of the land of Egypt.' C. dated the poem to 1846–7 (*Corr.* i, 245), and it should be seen in the context of John Henry Newman's decision to convert to Roman Catholicism, taken the previous year, which effectively put an end to the Oxford Movement. C. had been interested in the fortunes of the Movement, which sought to recall the Church of England to its 'Catholic' heritage, ever since his arrival at Oxford in October 1837; but in this poem he revives the traditional Protestant complaint of idolatry against the Church of Rome as a way of criticising Newman's premature abandonment of the questioning spirit.

The day behold, at first foretold,
    Of atheist unbelief:
Take better part, with manly heart,
    Thine adult spirit can;   10
Receive it not, believe it not,
    Believe it not, O Man!

As men at dead of night awaked
    With cries, 'The king is here,'
Rush forth and greet whome'er they meet,   15
    Whoe'er shall first appear;
And still repeat, to all the street,
    ''Tis he, – the king is here;'
The long procession moveth on,
    Each nobler form they see   20
With changeful suit they still salute,
    And cry, ''Tis he, 'tis he!'

So, even so, when men were young,
    And earth and heaven was new,
And His immediate presence He   25
    From human hearts withdrew,
The soul perplexed and daily vexed
    With sensuous False and True,
Amazed, bereaved, no less believed,
    And fain would see Him too: 30
He is! the prophet-tongues proclaimed;
    In joy and hasty fear,
He is! aloud replied the crowd,
    Is, here, and here, and here.

He is! They are! in distance seen   35
    On yon Olympus high,
In those Avernian woods abide,
    And walk this azure sky:
They are, They are! to every show
    Its eyes the baby turned,   40
And blazes sacrificial tall
    On thousand altars burned:

---

13 et seq.] C. gives an anthropological account of the development of human religion, seeing it as a progression from primitive polytheism to Judaeo-Christian monotheism.

36] Mount Olympus was the home of the Greek gods.

37. Avernian woods] The woods surrounding Lake Averno near Rome, held in antiquity to be one of the entrances to the underworld; C.'s account encompasses both Greek and Roman versions of polytheism.

They are, They are! – On Sinai's top
    Far seen the lightnings shone,
The thunder broke, a trumpet spoke,   45
    And God said, I am One.

God spake it out, I, God, am One;
    The unheeding ages ran,
And baby-thoughts again, again,
    Have dogged the growing man: 50
And as of old from Sinai's top
    God said that God is One,
By science strict so speaks He now
    To tell us, There is None!
Earth goes by chemic forces; Heaven's   55
    A Mécanique Céleste!
And heart and mind of human kind
    A watch-work as the rest!

Is this a Voice, as was the Voice
    Whose speaking spoke abroad,   60
When thunder pealed, and mountain reeled,
    The Ancient Truth of God?
Ah, not the Voice; 'tis but the cloud,
    The cloud of darkness dense,
Where image none, nor e'er was seen   65
    Similitude of sense.
'Tis but the cloudy darkness dense
    That wrapt the Mount around;
With dull amaze the people stays,
    And doubts the Coming Sound.   70

Some chosen prophet-soul the while
    Shall dare, sublimely meek,
Within the shroud of blackest cloud
    The Deity to seek:
'Midst atheistic systems dark,   75

43–5] Exodus 19:16: 'And it came to pass on the third day in the morning, that there were thunders and lightnings, and a thick cloud upon the mount, and the voice of the trumpet exceeding loud[.]'
46] Exodus 20:2–5.
56. Mécanique Céleste] Carlyle refers to 'Laplace's *Mécanique Céleste*' in *Sartor Resartus*, Bk 1, ch. iv; used here as a typical example of the mechanistic thinking of the Enlightenment.
59–70] Atheistic 'Science' is not a rival to the revelation given to Moses on Mount Sinai, but a part of the 'cloudy darkness dense' currently obscuring the truth.

And darker hearts' despair,
    That soul has heard his very word,
        And on the dusky air
His skirts, as passed He by, to see
        Has strained on their behalf,   80
Who on the plain, with dance amain,
        Adore the Golden Calf.

'Tis but the cloudy darkness dense;
    Though blank the tale it tells,
No God, no Truth! yet He, in sooth,   85
    Is there – within it dwells;
Within the sceptic darkness deep
        He dwells that none may see,
Till idol forms and idol thoughts
        Have passed and ceased to be: 90
No God, no Truth! ah though, in sooth,
        So stand the doctrine's half;
On Egypt's track return not back,
        Nor own the Golden Calf.

Take better part, with manlier heart,   95
    Thine adult spirit can;
No God, no Truth, receive it ne'er –
    Believe it ne'er – O Man!
But turn not then to seek again
        What first the ill began;   100
No God, it saith; ah, wait in faith
        God's self-completing plan;
Receive it not, but leave it not,
        And wait it out, O Man!

The Man that went the cloud within   105
    Is gone and vanished quite;
He cometh not, the people cries,
    Nor bringeth God to sight:
Lo these thy gods, that safety give,
        Adore and keep the feast!   110
Deluding and deluded cries
    The Prophet's brother-Priest:
And Israel all bows down to fall
    Before the gilded beast.

112] The 'Prophet's brother-Priest' is Aaron.

Devout, indeed! that priestly creed,   115
　　O Man, reject as sin;
The clouded hill attend thou still,
　　And him that went within.
He yet shall bring some worthy thing
　　For waiting souls to see;   120
Some sacred word that he hath heard
　　Their light and life shall be;
Some lofty part, than which the heart
　　Adopt no nobler can,
Thou shalt receive, thou shalt believe,   125
　　And thou shalt do, O Man!

———————

I

Why should I say I see the things I see not,
　　Why be and be not?
Show love for that I love not, and fear for what I fear not?
And dance about to music that I hear not?
　　　Who standeth still i' the street   5
　　　Shall be hustled and justled about;
And he that stops i' the dance shall be spurned by the dancers'
　　　feet, –
Shall be shoved and be twisted by all he shall meet,
　　　And shall raise up an outcry and rout;
　　　　And the partner, too, –   10
　　　　What's the partner to do?
While all the while 'tis but, perchance, an humming in mine ear,
　　　That yet anon shall hear,
　　　And I anon, the music in my soul,
　　　In a moment read the whole;   15

1. 'Why should I say I see the things I see not?'] The title used in posthumous
reprintings of this poem, 'The Music of the World and of the Soul', seems to
have been invented by C.'s editors. The metaphor upon which the poem is
based is prefigured in John Henry Newman's *Loss and Gain* (1848): ' "You are
like the man in one of Miss Edgeworth's novels, who shut his ears to the music
that he might laugh at the dancers." ' In the same chapter Newman's hero
Charles Reding laments ' "the misery I have endured having to stand up to
dance, and to walk about with a partner! – everybody looking at me, and I so
awkward" ' (part 1, ch. 4). Matthew Arnold appears to have regarded the poem
as nothing more than an unsuccessful 'metrical curiosity' (see Lowry 1932: 61).
12. an humming in mine ear] C. later suggested 'a torpor' (*B*), a reading which
makes the sense clearer.

The music in my heart,
Joyously take my part,
And hand in hand, and heart with heart, with these retreat,
 advance;
   And borne on wings of wavy sound,
   Whirl with these around, around,   20
  Who here are living in the living dance!
   Why forfeit that fair chance?
   Till that arrive, till thou awake,
   Of these, my soul, thy music make,
   And keep amid the throng,   25
And turn as they shall turn, and bound as they are bounding, –
Alas! alas! alas! and what if all along
   The music is not sounding?

II

Are there not, then, two musics unto men? –
   One loud and bold and coarse,   30
   And overpowering still perforce
   All tone and tune beside;
   Yet in despite its pride
Only of fumes of foolish fancy bred,
And sounding solely in the sounding head: 35
   The other, soft and low,
   Stealing whence we not know,
Painfully heard, and easily forgot,
With pauses oft and many a silence strange,
(And silent oft it seems, when silent it is not)   40
Revivals too of unexpected change:
Haply thou think'st 'twill never be begun,
Or that 't has come, and been, and past away;
   Yet turn to other none, –
   Turn not, oh, turn not thou!   45
But listen, listen, listen, – if haply be heard it may;
Listen, listen, listen, – is it not sounding now?

III

Yea, and as thought of some beloved friend
By death or distance parted will descend,
Severing, in crowded rooms ablaze with light,   50
As by a magic screen, the seer from the sight,
(Palsying the nerves that intervene

The eye and central sense between;)
    So may the ear,
      Hearing, not hear,   55
Though drums do roll, and pipes and cymbals ring;
So the bare conscience of the better thing
Unfelt, unseen, unimaged, all unknown,
May fix the entranced soul 'mid multitudes alone.

Duty – that's to say complying
    With whate'er's expected here;
On your unknown cousin's dying,
    Straight be ready with the tear;
Upon etiquette relying,   5
Unto usage nought denying,
Lend your waist to be embraced,
    Blush not even, never fear;
Claims of kith and kin connection,
    Claims of manners honour still,   10
Ready money of affection
    Pay, whoever drew the bill.
With the form conforming duly,
Senseless what it meaneth truly,
Go to church – the world require you,   15
    To balls – the world require you too,
And marry – papa and mama desire you,
    And your sisters and schoolfellows do.
Duty – 'tis to take on trust
What things are good, and right, and just;   20
    And whether indeed they be or be not,
    Try not, test not, feel not, see not:
    'Tis walk and dance, sit down and rise
    By leading, opening ne'er your eyes;
Stunt sturdy limbs that Nature gave,   25
And be drawn in a Bath chair along to the grave.

    'Tis the stern and prompt suppressing,
      As an obvious deadly sin,

---

1. 'Duty – that's to say complying'] Cp 'The human spirits' with this more
sceptical reflection on the value of duty.
7] Omitted in 1862 as indelicate.
23–4] Another use of the dance as an image for participation in social convention.
26. Bath chair] A large wheeled chair for use by disabled people.

All the questing and the guessing
  Of the soul's own soul within: 30
'Tis the coward acquiescence
  In a destiny's behest,
  To a shade by terror made,
Sacrificing, aye, the essence
  Of all that's truest, noblest, best: 35
'Tis the blind non-recognition
  Either of goodness, truth, or beauty,
Except by precept and submission;
  Moral blank, and moral void,
  Life at very birth destroyed,   40
Atrophy, exinanition!
Duty! –
Yea, by duty's prime condition
  Pure nonentity of duty!

I have seen higher holier things than these,
  And therefore must to these refuse my heart,
Yet am I panting for a little ease;
  I'll take, and so depart.

Ah hold! the heart is prone to fall away,   5
  Her high and cherished visions to forget,
And if thou takest, how wilt thou repay
  So vast, so dread a debt?

How will the heart, which now thou trustest, then
  Corrupt, yet in corruption mindful yet,   10
Turn with sharp stings upon itself! Again,
  Bethink thee of the debt!

– Hast thou seen higher holier things than these,
  And therefore must to these thy heart refuse?
With the true best, alack, how ill agrees   15
  The best that thou wouldst choose!

41. exinanition] The action or process of emptying or exhausting, whether in a material or immaterial sense; emptied or exhausted condition. (OED)
1. 'I have seen higher holier things than these'] From the sequence entitled *'Blank Misgivings of a Creature moving about in Worlds not realized'* (Wordsworth, 'Ode: Intimations of Immortality from Recollections of Early Childhood', ix). Printed as a separate poem from 1862 onwards and entitled τὸ καλόν ('The good or beautiful'). C. does not seem to have regarded the sequence as an indivisible whole; in the letter of December 1858 to C.E. Norton mentioned above (p. 32) he suggested printing only one extract from it in the projected edition of his poems.

The Summum Pulchrum rests in heaven above;
    Do thou, as best thou may'st, thy duty do:
Amid the things allowed thee live and love;
    Some day thou shalt it view.   20

Qua cursum ventus

As ships becalmed at eve that lay
    With canvass drooping, side by side,
Two towers of sail at dawn of day
    Are scarce long leagues apart descried;

When fell the night, upsprung the breeze,   5
    And all the darkling hours they plied,
Nor dreamt but each the self-same seas
    By each was cleaving, side by side:

E'en so – but why the tale reveal
    Of those, whom year by year unchanged,   10
Brief absence joined anew to feel,
    Astounded, soul from soul estranged.

At dead of night their sails were filled,
    And onward each rejoicing steered –
Ah, neither blame, for neither willed,   15
    Or wist, what first with dawn appeared!

To veer, how vain! On, onward strain,
    Brave barks! In light, in darkness too,
Through winds and tides one compass guides –
    To that, and your own selves, be true.   20

But O blithe breeze! and O great seas,
    Though ne'er, that earliest parting past,
On your wide plain they join again,
    Together lead them home at last.

---

17. *Summum Pulchrum]* The highest beauty.
Title. Qua Cursum Ventus] Adapted from Virgil, *Aeneid* III.268–9: 'fugimus
spumantibus undis,/ qua cursum ventusque gubernatorque vocabat' – 'The
south wind filled the canvas, and wind and helmsman each set the same course
for us as we flew over the foaming waves.' The title was added to C.'s proof-
copy (*A*).

One port, methought, alike they sought,   25
    One purpose hold where'er they fare, –
O bounding breeze, O rushing seas!
    At last, at last, unite them there!

Natura naturans

Beside me, – in the car, – she sat,
    She spake not, no, nor looked to me:
From her to me, from me to her,
    What passed so subtly stealthily?
As rose to rose that by it blows   5
    Its interchanged aroma flings;
Or wake to sound of one sweet note
    The virtues of disparted strings.

Beside me, nought but this! – but this,
    That influent as within me dwelt   10
Her life, mine too within her breast,
    Her brain, her every limb she felt:
We sat; while o'er and in us, more
    And more, a power unknown prevailed,
Inhaling, and inhaled, – and still   15
    'Twas one, inhaling or inhaled.

Beside me, nought but this; – and passed;
    I passed; and know not to this day
If gold or jet her girlish hair,
    If black, or brown, or lucid-grey   20
Her eye's young glance: the fickle chance
    That joined us, yet may join again;
But I no face again could greet
    As hers, whose life was in me then.

As unsuspecting mere a maid   25
    As, fresh in maidhood's bloomiest bloom,

Title. Natura naturans] A term from scholastic philosophy meaning 'creating nature' as opposed to '*natura naturata*', 'created nature'; used in Coleridge 1949: 371. Mrs C. strongly disliked the poem, and insisted that C.E. Norton omit it from his collection of C.'s poems: 'The only thing I particularly desire is to leave out Natura naturans which is abhorrent to me' (25 April 1862; Harvard bMS Am 1088 No. 1366).
1. in the car] i.e. the railway carriage.
8. virtues] Inherent powers.

In casual second-class did e'er
  By casual youth her seat assume;
Or vestal, say, of saintliest clay,
  For once by balmiest airs betrayed   30
Unto emotions too too sweet
  To be unlingeringly gainsaid:

Unowning then, confusing soon
  With dreamier dreams that o'er the glass
Of shyly ripening woman-sense   35
  Reflected, scarce reflected, pass,
A wife may-be, a mother she
  In Hymen's shrine recals not now,
She first in hour, ah, not profane,
  With me to Hymen learnt to bow.   40

Ah no! – Yet owned we, fused in one,
  The Power which e'en in stones and earths
By blind elections felt, in forms
  Organic breeds to myriad births;
By lichen small on granite wall   45
  Approved, its faintest feeblest stir
Slow-spreading, strengthening long, at last
  Vibrated full in me and her.

In me and her – sensation strange!
  The lily grew to pendent head,   50
To vernal airs the mossy bank
  Its sheeny primrose spangles spread,
In roof o'er roof of shade sun-proof
  Did cedar strong itself outclimb,
And altitude of aloe proud   55
  Aspire in floreal crown sublime;

Flashed flickering forth fantastic flies,
  Big bees their burly bodies swung,
Rooks roused with civic dins the elms,
  And lark its wild reveillez rung;   60

---

29. vestal] The vestals were a celibate female religious order in Ancient Rome dedicated to Vesta, goddess of the hearth.
38. Hymen] The Roman god of marriage.
41–4] The 'Power' is the force of '*natura naturans*'; C. is suggesting that the sexual instinct in human beings is continuous with the creative and generative forces apparent in the rest of organic nature.
57–64] The alliteration here is doubtless intended to suggest boundless fecundity.

In Libyan dell the light gazelle,
    The leopard lithe in Indian glade,
And dolphin, brightening tropic seas,
    In us were living, leapt and played:

Their shells did slow crustacea build,   65
    Their gilded skins did snakes renew,
While mightier spines for loftier kind
    Their types in amplest limbs outgrew;
Yea, close comprest in human breast,
    What moss, and tree, and livelier thing,   70
What Earth, Sun, Star of force possest,
    Lay budding, burgeoning forth for Spring.

Such sweet preluding sense of old
    Led on in Eden's sinless place
The hour when bodies human first   75
    Combined the primal prime embrace,
Such genial heat the blissful seat
    In man and woman owned unblamed,
When, naked both, its garden paths
    They walked unconscious, unashamed: 80

Ere, clouded yet in mistiest dawn,
    Above the horizon dusk and dun,
One mountain crest with light had tipped
    That Orb that is the Spirit's Sun;
Ere dreamed young flowers in vernal showers   85
    Of fruit to rise the flower above,
Or ever yet to young Desire
    Was told the mystic name of Love.

Is it true, ye gods, who treat us
As the gambling fool is treated,
O ye, who ever cheat us,
And let us feel we're cheated!
Is it true that poetical power,   5

67–8] This looks like a glancing allusion to the pre-Darwinian theory of evolution put forward in Chambers' 1844 *Vestiges of the Natural History of Creation*; cp *Amours* III.59 and note.
73–80] On the significance of the motif of the Fall, see Introduction, pp. 10–11.
1. 'Is it true, ye gods, who treat us'] This poem does not appear in *A*; it was included in the volume as a late replacement for the omitted 'Homo Sum, Nihil Humani –'.

The gift of heaven, the dower
Of Apollo and the Nine,
The inborn sense, 'the vision and the faculty divine',
All we glorify and bless
In our rapturous exaltation,   10
All invention, and creation,
Exuberance of fancy, and sublime imagination,
All a poet's fame is built on,
The fame of Shakespeare, Milton,
Of Wordsworth, Byron, Shelley,   15
Is in reason's grave precision,
Nothing more, nothing less,
Than a peculiar conformation,
Constitution, and condition
Of the brain and of the belly?   20
Is it true, ye gods who cheat us?
And that's the way ye treat us?

Oh say it, all who think it,
Look straight, and never blink it!
If it is so, let it be so,   25
And we will all agree so;
But the plot has counterplot,
It may be, and yet be not.

---

7. Apollo and the Nine] Apollo was the God of the Sun and the Patron of the
nine muses in Greek mythology.
8. 'the vision and the faculty divine'] From *The Excursion* i.79.
17–20] Cp Carlyle, 'Signs of the Times' (1829), in which he cites the opinion
of one Cabanis that poetry and religion are ' "a product of the smaller
intestines"!' (Carlyle 1899: xxvii, 65). See also Southey's quotation of Beattie's
quatrain on Milton in *Omniana*, no. 212: 'A certain High Priest could explain/
How the soul is but nerve at the most,/ And how Milton had glands in his
brain/ Which secreted the Paradise Lost.'

Adam and Eve

Publication: *Fragments of The Mystery of the Fall*, 1869; *Adam and Eve*, 1974.

Text and MSS: There are five MSS: *1. Roma* Notebook (2, 3, 4, 5, 13.77–95); *2. Venice* Notebook (8, 10, 11, 13.1–77); *3.* Bod. MS. Eng. poet. d.124 (1, 6, 7, 12, 14); *4.* Bod. MS. Eng. poet. d.125; a fair copy of 1 and 2.1–78; *5.* A draft of scene 11. Scene 9 is written on the back of one version of the 'Envoi' to *Amours de Voyage*.

Mrs C., the poem's first editor, notes that the MSS of *Adam and Eve* are 'singularly fragmentary', with scenes 'scattered up and down more than one notebook, written chiefly in pencil with no indications as to date, and nothing but the sense to guide us as to their order', but that 'in spite of the roughness and imperfection of expression, the perfect coherence of thought is very curiously felt in all the scattered pieces' (Mulhauser 1974: 663). This has been the consensus among editors until recently, and all previous versions of the poem have followed Mrs C.'s ordering of the scenes. Patrick Scott has, however, recently suggested that the poem should be regarded as an imperfectly achieved attempt to weld together two fragmentary dramas (on Adam and Eve, and on Cain and Abel respectively) composed at different times, and has discovered among the manuscripts a draft order of scenes for the poem which implies the omission of current scenes 5, 7 and 12, and the repositioning of scene 10 (Scott 1981: 98). In spite of Scott's arguments I have decided to retain the traditional arrangement of scenes, as the draft order does not seem to represent C.'s final thoughts on the matter, and its adoption would entail the omission of a number of scenes in a poem which remains a collection of fragments whatever the order adopted.

The poem has been re-edited from the various MSS. Where there are competing versions of the same scene – ie with scenes 1, 2 and 11 – I have followed what seems to be the later of the two MSS; that is, MS*4* for scenes 1 and 2.1–78, and MS*5* for scene 11.

The most important poetic precursor for *Adam and Eve* is, of course, *Paradise Lost* (on which see Introduction above p. 9 *et seq.*). There were, in addition, a number of poetic treatments of this theme during the early nineteenth century, including Byron's *Cain, A Mystery* (1821) and Elizabeth Barrett's *A Drama of Exile* (1844). C.'s poem is, however, the first to attempt to incorporate the results of advanced biblical criticism into this poetic tradition. Suggestions that

the narrative of the Fall might not be 'true' in the literal sense had been around
for over a century by the time the poem was written; the eighteenth-century
English theologian Conyers Middleton wrote:

> I have ever been inclined to consider the particular story of the fall of man, as a moral
> fable or allegory . . . in which certain religious duties and doctrines, with the genuine
> nature and effects of them, are represented as it were to our senses, by a fiction of per-
> sons and facts, which had no real existence.   (Frei 1974: 120)

The German critics, Eichhorn and Gabler, developed these suggestions further, treating the opening chapters of Genesis 'as authentic records of the
experiences of the earliest human beings, once allowance was made for the
primitive or oriental thought forms in which the narrative was expressed'. In
their view what lay behind the narrative of the Fall was 'the experience of a
human couple who had become aware of their sexual differences as a result of
eating slightly poisonous fruit from a tree' (Rogerson 1984: 17–18). Later still
De Wette argued that Genesis was purely mythical, with the narratives arising
from etymological puns on names or from later political relationships between
the Israelites and their neighbours (De Wette 1843: ii,   33). C.'s notebooks
show that he read widely in contemporary biblical criticism, including sum-
maries of the arguments of Hume, the Rev. E. Channing, De Wette,
Schleiermacher and Hermann Olshausen, among others. In 1845 he wrote:

> (Is there anything in the notion) of a Fall & a Redemption which is not conveyed in
> the common philos[ophical] expressions of Atonement & Grace –
> And 2dly if so, = is it essential to connect these truths of human nature with the his-
> torical phenomena of Christ, & his life. May not Adam & Christ & their stories be but
> a Time-Effigiation of the Untemporal Truth?   (*Roma* Notebook)

This would appear to suggest a 'mythological' approach similar to De Wette's,
but the poem itself seems closer to the Eichhorn–Gabler hypothesis; Adam and
Eve are seen generating 'the mighty Mythus of the Fall' from the attempt to
understand a sudden and drastic change in their situation. C.'s poem is not,
however, simply a psychologically plausible dramatisation of the rationalistic
reading of the story of the Fall; it also implies the possibility of translating the
traditional doctrinal categories associated with the event into moral and existential terms. For Adam, the Fall leads directly to the discovery of moral
autonomy and individual conscience; it is, to borrow Coleridge's formulation,
'the dissociation of finite, self-conscious individuals from the Absolute One'
(Veyriras 1964: 362). This 'original sin' is, moreover, replicated in Cain's murder of Abel, and by implication whenever human beings recognise what C.'s
Danish contemporary Soren Kierkegaard calls 'the alarming possibility of
being able' (see VII 12–16 below).

The poem was begun between 1845 and 1848 (see Scott 1981), during the
period when C. was in the process of resigning his post at Oriel due to his
inability to subscribe to the XXXIX Articles of the Church of England, and it
can, as Houghton suggests, be seen as his *apologia pro abdicatione sua* in its
dramatisation of the conflict between the claims of the individual conscience and
those of dogma and ritual (Houghton 1963: 80). It can also be seen as an expression of C.'s profound ambivalence about the likely consequences of this 'fall'
from the safety and security of Oxford (see I.13–16 and Introduction, p. 11).

SCENE 1

Adam: Since that last evening we have fallen indeed
      Yes we have fallen my Eve Oh yes –
      One, two, and three, and four; – the Appetite,
      The enjoyment, the aftervoid, the thinking of it
      Specially the latter two, most specially the last   5
      There in synopsis see you have it all.
      Come, let us go and work!
                                Is it not enough?
      What is there three, four, five?

Eve: Oh guilt, guilt, guilt.

A: Be comforted; muddle not your soul with doubt[;]
      'Tis done; it was to be done; if indeed   10
      Other way than this there was, I cannot say;
      This was one way, and a way was needs to be found.
      That which we were, we could no more remain
      Than in the moist provocative vernal mould
      A seed its suckers close, and rest a seed.   15
      We were to grow. Necessity on us lay
      This way or that to move; necessity too
      Not to be over-careful this or that
      So only move we should.
                          Come, my wife;
      We were to grow, and grow I think we may,   20
      And yet bear goodly fruit.

E: Oh guilt, oh guilt!

A: You weary me with your 'Oh guilt, oh guilt!'
      Peace to the senseless iteration. What!
      Because I plucked an apple from a twig
      Be damned to death eterne! parted from Good,   25
      Enchained to Ill! No, by the God of Gods,

1.3–5] Adam's description of the event – appetite, enjoyment, aftervoid, thinking of it – could refer to the eating of the forbidden fruit, but the careful ambiguity of the language also suggests that C. is alluding here to the tradition which identified the Fall with sexual intercourse; cp Eichhorn and Gabler's interpretation of the myth above, and Introduction, pp. 10–11.

1.13–16] A crucial instance of the figure of growth; see Headnote above and Introduction p. 11.

1.16–19] Cp *Dipsychus* 2.34–6: 'What we call sin,/ I could believe a painful opening out/ Of paths for ampler virtue.'

1.24–5] Notice that Adam suggests it is he, rather that Eve, who plucked the apple from the tree.

No, by the living will within my breast,
It cannot be and shall not; and if this,
This guilt of your distracted fantasy,
Be our experiment's sum, thank God for guilt!   30
Which makes me free! –
But thou, poor wife, poor mother shall I say?
Big with the first maternity of Man,
Draw'st from thy teeming womb thick fancies fond
That with confusion mix thy delicate brain;   35
Fondest of which and cloudiest call the dream
(Yea, my beloved, hear me, it is a dream)
Of the serpent, and the apple and the curse
Fondest of dreams and cloudiest of clouds.
    Well I remember in our marriage bower   40
How in the dewiest balminess of rest
Inarmed as we lay, sudden at once
Up from my side you started, screaming 'Guilt'
And 'Lost, lost, lost.' I on my elbow rose,
And rubbed unwilling eyes, and cried Eve, Eve!   45
My love! my wife! and knit anew the embrace,
And drew thee to me close, and calmed thy fear,
And woo'd thee back to sleep: In vain; for soon
I felt thee gone, and opening widest eyes
Beheld thee kneeling on the turf; hands now   50
Clenched and uplifted high; now vainly outspread
To hide a burning face and streaming eyes
And pale small lips that muttered faintly 'Death.'
And thou would'st fain depart; thou said'st the place
Was for the like of us too good; we left   55
The pleasant woodland shades, and passed abroad
Into this naked champaign, glorious soil
For digging and for delving, but indeed,
Until I killed a beast or two, and spread
Skins upon sticks to make our palace here   60
A residence sadly exposed to wind and rain.
But I in all submit to you: and then
I turned out too; and trudged a furlong space
Till you fell tired, and fain would wait for morn.
So as our nightly journey we began   65
Because the autumnal fruitage that had fallen
From trees whereunder we had slept, lay thick,
And we had eaten overnight, and seen

1.40–80] C.'s approach here is very close to the rationalism of Eichhorn and Gabler (see Headnote); Eve generates 'the mighty mythus of the Fall' by reading her own fears into a series of chance external events.

And saw again by starlight when you woke me
A sly and harmless snake glide by our couch;   70
And because some few hours before a lamb
Fell from a rock and broke its neck, and I
Had answered to your wonder, that 'twas dead,
Forsooth the molten lava of your fright
Forth from your brain, its crater, hurrying down   75
Took the chance mould; the vapour blowing by
Caught and reflected back some random shapes;
A vague and queasy dream was obstinate
In waking thoughts to find itself renewed,
And lo, the mighty mythus of the Fall!   80
Nay smile with me, sweet mother!

E: Guilt, oh, guilt!

A: Peace, woman, peace; I go[.]

E: Nay, Adam, nay;
Hear me, I am not dreaming, am not crazed.
Did not yourself confess that we are changed?
Do not you too – ?   85

A: Do not I too? Well, well!
Listen! I too when homeward weary of toil
Through the dark night I have wandered in rain and wind,
Bewildered, haply, scared, – I too have lost heart,
And deemed all space with angry power replete,
Angry, almighty; and panic-stricken have cried,   90
'What have I done! What wilt thou do to me?'
Or with the coward's 'No I did not, I will not,'
Belied my own soul's self. I too have heard
And listened too to a Voice that in my ear
Hissed the temptation to curse God, or worse   95
And yet more frequent, curse myself, and die.
Until in fine I have begun to half-believe
Your dream *my* dream too, and the dream of both
No dream but dread reality; have shared
Your fright; e'en so, share thou, sweet life, my hope.   100
I too again when weeds with growth perverse
Have choked my corn, and marred a season's toil,
Have deemed I heard in heaven abroad a cry
'Cursed is the ground for thy sake; thou art curst',
But oftener far and stronger also far,   105

1.93–121] The competing voices in Adam's head indicate the onset of individual conscience and moral autonomy.
1.104] Genesis 3:17.

In consonance with all things out and in,
I hear a Voice, more searching, bid me, On,
On, on; it is the folly of the child
To choose his path and straightway think it wrong,
And turn right back, or lie on the ground to weep.   110
Forward; go, conquer! work and live! Withal
A Word comes half-command, half-prophecy,
'Forgetting things behind thee, onward press
Unto the mark of your high calling.' Yea,
And voices too in woods and flowery field,   115
Speak confidence from budding banks and boughs,
And tell me, Live and Grow, and say, Look still
Upward, spread outward. Trust, be patient, live!
Therefore, if weakness bid me, curse and die
I answer, No. I will nor curse myself   120
Nor aught beside; I shall not die but live.

E: Ah me. Alas: – Alas!
More dismally in my face stares the doubt,
More heavily on my heart weighs the world.
Methinks   125
The questionings of ages yet to be,
The thinkings and cross-thinkings, self-contempts,
Self-horror; all despondencies, despairs
Of mutitudinous souls on souls to come
In me imprisoned fight, complain, and cry.   130
Alas.
Mystery, mystery, mystery evermore.

SCENE 2

Adam alone

Misery, O my misery; O God, God!
How could I ever, ever, could I do it?

1.113–14] An anachronistic allusion to St Paul (Philippians 3:13–14):
'Brethren, I count not myself to have apprehended: but *this* one thing *I do*, forgetting those things which are behind, and reaching forth unto those things
which are before,/ I press toward the mark for the prize of the high calling of
God in Christ Jesus.'
2. Adam alone] Adam gives way to much bleaker reflections when alone; cp
Act II of Arnold's *Empedocles on Etna*.
2.1–45] Adam wavers between acceptance of Eve's 'catastrophic' version of
events and a cooler appraisal of their circumstances.

Whither am I come? where am I? O me miserable!
My God, my God, that I were back with thee[.]
O fool, O fool! O irretrievable act.   5
    Irretrievable what, I should like to know.
What act, I wonder; what is it I mean? –
    O heaven! the spirit holds me; I must yield;
Up in the air he lifts me, casts me down.
I writhe in vain, with limbs convulsed in the void.   10
Well, well! go, idle words, babble your will:
I think the fit will leave me, ere I die.
    Fool, fool; where am I? O my God! Fool, fool!
Why did we do't? Eve, Eve, where are you? Quick.
His tread is in the Garden! hither it comes!   15
Hide us, O bushes, and ye thick trees hide[.]
He comes on, on; alack and all these leaves,
These petty quivering and illusive blinds,
Avail us nought. The light comes in and in,
Displays us to ourselves; displays, ah shame,   20
Unto the inquisitive day our nakedness.
He comes. He calls. The large eye of his truth
His full severe all comprehending view
Fixes itself upon our guiltiness –
O God, O God, what are we, what shall we be?   25
    What is all this about, I wonder now.
Yet I am better too – I think it will pass.
    'Tis going now, unless it comes again;
A terrible possession while it lasts;
Terrible surely; and yet indeed 'tis true   30
E'en in my utmost impotence I find
A fount of strange persistence in my soul
Also, and that perchance is stranger still,
A wakeful, changeless touchstone in my brain
Receiving, noting, testing all the while   35
These passing, curious, new phenomena,
Painful, and yet not painful unto it.
Though tortured in the crucible I lie
Myself my own experiment, yet still
I or a something that is I indeed,   40

2.15–21] Cp Genesis 3:6–11.
2.33–7] The serpent says to Eve: 'God doth know that in the day ye eat thereof, then your eyes shall be opened, and ye shall be as gods, knowing good and
evil' (Genesis 3:5); the Fall gives rise to knowledge.
2.38–45] Adam describes himself as his own experiment because he is observing
his own transformations and reactions from an unassailable central vantage point,
a 'living central and more inmost I' which persists in spite of these changes.

A living central and more inmost I
Within the scales of mere exterior me's,
I – seem eternal, O thou God, as thou.
Have knowledge of the Evil and the Good,
Superior in a higher Good to both.   45
    Well, well, well! it has gone from me; though still
Its images remain upon me whole:
And undisplaced upon my mind I view
The reflex of the total seizure past.
Really now, had I only time and space,   50
And were not troubled with this wife of mine,
And the necessity of meat and drink
I really do believe,
With time and space and proper quietude
I could resolve the problem on my brain   55
But no: I scarce can stay one moment more
To watch the curious seething process out.
If I could only dare to let Eve see
These operations – it is like enough
Between us two we two could make it out.   60
But she would be so frightened, think it proof
Of all her own imaginings. 'Twill not do.
So as it is
I must e'en put a cheery face on it;
Suppress the whole; rub off the unfinished thoughts   65
For fear she read them. O 'tis pity indeed
But confidence is the one and main thing now.
Who loses confidence, he loses all.
A demi-grain of cowardice in me
Avowed were poison to the whole mankind.   70
When men are plentier 'twill be time to try.
At present, no.
No.
Shake it all up and go
That is the word and that must be obeyed.   75
I must be off. But yet again some day
Again will I resume it; if not I,
I in some child of late posterity.
Yes yes, I feel it – it is here the seed
Here in my head – but O thou power unseen   80
In whom we live and move and have our being
Let it not perish – grant unlost unhurt

2.46–75] An explanation of Adam's failure to prevent 'the mighty mythus of
the fall' from hardening into historical fact for future generations.
2.81] Acts 17:28: 'For in him we live, and move, and have our being.'

In long transmission this rich atom some day
In some futurity of distant years
How many thou intend'st to have I know not   85
In some matured and procreant human brain may
Germinate, burst, and rise into a tree.
No and I don't tell Eve –

SCENE 3

'Now the birth of Cain was in this wise'
(Adam and Eve)

E: Oh Adam I am comforted indeed
Where is he[?] – O my little one –
My heart is in the garden as of old
And Paradise come back. –

A: My Eve,
Blessed be this good day to thee indeed,   5
Blessed the balm of joy unto thy soul:
A sad unskilful nurse was I to thee,
But nature teaches mothers I perceive.

E: But you my husband, you meantime I feel
Join not your perfect Spirit in my joy.   10
No: your Spirit mixes not I feel with mine.

A: Alas sweet Eve for many a weary day
You and not I have borne this heavy weight
How can I, should I, might I feel your bliss,
Now heaviness is changed to glory – long   15
In long and unparticipated pangs
Your heart hath known its own great bitterness:
How should in this its jubilant release
A stranger intermeddle with its joy[?] –

E: My husband, there is more in it than this   20
Nay you are surely positively sad.

A: What if I were (and yet I think I am not)
'Twere but the silly and contrarious mood
Of one whose sympathies refuse to mix
In aught not felt immediate from himself –   25
But of a truth –

---

3. 'Now the birth of Cain was in this wise'] Cp Matthew 1:18: 'Now the birth of
Jesus Christ was on this wise' – a hint that the New Testament's nativity sto-
ries might be as 'mythological' as the narrative of the Fall and its aftermath.

Your joy is greater, mine seems therefore none.

E: Nay neither this I think nor that is true[.]
      Evermore still you love to cheat me, Adam
      You hide from me your thoughts like evil beasts   30
      Most foolishly; for I thus left to guess,
      Catch at all hints and where perchance one is
      People the forest with an hundred ills
      Each worse perhaps an hundred times than it.
      No you have got some fearful thoughts: no no   35
      Look not in that way on my baby Adam –
      You do it harm: you shall not[.]

A: Hear then Eve
      If hear you will, and speak I think I must
      Hear me. Yet think not too much of my word.
      What is it would say – I shrink,   40
      And yet I must – so hear me, Mother blest
      That sittest with thy [nursling] at thy heart.
      Hope not too greatly neither fear for him
      Feeding on thy breast his small compressing lips.
      And glorying in the gift they draw from thee[;]   45
      Hope not too greatly in thyself and him
      And hear me O young Mother – I must speak.
      This child is born of us and therefore like us
      Is born of us and therefore is as we,
      Is born of us, and therefore is not pure,   50
      Earthy as well as godlike: bound to strive
      Not doubtfully I augur from the past
      Through the same straits of Anguish and of Doubt,
      'Mid the same storms of terror and alarm:
      To the Calm Ocean which he yet shall reach   55
      He of himself or in his sons hereafter,
      Of consummated consciousness of self.
      The selfsame stuff which wrought in us to grief
      Runs in his veins, and what to work in him?
      What shape of unsuspected deep disguise   60
      Transcending our experience our best cares
      Baffling, evading all preventive thought

3.48 et seq.] A rewriting of the doctrine of original sin; the compound nature of human life means that the Fall will inevitably repeat itself in subsequent generations. With this understanding of the Fall as an existential imperative compare Soren Kierkegaard (1964) *The Concept of Dread* (see note to 7.15–16 below).

3.57. consummated consciousness of self] The idea that complete self-consciousness represents the final stage of human development is a Hegelian one; Veyriras notes the similarities between C.'s theology and Hegel's, and argues that C. 'conceived his poem according to a Hegelian plan' – Veyriras 1964: 362.

Will the old mischief choose I wonder here[?]
O born to human trouble – also born
Else wherefore born to some [ ]   65
Live and may Chance treat thee no worse than us.
There I have done – the dangerous stuff is out
My mind is freed – And now my gentle Eve
Forgive thy foolish spouse and let me set
A father's kiss upon these budding lips   70
A husband's on the mother's, the full flower.
There – There: and so my own and only wife
Believe me, my worst thought is now to count
How best and most to serve this child and thee.

E: This child is born of us and therefore like us –   75

A: Most true, mine own and if a man like me
      Externally, internally I trust
      Most like (his best original) to thee.

E: Is born of us and therefore is not pure.

A: Did I say that[?] – I know not what I said,   80
      It was a foolish humour, but indeed
      Whatever you may think I have not learnt
      The trick of deft suppression, e'en the skill
      To sort my thoughts and sift my words enough.
      Not pure indeed; and if it is not pure   85
      What is? – Ah well, but most I look to the days
      When these small arms, with pliant thewes filled out
      Shall at my side break up the fruitful glebe
      And aid the cheery labours of the year.
      Aid or in feebler wearier years, replace   90
      And leave me longer hours for home and Eve.

SCENE 4

(Adam and Eve)

E: O Adam it was I was godless then
      [   ]

3.67–8] An allusion to the therapeutic theory of utterance; cp *Amours* V.70–1,
Dipsychus 1.1.11–15.
3.82–4] Cp 2.46–75 above.
4. After line 1] There is a large space in the MS: Eve is clearly meant to say
more. Lines 1–16 look like the opening to a scene which C. never completed;
see Scott 1981.

But you were mournful, heavy, but composed,
At times would somewhat fiercely bite your lip
And pass your hand about your brow: but still
Held out, denied not God, acknowledged still   5
Those glories that were gone. No – I never
Felt all your worth to me before. I feel
You did not fall as I did.

A: Nay, my child
About our falls I don't profess to know.
If yours indeed as you will have it so   10
Were a descent more lengthy than was mine
It is not that your place is lower now
But at the first your place was higher up[;]
I know I ne'er was innocent as thou.
It is that, I being bestial, you divine,   15
We now alike are human beings both.

Moping again my love[?] – Yes I dare swear
All the day long while I have been at work
With some religious crotchet in your head.

E: No, Adam, I am cheerful quite today   20
I vary much indeed from hour to hour –
But since my baby's birth I am happier far.
And I have done some work as well as you.

A: What is it though[?] - for I will take my oath
You've got some fancy stirring now within.   25

E: Nay but it vexes me for ever more
To find in you no credence to my thought.
You do not think then Adam
We have been disobedient to God[?]

A: My child, how should I know, and what do you mean[?]   30
Your question's not so simple as it looks.
For if you mean that God said this or that
As that You shall not touch those apples there
And that we did: – Why all that I can say
Is that I can't conceive the thing to be.   35
But if it were so, I should then believe
We had done right – at any rate no harm[.]

E: O Adam, I can scarcely think I hear –
For if God said to us, God being God,
You shall not is not His commandment His   40
And are not we the Creatures He hath made[?]

A: My child God does not speak to Human minds
       In that unmeaning arbitrary way
       God were not God, if so and Good not Good.
       Search in your heart and if you tell me there   45
       You find a genuine Voice, no fancy mind you,
       Declaring to you this or that is Evil
       Why, this or that I dare say evil is.
       Believe me I will listen to the Word.
       For not by observation of without   50
       Cometh the Kingdom of the Voice of God:
       It is within us. Let us seek it there.

E: Yet I have Voices surely in my heart.
       Often you say I heed them overmuch.

A: God's Voice is of the heart I do not say   55
       All voices therefore of the heart are God's.
       And to discern the Voice amidst the voices
       Is that hard task my love that we are born to.

E: Ah me, in me I am sure the one one Voice
       Goes somehow to the sense of what I say,   60
       The sense of disobedience to God.
       O Adam some way, some time we have done wrong
       And when I think of this, I still must think
       Of Paradise and of the stately tree
       Which in the middle of the garden grew   65
       The golden fruit that hung upon its bough.
       Of which, but once, we ate, and I must feel
       That whereas once in his continual sight
       We lived – in daily communing with Him
       We now are banished, and behold not Him.   70
       Our only present communing, alas,
       Sad penitential mourning, and the gaze
       Of the abased and prostrate prayerful soul[.]
       But you yourself, my Adam you at least
       Acknowledge some time somehow we did wrong.   75

A: My child I never granted even that.

E: Oh but you let strange words at times fall from you[.]
       They are to me like thunderbolts from Heaven

4.42–4] Adam insists that God's must be a rational service; he rejects the idea that eternal punishment might be inflicted for the breach of an apparently arbitrary rule.
4.45–8] The 'Voice' is, of course, conscience; deprived of immediate contact with God, human beings must judge their actions for themselves.
4.50–2] An anticipation of Jesus's words in Luke 17:20–1: 'The kingdom of God cometh not with observation:/ Neither shall they say, Lo here! or, lo there! for, behold, the kingdom of God is within you.'

I watch terrified and sick at heart
Then hastè and pick them up and treasure them.   80
What was it that you said when Cain was born[?]
'Is born of us and therefore is not pure'
O you corrected well my husband then
My foolish, fond exuberance of delight.

A: My child – believe me, truly I was the fool   85
But a first baby is a strange surprise[;]
I shall not say so when another comes[.]
And I beseech you treasure up no words –
You know me. I am loose of tongue and light.
I beg you Eve remember nought of this.   90
Put not at least, I pray you, nay command
Put not when days come on, your own strange whim
And misconstruction of my idle words
Into the tender brains of our poor young ones.

SCENE 5

Adam: Cain beware
Strike not your brother – I have said, beware:
A heavy curse is on this thing, my son:
With Doubt and Fear,
Terror and Toil and Pain already here   5
Let us not have injustice too, my son.
So Cain beware:
And Abel too see you provoke him not.

SCENE 6

(Abel alone)
        At times I could believe
My father is no better than his son;
If not as overbearing, proud and hard,
Yet prayerless, worldly almost more than Cain.
Enlighten and convert him ere the end   5
My God! spurn not my mother's prayer and mine.
Since I was born, was I not left to thee,
In an unspiritual and godless house
Unfathered and unbrothered; Thine and hers?

6.6] Abel continues Eve's attitude of prayerful repentance while Cain, as we
shall see, inherits his father's defiant and wilful attitude.

They think not of the Fall: e'en less they think   10
Of the Redemption, which God said should be,
Which, for we apprehend it by our faith
And by our strong assurance
Already is, is come for her and me
Yea though I sin, my sin is not to death.   15
In my repentance I have joy, such joy
That almost I could sin to seek for it.
Yea, if I did not hate it and abhor
And know that thou abhorr'st and hatest it –
And will'st for an example to the rest   20
That thine elect should keep themselves from it.
Alas. –
My mother calls the Fall a Mystery
Redemption is so too. But oh, my God,
Thou wilt bring all things in the end to good.   25
Yea, though the whole earth lie in wickedness, I
Am with thee, with thee, with thee evermore.
Ah, yet I am not satisfied with this
Am I not feeding spiritual pride
Rejoicing over sinners, inelect   30
And unadmitted to the fellowship
Which I unworthy, most unworthy share –
What can I do – how can I help it then?
O God remove it from my heart – pluck out
Whatever pain, what [wrench] to me   35
These sinful roots and remnants, which whate'er
I do, how high soe'er I soar from earth
Still, undestroyed, still germinate within.
Take them away in thy good time, O God,
Meantime for that atonement's precious sake   40
Which in thy counsels predetermined works
Already to the saving of the saints

6.11–21] Abel uses the language of Protestant theology. According to Calvin,
the French Reformer, God had chosen a certain number of souls – the 'elect' –
to be saved from the beginning of time; this position implies that actions performed during one's lifetime cannot affect one's prospects of salvation. Hence
Abel's 'assurance' that he is free to act however he chooses, even to sin.
Veyriras sees Abel as a parody of the 'arrogant humility' of contemporary
Puritanism (Veyriras 1964: 360).
6.23] See above, 1.132.
6.40–2] Jesus Christ's 'atonement' for the sins of humanity is, of course, in
the future, but Abel feels free to invoke it because it is part of God's 'predetermined' plan for humanity, and therefore capable of producing retrospective
justification for the elect.

O Father, view with Mercy and forgive –
Nor let my vexed perception of my sin,
Nor any multitude of evil thoughts   45
Crowding like demons in the [   ] house
Nor life nor death, things here or things below
Cast out the sweet assurance of my soul
That I am thine, and thou art mine, my God.

SCENE 7

(Cain alone)

Am I or am I not this which they think me[?]
My mother loves me not: my brother Abel
Spurning my heart, commends my soul to God[.]
My father does not spurn me; there's my comfort[.]
Almost I think they look askance on him –   5
Ah, but for him
I know not what might happen; for at times
Ungovernable angers take the waves
Of my deep soul and sweep them who knows whither
And a strange impulse struggling to the truth   10
Urges me onward to put forth my strength,
No matter how – Wild curiosity
Possesses me moreover to essay
This world of Action round me so unknown.
And to be able to do this or that   15
Seems cause enough, without a cause, for doing it –
My father he is cheerful and content
And leads me frankly forward – Yet, indeed,
His leading, – or (more truly) to be led
At all, by any one, and not myself   20
Is mere dissatisfaction evermore
Something I must do, individual
To vindicate my nature, to give proof
I also am, as Adam is, a man.

7.15–16] Cain is here in the state of 'dread' described by Kierkegaard, driven into action of any kind by 'the alarming possibility of *being able*' (Kierkegaard 1964: 40).

SCENE 8

Adam: These sacrificings, O my best beloved
            These rites and forms which you have taught our boys
            Which I nor practice nor can understand
            Will turn I trust to good – but I much fear,
            Besides the superstitious search of signs   5
            In merest accidents of earth and air
            They cause, I think, a sort of jealousy
            Ill blood – Hark now[!]

Eve: O God whose cry is that:
            Abel – where is my Abel[?]

A: Cain, what Cain[!]

SCENE 9

(Cain alone with the body of Abel)

What? fallen? so quickly down – so easily felled,
And so completely? Why, he does not move!
Will not he stir – will he not breathe again?
Still as a log, still as his own dead lamb –
Dead is it then? – Oh wonderful – O strange.   5
Dead – dead. And we can slay each other then?
If we are wronged, why we can right ourselves,
If we are plagued and pestered with a fool
That will not let us be, nor leave us room
To do our will and shape our path in peace,   10
We can be rid of him – There, he is gone;
Victory – Victory – Victory – My heaven
Methinks from infinite distances borne back

8.1. sacrificings] The 'sacrificings' of Cain and Abel are described in Genesis
4:3-5: 'And in process of time it came to pass, that Cain brought of the fruit of
the ground an offering unto the LORD./ And Abel, he also brought of the
firstlings of the flock and of the fat thereof. And the LORD had respect unto
Abel and to his offering:/ But unto Cain and to his offering he had not respect.
And Cain was very wroth, and his countenance fell.'
8.2] C.'s invention; there is no hint in Genesis that Eve was the progenitor of
the ritualistic aspects of the Jewish religion.
9.12–16] Cp *Amours* II.vi; this scene was in fact written on the back of a sheet
used for *Amours*, and is 'not by this mark alone to be recognized as written at
Rome' according to Mrs C. (Mulhauser 1974: 663).

It comes to me reborn in multitude,
Echoed, re-echoed, and re-echoed again.   15
Victory – Victory – distant yet distinct,
Uncountable times repeated – O ye gods
Where am I come, and whither am I borne?
    I stand upon a pinnacle of earth,
And hear the wild seas laughing all about;   20
Yet I could wish that he had struggled more –
That passiveness was disappointing. Ha!
He should have writhed and wrestled in my arms,
And all but overcome, and set his knee
Hard on my chest, till I – all faint, yet still   25
Holding my fingers at his throat – at last,
Inch after inch, had forced him to relax:
But he went down at once, without a word,
Almost without a look. –
                              Ah, hush, my God,
Who was it spoke, what is this questioner?   30
Who was it asked me where my brother is?
Ha, ha, was I his keeper? I know not!
Each for himself; he might have struck again.
Why did he not? I wished him to – was I
To strike for both at once? No! – Yet, ah   35
Where is thy brother? – Peace, thou silly Voice –
Am I my brother's keeper? – I know not,
I know not aught about it – let it be.
Henceforth I shall walk freely upon earth
And know my will and do it by my might.   40
My God – it will not be at peace – My God
It flames, it bursts to fury in my soul.
What is it I have done? – Almighty God
What is it that will come of this? –
I see it, I behold it as it is,   45
As it will be in all the times to come:
Slaughter on slaughter, blood for blood – and death
For ever ever ever evermore. –

9.19–20] Striking the pose of the Byronic hero, soaring above humanity and
defying the gods.
9.30–2] Genesis 4:9: 'And the LORD said unto Cain, Where *is* Abel thy
brother? And he said, I know not: *Am* I my brother's keeper?' Note that C.
represents this voice as an internal one; at no point in the poem does he introduce supernatural characters.
9.33. *Each for himself*] Cp *In stratis viarum* I; Cain aligns himself with the philosophy of self-gratification.

And all for what?
        O Abel, brother mine,
Where'er thou art, more happy far than me!   50

SCENE 10

Adam: Abel is dead, and Cain, ah what is Cain[?]
      Is he not even more than Abel dead[?]
      Well we must hope in Seth – this merest man
      This unambitious commonplace of life
      Will after all perhaps mend all – and though   5
      Record shall tell unto the aftertime
      No wondrous tales of him – in him at last
      And in his seed increased and multiplied,
      Earth shall be blest and peopled and subdued
      And what was meant to be be brought to pass –   10
      Ah but my Abel and my Cain, e'en so
      You shall not be forgotten nor unknown.

SCENE 11

Cain: I am come – Curse me
     Curse Cain, my Mother, ere he goes: He waits.

Eve: Who? What is this –
     Oh Abel, O my gentle, holy child,
     My perfect son   5
     Monster! and did I bear thee too –

C: He was so good, his brother hated him,
     And slew him for't – Go on my mother on[.]

E: For there are rites and holy means of grace
     Of God ordained for man's eternal [weal].   10
     With these my son address thyself to Him
     And seek atonement from a gracious God
     With whom is balm for every wounded heart[.]

C: I ask not for atonement, mother mine.

10.3. Seth] Adam's third son; see Genesis 4:25.
11. After 8] There is a large space in the MS here. Eve's words suggest that C.
might have intended her to say more at this point.

I ask but one thing – never to forget   15
I ask but – not to add to one great crime
Another, self-delusion, scarcely less.
I *could* ask more – but more I know is sin
I could ask back again
(If sacrifices and the fat of lambs   20
And whole burnt-offerings upon piles of turf
Will bring me this I'll fill the heaven with smoke,
And deface earth with million fiery scars)
I could ask back (and think it but my right,
And passionately claim it as my right)   25
That precious life which one misguided blow
Which one scarce conscious momentary [act],
One impulse blindly followed to its end
Ended – for ever – but that I know this vain.
If they shall only keep my sin in mind   30
I shall not, be assured, neglect them either.

E: You ask not for atonement – O my son,
Cain you are proud and hard of heart e'en now[.]
Beware – prostrate your soul in penitential prayer
Humble your heart beneath the mighty hand   35
Of God whose gracious guidance oft shall lead
Through sin and crime the changed and melted heart
To sweet repentance and the sense of Him.
You ask not for Atonement, O my son
What, to be banished from the sight of God   40
To dwell with wicked spirits, be a prey
To them and prey yourself on human souls
What, to be lost in wickedness and sink
Deeper and deeper down –
What Cain do you choose this[?]   45

C: Alas, my mother.
I know not – there are mysteries in your heart
Which I profess not knowledge of – it may be
That this is so; if so, may God reveal it.
Have faith you too in my heart's secrets, yea,
All I can say, alas, is that to me   50
As I now comprehend it, this were sin.

---

ll.15–17] For Cain, the 'rites and holy means of grace' designed to expunge
past actions are simply means of 'self-delusion', attempts to evade responsibili-
ty for one's own actions.
ll.35–36] Scott 1981 notes the similarity to 1 Peter 5:6.

Atonement no not that, but punishment
But what avails to talk – talk as we will
As yet, we shall not know each other's hearts[;]
Let me not talk, but act – Farewell – For ever.   55

SCENE 12

(Adam and Cain conversing)

C: This is the history then, my father, is it?
    This is the perfect whole.

A: My son, it is:
    And whether a dream, and if it were a dream
    A transcript of an inward spiritual fact
    (As you suggest, and I allow, might be)   5
    Not the less true because it was a dream.
    I know not, O my Cain, I cannot tell.
    But in my soul I think it was a dream,
    And but a dream: a thing, whence e'er it came
    To be forgotten and considered not.   10
    For what is life, and what is pain, or death?
    You have killed Abel: Abel killed the lamb.
    An act in him prepense in you unthought of.
    One step you stirred, and lo you stood entrapped.

C: My father this is true: I know: but yet   15
    There is some truth beside – I cannot say
    But I have heard within my soul a Voice
    Asking Where is thy brother and I said
    That is the evil heart within me said
    Am I my brother's keeper[?] Go ask him   20
    Who was it that provoked me: should he rail

12] The positioning of this scene is problematic; see Scott 1981.
12.1–2] Adam reveals the story of the Fall to Cain, aware now that it can do
him no further harm.
12.4–6] Even if the Fall is not factually true as an event, it might still possess
truth as the 'transcript of an inward spiritual fact', that is to say as the representation of a genuine spiritual transformation; cp C.'s notebook comment
describing Adam's story as 'a Time-Effigiation of the Untemporal Truth'
(see Headnote above).
12.13. prepense] Premeditated.
12.15–24] Cain's action, like Adam's, gives rise to the the dilemmas of moral
autonomy.

And I not smite? his death be on his head!'
But the voice answered in my soul again
So that the other ceased and was no more.

SCENE 13

Cain: Curse me my father ere I go – your curse
      Will go with me for good – your curse
      Will make me not forget – Abel is dead.

Adam: My son, 'tis done, it was to be done; some good end
        Thereby to come, or else it had not been[.]   5
        Go, for it must be, Cain – I know your heart
        You cannot be with us – Go then, depart
        But be not over-[scrupulous], my son.

C: Alas I am not of that pious kind
      Who, when the blot has fallen upon their life   10
      Can look to heaven and think it white again –
      Look up to heaven and find a something
      To make what is not be although it is[.]
      My mother – ah how you have spoke of this
      The dead – to him 'twas innocence and joy   15
      And purity and safety from the world –
      To me the thing seems sin – the worst of sin.

      If it be so – why are we here; the world,
      Why is it as I find it[?] – the dull stone
      Cast from my hand why comes it not again[?]   20
      The broken flow'ret why does it not live[?]
      Shall this be true
      Of stocks and stones and mere inanimate clay,
      And not in some sort also hold for us?
      If it be so –   25
      Why are we here and why is Abel dead[?]

13] Scott's conjectural re-ordering of the lines in Scene 13 has been adopted
here.
13.4] Cp 1.10; Adam's use of the same words he had used to Eve concerning
the Fall highlights the parallel between the two events.
13.9–11] Another rejection of the idea of atonement; see also 13.35–42.
13.18–26] Cain's line of reasoning is not altogether clear here; he seems to
suggest that the ideas of repentance and atonement, according to which
unwanted events can be erased, are false to the sequential nature of reality.

A: My son Time healeth all
       Time and great Nature heed her speech and learn –

C: My father, you are learned in this sort
       You read the Earth, as does my mother Heaven   30
       Both books are dark to me – only I feel
       That this one thing
       And this one word in me must be declared
       That to forget is not to be restored
       To lose with time the sense of what we did   35
       Cancels not that we did: what's done remains
       I am my brother's murderer – Woe to me
       Abel is dead – No prayers to empty heaven,
       No vegetative kindness of the Earth
       Will bring back into his clay again   40
       The gentleness of love into his face[.]
       Therefore for me farewell
       Farewell for me, the soft
       The balmy influences of night and sleep
       The satisfactions of achievement done   45
       The restorative pulsing of the blood
       That changes all and changes e'en the soul
       And natural functions moving as they should
       The sweet good nights – the sweet delusive dreams
       That lull us out of old things into new   50
       But welcome Fact – and fact's best brother Work
       Welcome, the conflict of the stubborn soil
       To toil the livelong day, and at its end
       Instead of rest, re-carve into my brow
       The dire memorial mark of what still is –   55
       Welcome this worship – which I feel is mine.
       Welcome this duty –
                   – the solidarity of life
       And unity of individual soul
       That which I did, I did, I who am here   60

13.28] There is a space in the MS here – judging by Cain's next speech,
Adam was clearly meant to say something about the decomposition and regeneration of organic matter at this point.
13.51] One of many such statements in C.'s work; cp e.g. *Amours* V.101–2 and
Dipsychus 2.4.159–62.
13.54–5] A reference to the mark placed upon Cain by God; Genesis 4:15.

There is no safety but in this and when
I shall deny the thing that I have done
I am a dream –

A: My son, what shall I say –
That which your soul in marriage with the world
Imbreeds in you, accept; – how can I say   65
Refuse the revelations of the soul[?]
Yet be not over scrupulous my son
And be not over proud to put aside
The due consolements of the circling years
What comes receive; be not too wise for God.   70
The Past is something, but the Present more
Will not it too be past – nor fail withal
To recognise the future in our hopes.
Unite them in your manhood each and all
Nor mutilate the perfectness of life   75
You can remember[,] you can also hope
For doubtless with the long instructive times
Comfort will come to you, my son; to me;
Even to your Mother comfort, but to us
Knowledge at least; the certainty of things,   80
Which as I think is consolation's sum.
For truly now, today, tomorrow, yes
Days many more to come alike to you
Whose earliest revelation of the world
Is, horrible indeed, this fatal fact   85
And unto me – who knowing not much before
Look gropingly and idly into this,
And recognise no figure seen before
Alike my son to me and to yourself
Much is dark now which one day will be light.   90
With strong assurance fortify your soul
Of this – and that you meet me here again
Promise me, Cain. So for five years farewell
To meet again.

13.80–1] Cp Claude's commitment to knowledge at the end of *Amours*.

SCENE 14

(Adam's Vision)

A: O Cain the words of Adam shall be said
Come near and hear your father's words my son.
I have been in the spirit, as they call it
Dreaming, as others say, which is the same.
I sat and you [were] with me Cain and Eve.   5
(We sat as in a Picture people sit
Great figures silent, with their place content.)
And Abel came and took your hand, my son,
And wept and kissed you, saying Forgive me, Cain.
Ah me, my brother, sad has been thy life,   10
For my sake, all through me – how foolishly:
Because we knew not both of us were right[.]
And you embraced and wept and we too wept[.]
Then I beheld through eyes with tears suffused,
And deemed at first 'twas blindness thence ensuing   15
Abel was gone and you were gone, my son
Gone and yet not gone – yea I seemed to see
The decomposing of those coloured lines
Which we called you – their fusion into one
And therewithal their vanishing and end.   20
And Eve said to me – Adam in the day
When in the inexistent void I heard God's Voice,
An awful whisper bidding me to be –
How sad how slow to come how loth to obey –
As slow, as sad as lingeringly loth   25
By the same sovran strong compulsion borne
I fade I vanish, sink and cease to be[.]
Ah if I vanish, be it into thee.
She spoke nor speaking ceased, I listening – but,
I was alone – yet not alone – with her   30
And she with me, and you with us, my sons,
As at the first, and yet not wholly: – yea,
And that which I had witnessed thus in you
This fusion and mutation and return
Seemed in my substance working too – I slept   35
I did not dream – my sleep was sweet to me:
Yes in despite of all disquietudes
For Eve, for you, for Abel, which indeed
Impelled in me that gaiety of soul

14.6–7] A bizarre anachronism.

Without your fears I had listened to my own   40
In spite of doubt despondency and death,
Though lacking knowledge alway, lacking faith
Sometimes, and hope; with no sure trust in aught
Except a kind of impetus within
Whose sole credentials were that trust itself   45
Life has been beautiful to me, my Son,
And I if I am called will come again.
But sleep is sweet and I would sleep, my son.
Behold, the words of Adam have an end.

Amours de Voyage

Publication: *Atlantic Monthly (AM)*, February–May 1858.

Text and MSS: There are 8 MSS: (*A*) The earliest substantial draft of the poem; it is considerably longer than the version eventually published in *AM*, and material from it was restored to the poem in 1859 Corrections. (*B*) Loose sheets containing early drafts of a number of letters, possibly composed *in situ*. (*C*) Drafts of some of the Trevellyns' letters in the 1850 (*Venice*) Notebook. *A*, *B* and *C* are located in the Bodleian Library. (*D*) The 1849 (*Roma*) Notebook in Balliol College Oxford. (*E*) A fair copy (in Mrs C.'s handwriting) entitled 'Roman Elegiacs and Roman Hexameters April to July 1849' sent by C. to C.E. Norton in 1854. This version omits the love-plot. (*F*) A fair copy of Canto I. (*G*) A draft of some letters in Canto III written on the back of an examination paper dated 1857. (*H*) The fair copies of Cantos I and II used by the *Atlantic Monthly*. *E*, *F*, *G* and *H* are located in the Houghton Library at Harvard University.

The text printed below is that of *AM*, incorporating the changes which C. made in his letters to C.E. Norton of March–April 1859 (1859 *Corrections*). Significant variants from the MSS are listed after each letter.

Historical and biographical background: C. arrived in Rome on 15 April 1849. Italy had been in a state of turmoil since the revolts of the previous year, with Piedmont and the Venetian Republic struggling unsuccessfully to retain control over the areas of northern Italy liberated from Austrian domination. Pope Pius IX, temporal ruler of the Papal States of Central Italy, had fled Rome in November 1848 amidst rising republican sentiment following his renunciation of the cause of Italian nationalism, and Mazzini had proclaimed the Roman Republic in February of the following year. When C. arrived the new Republic was generally friendless but not yet in immediate danger. He paid a visit to Mazzini on 22 April, finding him 'a less fanatical fixed-idea sort of man than I had expected'; they discussed the Republic's prospects, and Mazzini confessed that he expected it to fall in the end through foreign intervention (*PR* 147–8). His expectation was soon realised. France, increasingly alarmed at Austria's military successes in the northern campaign, decided to take the Papal States into protective custody, and landed an expeditionary force under General Oudinot at Civita Vecchia on 25 April 1849 (see II.29). C.'s account of the subsequent battle of 30 April, in which Garibaldi and his irregulars inflicted an embarrassing defeat on the French troops, was eventually transformed into letter II.v. There followed a month of negotiations, and then a renewed French assault on the night of 2–3 June. This attack was more successful than the first, and allowed the French to establish a position from which to bombard the city. The siege proper lasted until 30 June, when a final French push forced the capitulation of the Republic. The victorious French troops entered on 3 July. C. thought about leaving Rome during May and June – see below – but in the event he was forced to stay, 'le citoyen malgré lui', until 17 July. C.'s letters from Rome are in *Corr.* i, 252–68 and *PR* 144–69; there is an itinerary listing his day-to-day activities in the *Roma* Notebook, part of which is reprinted in Scott 1974: 77–8.

Claude's adventures are clearly modelled on C.'s, but should not be taken as strictly autobiographical. Attempts to find a prototype for Mary Trevellyn, in particular, have so far proved unsuccessful; Scott shows that the already-married Margaret Fuller is a very unlikely candidate (Scott 1974: 6–7). There are, however, intriguing parallels between C.'s letters and certain aspects of the poem. In a letter of 11 May to his mother C. mentions 'an acquaintance who left for Florence about a week ago' and announces his intention of going there himself. On 27 May he is still intending to go, but by 9 June there has been a change of plan: 'On Saturday I all but started for Florence, but now I think I shall stay: ultimately, whether by way of Naples, or direct, I shall go and enquire for letters there.' A few days later he changes his mind again: 'Sunday June 17th. Here still, commencing the 3rd week of our siege. But (D.V.) I shall get away on Tuesday, and abandoning all thoughts of Naples, betake myself to Florence. I wish I had done so earlier, but one thing or other withheld me.' (All quotations from unpublished letters in Bod. MS Eng. Lett. d.176.) When C. eventually left Rome on 17 July, however, he headed not for Florence but for Naples, and returned home to England via Genoa, Turin and Geneva. This hesitation about whether or not to go to Florence parallels Claude's behaviour in Cantos III and IV, but C.'s letters give no definite clues about the motivation behind it. He mentions, in passing, the wife and daughter of Bishop Jonathan Wainwright of Trinity Church, New York, who stayed in the same lodgings as him during his first few weeks in the city, but there is no direct evidence in the letters that the Wainwrights visited Florence during May–June 1849.

Others have suggested that *Amours* might be based on one of Matthew Arnold's unsuccessful amorous liaisons rather than one of C.'s. This speculation was prompted by Park Honan's argument that the original of Arnold's 'Marguerite' was a Lakeland neighbour called Mary Claude. For a thorough discussion of the evidence see Eugene R. August, '*Amours de Voyage* and Matthew Arnold in Love: An Inquiry', *Victorian Newsletter* 60 (1981): 15–20. An interesting comparative study of *Amours* and Arnold's 'Marguerite' lyrics is provided by Patricia M. Ball (1976) *The Heart's Events* (Athlone Press), ch. 2.

Literary Antecedents: There is no direct precedent in English poetry for *Amours de Voyage*'s eclectic mixture of styles and genres; it is a hybrid of ancient and modern, formal and colloquial, poem and novel. Clough employs the hexameter, the epic metre of Latin and Greek poetry, but does so in a loose, irregular way which emphasises the impossibility of 'translating' ancient into modern in any simple way. Moreover, he divides his classical verses into the 'cantos' used by the Christian epic poets of medieval Italy, thereby echoing in the poem's form Rome's incongruous combination of Christian and Pagan elements. The idea of combining poetry with the newly hegemonic literary form of the novel was one which appealed to several poets in the 1850s; Tennyson's *Maud* (1854) and Elizabeth Barrett Browning's *Aurora Leigh* (1856) are comparable attempts to fuse the narrative interest and contemporary relevance of the novel with the lyric intensity of poetry. Clough's employment of the epistolary form for this venture is, however, unique, and might possibly owe something to his small part in helping his friend Richard Monckton Milnes prepare the first edition of Keats's *Life, Letters and Literary Remains* in 1848 (see esp. III.vi below and notes).

Perhaps the closest thing to a direct precursor for *Amours* (as for so much else in nineteenth-century poetry) is Byron's *Childe Harold's Pilgrimage*, especially the fourth canto of that poem. Like Byron's hero, Claude combines personal reflections with musings on human history prompted by his presence in the consecrated landscapes of ancient Rome. The relation between the two poems is, however, an ironic and unstable one. Claude's hesitations and uncertainties can be seen as the kind of bathetic re-enactment of Byron's feats appropriate to 'feeble and restless youths born to inglorious days', but the irony works both ways; Claude's retreat from the Romantic ideals of love and action helps to puncture the rhetorical inflation of Byron's heroic poses.

OH, you are sick of self-love, Malvolio,
And taste with a distempered appetite! – SHAKSPEARE.

Il doutait de tout, même de l'amour. – FRENCH NOVEL.

Solvitur ambulando. – SOLUTIO SOPHISMATUM.

Flevit amores
Non elaboratum ad pedem. – HORACE.

Mottoes: 1. *Twelfth Night* I.v.89–90. 2. 'He doubted everything, even love' – source unknown. 3. 'It is solved by walking' – SOPHISTICAL SOLUTION. 4. 'Anacreon, who very often/ *in simple metres deplored his love*' – Horace, *Epodes* 14.10–11. C. misquotes 'amorem' as plural 'amores' to fit his title.

MS *A* suggests three further possibilities: 1. 'Nor digger him the gods had made, nor ploughman,/ Nor wise in aught beside' – attributed to Homer's lost *Margites* in Aristotle's *Ethics*, p. 211. 2. 'What you are looking for all the time is something that is, I should say, outside the range of ordinary experience, and yet you cannot even think straight about the facts of life that are before you' – from Cleon's ultrapragmatic speech on the revolt of the Mytilenians in Thucydides, *The Peloponnesian War*, p. 182. 3. 'He who despairs of himself is mad – Anglo-Saxon Proverb' (C.'s translation and attribution).

I.

Over the great windy waters, and over the clear crested summits,
  Unto the sun and the sky, and unto the perfecter earth,
Come, let us go, – to a land wherein gods of the old time wandered,
  Where every breath even now changes to ether divine.
Come, let us go; though withal a voice whisper, 'The world that
    we live in,   5
  Whithersoever we turn, still is the same narrow crib;
'Tis but to prove limitation, and measure a cord, that we travel;
  Let who would 'scape and be free go to his chamber and think;
'Tis but to change idle fancies for memories wilfully falser;
  'Tis but to go and have been.' – Come, little bark, let us go!   10

I. – CLAUDE TO EUSTACE.

DEAR EUSTATIO, I write that you may write me an
    answer,
Or at the least to put us again *en rapport* with each other.
Rome disappoints me much, – St. Peter's, perhaps, in
    especial;
Only the Arch of Titus and view from the Lateran please me:
This, however, perhaps, is the weather, which truly is horrid. 15
Greece must be better, surely; and yet I am feeling so spiteful,

5–10] These sentiments recall Horace's 'Coelum non animum mutant qui
trans mare currunt' – *Epistles* 1.11.27.
11–12] Cp C.'s remark in a letter of 26 May 1848 to A.P. Stanley: 'I suppose
after writing 2 letters one begins to desire an assurance of the existence of one's
(titular?) correspondent' – *Corr.* i, 210. Unanswered or unacknowledged letters
are seen by both C. and Claude as a form of self-communion analogous to
prayer or confession: 'What is the meaning of Prayer . . . Is it to obtain juxtaposition – en rapportite with – a Vacuum? –' (*Roma* Notebook f 38v). See also
V.vi below.
13] Disappointment with St Peter's had become proverbial in the early nineteenth century; see e.g. *Childe Harold's Pilgrimage* IV, stanzas 153–9, and
Thomas Arnold's *Introductory Lectures on Modern History* (Arnold 1842: 1).
14] '*Arch of Titus*, erected by the Senate and people in honour of Titus, to
commemorate the conquest of Jerusalem. It is the most elegant of all the tri-
umphal arches, and as a record of Scripture history is, beyond all doubt, the
most interesting ruin in Rome' (Murray 1843: 304).
14] The Lateran (Palazzo del Laterano) is the seat of the Roman Vicariate; it
adjoins the cathedral of St John Lateran.

That I could travel to Athens, to Delphi, and Troy, and
    Mount Sinai,
Though but to see with my eyes that these are vanity also.

Rome disappoints me much; I hardly as yet understand, but
Rubbishy seems the word that most exactly would suit it.   20
All the foolish destructions, and all the sillier savings,
All the incongruous things of past incompatible ages,
Seem to be treasured up here to make fools of present and
    future.
Would to Heaven the old Goths had made a cleaner sweep
    of it!
Would to Heaven some new ones would come and destroy
    these churches!   25
However, one can live in Rome as also in London.
Rome is better than London, because it is other than London.
It is a blessing, no doubt, to be rid, at least for a time, of
All one's friends and relations, – yourself (forgive me!)
    included, –
All the *assujettissement* of having been what one has been,   30
What one thinks one is, or thinks that others suppose one;
Yet, in despite of all, we turn like fools to the English.
Vernon has been my fate; who is here the same that you
    knew him, –
Making the tour, it seems, with friends of the name of
    Trevellyn.

17] A telescoped journey into ever-more ancient cultures; Delphi was the site
of the most famous oracle in ancient Greece, Troy the location for Homer's
Iliad, and Mount Sinai the place where Moses received the Ten
Commandments from God.
18] Cp Ecclesiastes 1:14: 'I have seen all the works that are done under the
sun; and, behold, all *is* vanity and vexation of spirit'; and *Hamlet* I.ii.133–4:
'How weary, stale, flat, and unprofitable/ Seem to me all the uses of this
world!'
24. old Goths] The Germanic tribe which sacked Rome in AD 410.
30. assujettissement] Constraint, subjection.
34] The choice of Trevellyn for the family's surname seems to lend support to
the idea that *Amours* contains allusions to Matthew Arnold's failed romance
with Mary Claude; Matthew Arnold's mother's maiden name was Trevenen
(see Headnote).

II. – Claude to Eustace.

ROME disappoints me still; but I shrink and adapt
    myself to it.   35
Somehow a tyrannous sense of a superincumbent oppression
Still, wherever I go, accompanies ever, and makes me
Feel like a tree (shall I say?) buried under a ruin of
    brick-work.
Rome, believe me, my friend, is like its own Monte Testaceo,
Merely a marvellous mass of broken and castaway wine-pots.   40
Ye gods! what do I want with this rubbish of ages departed,
Things that Nature abhors, the experiments that she has
    failed in?
What do I find in the Forum? An archway and two or
    three pillars.
Well, but St. Peter's? Alas, Bernini has filled it with
    sculpture!
No-one can cavil, I grant, at the size of the great Coliseum.   45
Doubtless the notion of grand and capacious and massive
    amusement,
This the old Romans had; but tell me, is this an idea?
Yet of solidity much, but of splendour little is extant:
'Brickwork I found thee, and marble I left thee!' their
    Emperor vaunted;
'Marble I thought thee, and brickwork I find thee!' the
    Tourist may answer.   50

III. – Georgina Trevellyn to Louisa ——.

AT last, dearest Louisa, I take up my pen to address you.
Here we are, you see, with the seven-and-seventy boxes,

---

44. Bernini] Gian Lorenzo Bernini (1598–1680), the sculptor charged with the decoration of the interior of St Peter's, whose baroque flourishes are deprecated by the austere Claude. Murray shares Claude's opinion, describing the statues as 'unworthy of St. Peter's': 'Many of them are deformed by allegorical figures in the worst style of the school of Bernini, and are entirely beneath criticism' (Murray 1843: 341).

47] Claude is here invoking the Platonic sense of 'Idea' (revived by nineteenth-century idealist philosophers); the Idea is the perfect and rational form imperfectly expressed in contingent reality.

49] The boast of the Emperor Augustus: '[He] so beautified [Rome] that he could justly boast that he had found it built of brick and left it in marble' (Suetonius, *Lives of the Caesars*, p. 167).

Courier, Papa and Mamma, the children, and Mary and
    Susan:
Here we all are at Rome, and delighted of course with St.
    Peter's,
And very pleasantly lodged in the famous Piazza di Spagna.   55
Rome is a wonderful place, but Mary shall tell you about it;
Not very gay, however; the English are mostly at Naples;
There are the A.s, we hear, and most of the W. party.
George, however, is come; did I tell you about his
    mustachios?
Dear, I must really stop, for the carriage, they tell me, is
    waiting.   60
Mary will finish; and Susan is writing, they say, to Sophia.
Adieu, dearest Louise, – evermore your faithful Georgina.
Who can a Mr. Claude be whom George has taken to be
    with?
Very stupid, I think, but George says so *very* clever.

IV. – CLAUDE TO EUSTACE.

NO, the Christian faith, as at any rate I understood it,   65
With its humiliations and exaltations combining,
Exaltations sublime, and yet diviner abasements,
Aspirations from something most shameful here upon
    earth and
In our poor selves to something most perfect above in
    the heavens, –
No, the Christian faith, as I, at least, understood it,   70
Is not here, O Rome, in any of these thy churches;

54] See above I.13 and note.
55] The Piazza di Spagna was a notorious haunt of the English in the nine-teenth century (see Varriano 1991: 139).
57] The first hint of the impending conflict; C. remarked to Palgrave soon after his arrival that 'the wicked mistrustful English' were 'all at Naples' (Bod. MS Eng. Lett. d. 176).
I.iv] This letter alludes to the contemporary polemic on the true nature of Christian architecture, inaugurated in England by A.W.N. Pugin, who argued that '*pointed* [i.e. Gothic] *architecture was produced by the Catholic faith,* and . . . destroyed in England by the ascendancy of Protestantism' (Pugin 1841: iii–v). Ruskin, in turn, suggested that Gothic architecture exhibited 'Christian humility', raising up 'a stately and unaccusable whole' from 'fragments full of imperfection', and denied the title of Christian edifices to the neo-classical churches of the Renaissance – Ruskin 1975: 10.

Is not here, but in Freiberg, or Rheims, or Westminster
    Abbey.
What in thy Dome I find, in all thy recenter efforts,[1]
Is a something, I think, more *rational* far, more earthly,
Actual, less ideal, devout not in scorn and refusal,   75
But in a positive, calm, Stoic-Epicurean acceptance.[2]
This I begin to detect in St. Peter's and some of the
    churches,
Mostly in all that I see of the sixteenth-century masters;
Overlaid of course with infinite gauds and gewgaws,
Innocent, playful follies, the toys and trinkets of childhood,   80
Forced on maturer years, as the serious one thing needful,
By the barbarian will of the rigid and ignorant Spaniard.
    Curious work, meantime, re-entering society: how we

72. *Freiberg, or Rheims]* Cities in which pre-eminent examples of Gothic architecture can be found.

73–8] Claude accepts the equation between Gothic architecture and Christian humility, but inverts its significance; the 'humiliations and exaltations' of Gothic are contrasted, seemingly to their detriment, with the '*rational*' and 'calm' character of classically inspired buildings. (Cp the cancelled line 77 given below.) C. suggested in a letter to Tom Arnold that Michelangelo rejected Gothic forms in the design of St Peter's because he wanted to '[assert] totality' – *Corr.* i, 256.

76] Stoicism is a doctrine of austere impassivity before pleasure and pain, Epicureanism a recommendation to live for the present moment; both are predicated on an acceptance of the present life as the only one. Interest in these two philosophical and ethical systems grew steadily throughout the nineteenth century as people sought a form of belief which could replace dogmatic Christianity; see, e.g. Matthew Arnold's essay 'Marcus Aurelius' in 1865 *Essays in Criticism* and Walter Pater's 1885 *Marius the Epicurean.*

79] *Gauds* are the large ornamental beads used in some forms of Catholic worship; *gewgaws* are worthless toys or baubles.

81. one thing needful] Luke 10:42; changed to 'one thing essential' in *AM* to avoid upsetting the religious sensibilities of the New England readers, and changed back by C. in his final emendations. Cp Matthew Arnold's use of the phrase in the fifth chapter of 1869 *Culture and Anarchy*, entitled 'Porro unum est necessarium'.

82. the rigid and ignorant Spaniard] Claude is here lamenting the whole range of Spanish cultural impositions on Italy during the period of the Counter-Reformation; see also the next letter below.

83–6] These lines were restored to the poem by 1859 *Corrections*; cp Emerson, 'Self-Reliance': 'With consistency a great soul has simply nothing to do. He may as well concern himself with his shadow on the wall' – Emerson 1984: 37.

---

[1] After 73: All thine unperverted and purely natural doings (*A E F*)

[2] After 76: Not to the infinite straining, but resting in finite completeness (*A E*)

Walk a live-long day, great Heaven, and watch our shadows!
What our shadows seem, forsooth we will ourselves be.   85
Do I look like that? you think me that: then I am that.

V. – CLAUDE TO EUSTACE.

LUTHER, they say, was unwise; like a half-taught
    German, he could not
See that old follies were passing most tranquilly out of
    remembrance;
Leo the Tenth was employing all efforts to clear out abuses;
Jupiter, Juno, and Venus, Fine Arts, and Fine Letters, the
    Poets,   90
Scholars, and Sculptors, and Painters, were quietly clearing
    away the
Martyrs, and Virgins, and Saints, or at any rate Thomas
    Aquinas:
He must forsooth make a fuss and distend his huge
    Wittenberg lungs, and
Bring back Theology once yet again in a flood upon Europe:
Lo you, for forty days from the windows of heaven it fell;
    the   95
Waters prevail on the earth yet more for a hundred and fifty;
Are they abating at last? the doves that are sent to explore
    are
Wearily fain to return, at the best with a leaflet of
    promise, –
Fain to return, as they went, to the wandering wave-tost
    vessel, –
Fain to re-enter the roof which covers the clean and the
    unclean –   100
Luther, they say, was unwise; he didn't see how things
    were going;

---

89. *Leo the Tenth]* The great Renaissance Pope (1513–21) under whose patronage many of the finest works of Italian art and architecture were produced.

92. *Thomas Aquinas]* The thirteenth-century theologian whose incorporation of Aristotelian metaphysics into Christian thinking laid the foundation for the subsequent development of scholastic theology.

95–100] This passage comparing the theological polemic generated by the Reformation to the Flood includes phrases from Genesis 7:11–12, 7:24, 8:8 and 8:11.

Luther was foolish, – but, O great God! what call you
    Ignatius?
O my tolerant soul, be still! but you talk of barbarians,
Alaric, Attila, Genseric; – why they came, they killed, they
Ravaged, and went on their way; but these vile, tyrannous
    Spaniards,   105
These are here still, – how long, O ye Heavens, in the
    country of Dante?
These, that fanaticized Europe, which now can forget
    them, release not
This, their choicest of prey, this Italy; here you see them, –
Here, with emasculate pupils and gimcrack churches of
    Gesu,
Pseudo-learning and lies, confessional-boxes and
    postures, –   110
Here, with metallic beliefs and regimental devotions, –
Here, overcrusting with slime, perverting, defacing,
    debasing,
Michael Angelo's dome, that had hung the Pantheon in
    heaven,
Raphael's Joys and Graces, and thy clear stars, Galileo!

---

102. Ignatius] Ignatius Loyola (1491–1556) was the Spanish founder of the Jesuit order which led the Counter-Reformation, the Catholic Church's fightback against the Protestant Reformation. The Oxford Movement was often compared to the Counter-Reformation during the nineteenth century; see, e.g., Pattison 1885: 61, and 'The Oxford Counter-Reformation' in Froude 1899, vol. iv.

104. Alaric, Attila, Genseric] Leaders of the Goths, Huns and Vandals respectively, Germanic tribes which sacked Rome in the fifth century AD. Claude is alluding here to the sack of Rome in 1527, at the height of the Renaissance, carried out by German mercenary troops under the auspices of the Spanish Emperor Charles V; his point is that this sack was followed by a Spanish cultural colonisation of Rome which still continues.

109. gimcrack churches of Gesu] The Gesù is the principal Jesuit church in Rome, containing the altar-tomb of Ignatius Loyola; it epitomises the Baroque style associated with the Counter-Reformation.

110–11] A fairly common view of Catholic ritual in the early nineteenth century; cp Browning, 'The Bishop orders his tomb at St Praxed's Church'.

113] When Michael Angelo took over the building of St Peter's he declared 'that he would raise the Pantheon in the air'; Murray 1843: 335.

VI. – CLAUDE TO EUSTACE.

WHICH of the three Misses Trevellyn it is that
    Vernon shall marry   115
Is not a thing to be known; for our friend is one of those
    natures
Which have their perfect delight in the general tender-
    domestic,
So that he trifles with Mary's shawl, ties Susan's bonnet,
Dances with all, but at home is most, they say, with
    Georgina,
Who is, however, *too* silly in my apprehension for Vernon.   120
I, as before when I wrote, continue to see them a little;
Not that I like them much, or care a *bajocco* for Vernon,
But I am slow at Italian, have not many English
    acquaintance,
And I am asked, in short, and am not good at excuses.
Middle-class people these, bankers very likely, not wholly   125
Pure of the taint of the shop; will at table d'hôte and
    restaurant
Have their shilling's worth, their penny's pennyworth even:
Neither man's aristocracy this, nor God's, God knoweth!
Yet they are fairly descended, they give you to know, well
    connected;
Doubtless somewhere in some neighbourhood have, and
    careful to keep, some   130
Threadbare-genteel relations, who in their turn are
    enchanted
Grandly among county people to introduce at assemblies
To the unpennied cadets our cousins with excellent
    fortunes.
Neither man's aristocracy this, nor God's, God knoweth!

---

122. bajocco] A *baiocco* was a coin of very small value in circulation in the Papal states; 'non vale un baiocco' was a proverbial expression for something worthless.
128] A Carlylean expression; Claude's disdain for the commercial middle classes clearly owes a good deal to Carlyle – see, e.g. 1843 *Past and Present*, Bk 1, ch. 5.
133. cadets] A cadet is the younger son of an aristocratic family (and therefore, under English laws of primogeniture, generally 'unpennied').

VII. – CLAUDE TO EUSTACE.

AH, what a shame, indeed, to abuse these most worthy
    people!   135
Ah, what a sin to have sneered at their innocent rustic
    pretensions!
Is it not laudable really, this reverent worship of station?
Is it not fitting that wealth should tender this hômage to
    culture?[3]
Is it not touching to witness these efforts, if little availing,
Painfully made, to perform the old ritual service of
    manners?   140
Shall not devotion atone for the absence of knowledge?
    and fervour
Palliate, cover, the fault of a superstitious observance?
Dear, dear, what do I say? but, alas, just now, like Iago,
I can be nothing at all, if it is not critical wholly;
So in fantastic height, in coxcomb exaltation,[4]   145

I.vii] Throughout this letter Claude plays on the social differences between
himself and the Trevellyns; their middle-class 'wealth' recognises in his aristocratic 'culture' its natural superior, and clumsily attempts to offer the requisite
deference.
140. the old ritual service of manners] By 'manners' Claude means social etiquette; cp Georgina's description of Claude below as 'an awkward youth, but
still with very good manners' (I.256), and *Dipsychus* 4.101–2.
141–2] Claude picks up the ecclesiastical connotations of the phrase 'ritual
service of manners' and expands on them, employing a panoply of theological
terms; the worship which he imagines the Trevellyns to be offering him is
'superstitious' because it is not founded on a correct apprehension of the object
of worship, but it can nevertheless be accepted because its 'fervour' and 'devotion' atone for this fault. The underlying comparison is with a Dissenting
family attempting to embrace High Anglicanism. The lines after 138 in *A*,
which were cancelled by Lowell, editor of the *Atlantic Monthly*, for fear of
offending his readers, continue this line of thought by parodying Isaiah 1:13;
the Trevellyns' 'offering' is not a 'vain oblation' or an 'abomination'.
143–4] Cp Iago's comment to Desdemona: 'I am nothing, if not critical';
Othello II.i.19.
145. coxcomb] A fool or fop.

---

[3] After 138:
    No! the Music, the cards, and the tea so genteel and insipid
    Are not, believe me, I think it, no, are not vain oblations;
    One can endure their whist, their assemblies one can away with,
    No, and it is not iniquity, even the solemn meeting. (*A*)
[4] Alt.: Yes, in artistic height, in coxcomb exaltation (*A*)

Here in the Garden I walk, can freely concede to the Maker
That the works of his hand are all very good: his creatures,
Beast of the field and fowl, he brings them before me;
    I name them;
That which I name them, they are, – the bird, the beast,
    and the cattle.
But for Adam, – alas, poor critical coxcomb Adam!   150
But for Adam there is not found an help-meet for him.

VIII. – CLAUDE TO EUSTACE.

NO, great Dome of Agrippa, thou art not Christian!
    canst not,
Strip and replaster and daub and do what they will with
    thee, be so!
Here underneath the great porch of colossal Corinthian
    columns,
Here as I walk, do I dream of the Christian belfries above
    them?   155
Or on a bench as I sit and abide for long hours, till thy
    whole vast

146–51] Genesis 2:19–20; on the significance of the prelapsarian state in C.'s poetry see Introduction.

I.viii] Claude again takes up the question of the relation between Christian and Pagan aspects of Rome. The Pantheon – 'great Dome of Agrippa' – was transformed into the Christian church of *Santa Maria Rotonda* or *ad Martyres* in AD 609; Murray notes that '[it] passed with little alteration from the Pagan into the present worship; and so convenient were its niches for the Christian altar, that Michael Angelo, ever studious of ancient beauty, introduced their design as a model in the Catholic church'; Murray 1843: 286. With the sentiment expressed in this letter and x below cp Froude 1838: i, 298–9: '[The] thing which most takes possession of one's mind [in Rome] is the entire absorption of the old Roman splendour in an unthought-of system; to see their columns, and marbles, and bronzes, which had been brought together at such an immense cost, all diverted from their first objects, and taken up by Christianity; St. Peter and St. Paul standing at the top of Trajan's and Antonine's columns, and St. Peter buried in the circus of Nero, with all the splendour of Rome concentrated in his mausoleum!'

154. Corinthian columns] The Corinthian is the latest and most highly decorated of the three orders of classical architecture.

155. the Christian belfries] 'The tasteless belfries which deform the portico were added by Bernini, at the command of Urban VIII, and are in every way worthy of a Pope who plundered the ruin of its ornaments' – Murray 1843: 287; these 'ass-ears of Bernini', as they were popularly known, were eventually removed in 1883.

Round grows dim as in dreams to my eyes, I repeople thy
    niches,
Not with the Martyrs, and Saints, and Confessors, and
    Virgins, and children,
But with the mightier forms of an older, austerer worship;
And I recite to myself, how   160
                Eager for battle here
Stood Vulcan, here matronal Juno,
    And with the bow to his shoulder faithful
He who with pure dew laveth of Castaly
His flowing locks, who holdeth of Lycia   165
The oak forest and the wood that bore him,
    Delos and Patara's own Apollo.*

         *Hic avidus stetit
Vulcanus, hic matrona Juno, et
    Nunquam humero positurus arcum,
Qui rore puro Castaliae lavat
Crines solutos, qui Lyciae tenet
Dumeta natalemque sylvam,
    Delius et Patareus Apollo.

IX. – CLAUDE TO EUSTACE.

YET it is pleasant, I own it, to be in their company;
    pleasant,
Whatever else it may be, to abide in the feminine presence.
Pleasant, but wrong, will you say? But this happy, serene
    coexistence   170
Is to some poor soft souls, I fear, a necessity simple,
Meat and drink and life, and music, filling with sweetness,
Thrilling with melody sweet, with harmonies strange
    overwhelming,
All the long-silent strings of an awkward, meaningless
    fabric.
Yet as for that, I could live, I believe, with children; to
    have those   175
Pure and delicate forms encompassing, moving about you,
This were enough, I could think; and truly with glad
    resignation

161–7] Horace, *Odes* 3.4.58–64, cited below by C.
172–4] Cp the image of the two musics in 'Why should I say' above, p. 41.
177] Claude's desire for 'resignation' could be a delicate allusion to Matthew
Arnold's poem of the same name; see Headnote.

Could from the dream of romance, from the fever of
    flushed adolescence,
Look to escape and subside into peaceful avuncular
    functions.
Nephews and nieces! alas, for as yet I have none! and,
    moreover,   180
Mothers are jealous, I fear me, too often, too rightfully;
    fathers
Think they have title exclusive to spoiling their own little
    darlings;
And by the law of the land, in despite of Malthusian
    doctrine,
No sort of proper provision is made for that most patriotic,
Most meritorious subject, the childless and bachelor uncle.   185

X. – CLAUDE TO EUSTACE.

YE, too, marvellous Twain, that erect on the Monte
    Cavallo
Stand by your rearing steeds in the grace of your
    motionless movement,
Stand with your upstretched arms and tranquil regardant
    faces,
Stand as instinct with life in the might of immutable
    manhood, –
O ye mighty and strange, ye ancient divine ones of Hellas,   190
Are ye Christian too? to convert and redeem and renew you,
Will the brief form have sufficed, that a Pope has set up on
    the apex

---

183. Malthusian doctrine] In his 1802 *Essay on the Principle of Population* the
Rev. Thomas Malthus argued that the rate of population growth would, if left
unchecked, always exceed the rate of growth of production; his arguments
were taken up by the Benthamites and used to justify the institution of the
workhouse.
I.x] 'The obelisk of the Monte Cavallo*, erected in 1786 by Antinori . . . [was]
brought from Egypt by Claudius, A.D. 57. [. . .] At the sides of this obelisk
stand the colossal equestrian group which have been called Castor and Pollux
by recent antiquaries. They are undoubtedly of Grecian workmanship' –
Murray 1843: 328. The Monte Cavallo is an alternative name for the Piazza del
Quirinale.
190. Hellas] Greece (see above).

Of the Egyptian stone that o'ertops you, the Christian
    symbol?
And ye, silent, supreme in serene and victorious marble,
Ye that encircle the walls of the stately Vatican chambers,   195
Juno and Ceres, Minerva, Apollo, the Muses and Bacchus,
Ye unto whom far and near come posting the Christian
    pilgrims,
Ye that are ranged in the halls of the mystic Christian
    pontiff,
Are ye also baptized? are ye of the Kingdom of Heaven?
Utter, O some one, the word that shall reconcile Ancient
    and Modern!   200
Am I to turn me for this unto thee, great Chapel of Sixtus?

XI. – CLAUDE TO EUSTACE.

THESE are the facts. The uncle, the elder brother, the
    squire, (a
Little embarrassed, I fancy,) resides in a family place in
Cornwall, of course; "Papa is in business," Mary informs
    me;
He's a good sensible man, whatever his trade is. The
    mother   205
Is – shall I call it fine? – herself she would tell you refined,
    and
Greatly, I fear me, looks down on my bookish and
    maladroit manners;
Somewhat affecteth the blue; would talk to me often of
    poets;
Quotes, which I hate, Childe Harold; but also appreciates
    Wordsworth;

---

193. the Christian symbol] Many of the obelisks in Rome have Christian symbols (crosses and orbs) placed on top of them; Claude is questioning the effectiveness of this act of cultural appropriation.
198. the mystic Christian Pontiff] The Popes assumed the title of 'Pontifex Maximus' from their pagan precursors; Claude's use of this title serves yet again to emphasise the Catholic Church's indebtedness to pre-Christian practices.
201. Chapel of Sixtus] The Sistine Chapel.
204. Cornwall, of course] Trevellyn is a recognisably Cornish surname.
208. affecteth the blue] A 'blue stocking' is a female intellectual – usually (as here) a pejorative term.

Sometimes adventures on Schiller; and then to religion
    diverges;   210
Questions me much about Oxford; and yet, in her loftiest
    flights, still[5]
Grates the fastidious ear with the slightly mercantile accent.
Is it contemptible, Eustace, – I'm perfectly ready to think
    so, –
Is it, – the horrible pleasure of pleasing inferior people?[6]
I am ashamed my own self; and yet true it is, if disgraceful,   215
That for the first time in life I am living and moving with
    freedom.
I, who never could talk to the people I meet with my
    uncle, –
I, who have always failed, – I, trust me, can suit the
    Trevellyns;
I, believe me, – great conquest, – am liked by the country
    bankers.
And I am glad to be liked, and like in return very kindly.   220

209–10] Mrs Trevellyn's list of enthusiasms wins Claude's partial approval. Byron had been out of fashion among the literary avant-garde since Carlyle's Teufelsdrockh had issued the following injunction to his contemporaries: 'Close thy *Byron*; open thy *Goethe*' (1838 *Sartor Resartus,* Bk 2, ch. 9). Wordsworth, in contrast, had become a revered figure, especially at the universities. The mention of Schiller indicates Mrs Trevellyn's desire to keep up with the newly fashionable literature of Germany, cheap translations of which began to appear during the 1840s.

211. Questions me much about Oxford] The questions about Oxford refer, as the cancelled lines after 211 indicate, to the fall-out from Newman's defection to Rome in 1845 (see also *When Israel came out of Egypt* above, pp. 36–9 and notes).

213–14] C. voiced similar sentiments on finding himself in the predominantly middle-class *milieu* of University Hall: 'There is a great blessing I sometimes think in being set down amongst uncongenial people' – *Corr.* i, 279.

---

5 Alt. to 211:
    Questions me much about Newman, deplores so extremely, &c,
    She had admired so devoutly – and yet in her loftiest flights still (*A*)
6 Alt. to 213–14:
    Ah, I despise myself, Eustace, and feel it is greatly the mean and
    Dirty ignoble pleasure of being a god to small people. (*A*)

So it proceeds; *Laissez faire, laissez aller,* – such is the
 watchword.
Well, I know there are thousands as pretty and hundreds
 as pleasant,
Girls by the dozen as good, and girls in abundance with
 polish
Higher and manners more perfect than Susan or Mary
 Trevellyn.
Well, I know, after all, it is only juxtaposition, –   225
Juxtaposition, in short; and what is juxtaposition?

XII. – CLAUDE TO EUSTACE.

BUT I am in for it now, – *laissez faire,* of a truth,
 laissez aller.
Yes, I am going, – I feel it, I feel and cannot recall it, –
Fusing with this thing and that, entering into all sorts of
 relations,
Tying I know not what ties, which, whatever they are,
 I know one thing,   230
Will, and must, woe is me, be one day painfully broken, –
Broken with painful remorses, with shrinkings of soul,
 and relentings,
Foolish delays, more foolish evasions, most foolish
 renewals.
But I have made the step, have quitted the ship of
 Ulysses,
Quitted the sea and the shore, passed into the magical
 island;   235

221. Laissez faire, laissez aller] 'Let things go or happen as they will' – a
watchword of contemporary economic doctrine among the anti-protectionists,
here used ironically by Claude.
225–6] On juxtaposition and affinity, see Introduction, p. 151.
I.xii] Claude realises that he is about to enter the enchanted realm of passion,
but is determined to retain his knowledge in order to prevent his descent into
action from leading to unforeseen consequences.
227–33] The rule for preventing the 'lower kind of juxtaposition' from
becoming permanent is 'to check or suppress inferior vital effluxes – and coa-
lescences – combinations' (*Roma* Notebook).
234–6] Claude compares his situation to that of Ulysses; he is entering the
enchanted realm of passion, the island of Circe, but he has with him the '*moly*'
or secret antidote which will enable him to resist its blandishments' (see
Odyssey, Bk 10).

Yet on my lips is the *moly*, medicinal, offered of Hermes.
I have come into the precinct, the labyrinth closes around
    me,
Path into path rounding slyly; I pace slowly on, and the
    fancy,
Struggling awhile to sustain the long sequences, weary,
    bewildered,
Fain must collapse in despair; I yield, I am lost, and know
    nothing;   240
Yet in my bosom unbroken remaineth the clue; I shall use
    it.
Lo, with the rope on my loins I descend through the
    fissure; I sink, yet
Inly secure in the strength of invisible arms up above me;
Still, wheresoever I swing, wherever to shore, or to shelf,
    or
Floor of cavern untrodden, shell-sprinkled, enchanting,
    I know I   245
Yet shall one time feel the strong cord tighten about me, –
Feel it, relentless, upbear me from spots I would rest in;
    and though the
Rope sway wildly, I faint, crags wound me, from crag unto
    crag re-
Bounding, or, wide in the void, I die ten deaths, ere the
    end I
Yet shall plant firm foot on the broad lofty spaces I quit,
    shall   250
Feel underneath me again the great massy strengths of
    abstraction,
Look yet abroad from the height o'er the sea whose salt
    wave I have tasted.

237–41] An alternative figure for his predicament; Theseus enabled himself to
escape from the labyrinth of the Minotaur by unwinding a thread as he
entered.
242–52] The sexual implications of Claude's language of '[descending]
through the fissure' are quite obvious to the post-Freudian reader, and highlight the role of sexual intercourse in C.'s thought as an emblem of the Fall
from innocence into experience; see Introduction, p. 14.
251. the great massy strengths of abstraction] Claude's commitment to 'abstraction', the life of the mind, constitutes the 'clue' which, he hopes, will
eventually rescue him from the labyrinth of emotional entanglement.

XIII. – GEORGINA TREVELLYN TO LOUISA ——.

DEAREST LOUISA, – Inquire, if you please, about
    Mr. Claude ——.
He has been once at R., and remembers meeting the H.'s.
Harriet L., perhaps, may be able to tell you about him.   255
It is an awkward youth, but still with very good manners;
Not without prospects, we hear; and, George says, highly
    connected.
Georgy declares it absurd, but Mamma is alarmed and
    insists he has
Taken up strange opinions and may be turning a Papist.
Certainly once he spoke of a daily service he went to.   260
'Where?' we asked, and he laughed and answered, 'At the
    Pantheon.'
This was a temple, you know, and now is a Catholic
    church; and
Though it is said that Mazzini has sold it for Protestant
    service,
Yet I suppose the change can hardly as yet be effected.
Adieu again, – evermore, my dearest, your loving
    Georgina.   265

P.S. BY MARY TREVELLYN

I AM to tell you, you say, what I think of our last new
    acquaintance.
Well, then, I think that George has a very fair right to be
    jealous.
I do not like him much, though I do not dislike being with
    him.
He is what people call, I suppose, a superior man, and
Certainly seems so to me; but I think he is frightfully
    selfish.   270

258–9] No doubt as a result of questioning Claude on matters concerning
Oxford – see above I.211 and note.
262–4] C. wrote to his mother that the 'story which went about here, that the
Pantheon was sold to the English for a Protestant chapel' was 'simply a joke' –
Corr. i, 252. As Scott notes, Georgina's willingness to believe this rumour
highlights her provinciality. See also II.28 below and note.

ALBA, *thou findest me still, and, Alba, thou findest me ever,*
  Now from the Capitol steps, now over Titus's Arch,
Here from the large grassy spaces that spread from the Lateran
    portal,
  Towering o'er aqueduct lines lost in perspective between,
Or from a Vatican window, or bridge, or the high Coliseum,   275
  Clear by the garlanded line cut of the Flavian ring.
Beautiful can I not call thee, and yet thou hast power to
    o'ermaster,
  Power of mere beauty; in dreams, Alba, thou hauntest me
    still.
Is it religion? I ask me; or is it a vain superstition?
  Slavery abject and gross? service, too feeble, of truth?   280
Is it an idol I bow to, or is it a god that I worship?
  Do I sink back on the old, or do I soar from the mean?
So through the city I wander and question, unsatisfied ever,
  Reverent so I accept, doubtful because I revere.

II.

Is it illusion? or does there a spirit from perfecter ages,
  Here, even yet, amid loss, change, and corruption, abide?
Does there a spirit we know not, though seek, though we find,
    comprehend not,
  Here to entice and confuse, tempt and evade us, abide?
Lives in the exquisite grace of the column disjointed and single,   5
  Haunts the rude masses of brick garlanded gayly with vine,
E'en in the turret fantastic surviving that springs from the ruin,
  E'en in the people itself? Is it illusion or not?

271. *Alba]* The Alban hills south of Rome.
272. *Capitol]* The site of the Temple of Jupiter, the most venerated shrine in ancient Rome.
276. *Flavian ring]* 'The [Coliseum] was originally called the *Flavian Amphitheatre* in honour of its founders' – Murray 1843: 294.
279–84] Cp C.'s remarks on Newman's conversion to the Church of Rome: 'Newman falls down and worships *because* he does not know, and knows he does not know. I think others are more right, who say boldly We don't understand it, and therefore we *won't* fall down and worship it' – *Corr.* i, 182.
1–4] The idea of a *genius loci* at work in Rome is also mooted by John Henry Newman (1864) *Apologia pro vita sua*, part V.

> *Is it illusion or not that attracteth the pilgrim transalpine,*
>   *Brings him a dullard and dunce hither to pry and to stare?*   10
> *Is it illusion or not that allures the barbarian stranger,*
>   *Brings him with gold to the shrine, brings him in arms to the*
>   *gate?*

I. – CLAUDE TO EUSTACE.

WHAT do the people say, and what does the government
      do? – you
Ask, and I know not at all. Yet fortune will favour your
      hopes; and
I, who avoided it all, am fated, it seems, to describe it.   15
I, who nor meddle nor make in politics, – I, who sincerely
Put not my trust in leagues nor any suffrage by ballot,
Never predicted Parisian milleniums, never beheld a
New Jerusalem coming down dressed like a bride out of
      heaven
Right on the Place de la Concorde,[7] – I, nevertheless, let
      me say it,   20
Could in my soul of souls, this day, with the Gaul at the
      gates, shed
One true tear for thee, thou poor little Roman republic!

11–12] With this notion of Rome as a site of both pilgrimage and plunder, cp
Goethe, *Roman Elegies*, II.
II.i] This letter represents Claude's first reaction to the news of the arrival of
General Oudinot's expeditionary force at Civita Vecchia – see Headnote.
16–20] Claude is alluding here to the French Revolution of the previous year
(1848) which some ardent young radicals had hailed as the dawn of a new era
of justice and equality. The 'New Jerusalem' is, of course, the location of the
millennium in the book of Revelation; in a letter from revolutionary Paris C.
described to Tom Arnold how he had 'walked around Jerusalem and told the
towers thereof with wonderful delight' (*Cor.* i, 200). (Cp Psalm 48:12, and
II.145 below and note.)
20. Place de la Concorde] The site of the execution of Louis XVI in 1793.
21. The Gaul] The French.

---

[7] At this point the following lines are cancelled in A:
                  . . . I who despise the Masses,
    Think that the Pharaoh was right to build the Great Pyramid let them
    Die by the million or billion in misery, I who hold that
    As God made draught cattle and partridges, sheep to be shorn, and
    Calves to be fatted and killed, – e'en so! – yes I who thus think . . .

France, it is foully done! and you, my stupid old England, –
You, who a twelvemonth ago said nations must choose
    for themselves, you
Could not, of course, interfere, – you now, when a nation
    has chosen –[8]   25
Pardon this folly! *The Times* will, of course, have
    announced the occasion,
Told you the news of to-day; and although it was slightly
    in error
When it proclaimed as a fact the Apollo was sold to a
    Yankee,
You may believe when it tells you the French are at Civita
    Vecchia.

II. – CLAUDE TO EUSTACE.

DULCE it is, and *decorum*, no doubt, for the country to
    fall, – to   30

23–5] A reference to England's supposedly non-interventionist foreign policy.
26–9] C.'s letters are full of contemptuous references to the inaccuracies and
distortions of all the foreign newspapers, especially *The Times*; see, e.g., *PR*
147, 155.
28] C. laughs off the story of the proposed sale of the Belvedere Apollo to the
Americans in a letter to his mother; see *Corr.* i, 252 and note to I.262–4 above.
Scott (1974) points out that this rumour was reported seriously in *The Times* of
9 April 1849.
II.ii] Claude's debate on whether or not to fight is not entirely fanciful; a number of foreign students and artists resident in Rome participated in the defence
of the Republic (Trevelyan 1919, ch. 7).
30. DULCE, decorum] Horace *Odes* 3.2.13: 'Dulce et decorum est pro patria
mori' – 'It is sweet and proper to die for one's country.'

---

[8] After 25:
    When with the guilt of a single ill-deed a most suffering people
    Rid them of three heavy Century loads of Confusion – but wherefore?
    What is the good of my talking? Yet Politics I will confess it,
    Yes, my political friends, I recant and acknowledge, have something
    Generous – something organic Creative and Art-like in them;
    Something at some great times which a man forgetting all else and
    Casting to moles and to bats his idols of thought and self-knowledge,
    Losing his soul for the gospel, with joy could embrace and die in –
    Could as it were, with quick fingers extinguish the light in the chamber,
    Enter the great bridal bed of the combat and conflict of men, and
    Know not, nor ask, whether morning should ever return to awake him. (*A*)

Offer one's blood an oblation to Freedom, and die for the
  Cause; yet
Still, individual culture is also something, and no man
Feels quite distinct the assurance that he of all others is
  called on,
Or would be justified, even, in taking away from the
  world that
Precious creature, himself. Nature sent him here to abide
  here;   35
Else why sent him at all? Nature wants him still, it is likely.
On the whole, we are meant to look after ourselves; it is
  certain
Each has to eat for himself, digest for himself, and in
  general
Care for his own dear life, and see to his own preservation;
Nature's intentions, in most things uncertain, in this are
  decisive: 40
These, on the whole, I conjecture the Romans will follow,
  and I shall.
    So we cling to our rocks like limpets; Ocean may bluster,
Over and under and round us; we open our shells to
  imbibe our
Nourishment, close them again, and are safe, fulfilling the
  purpose
Nature intended, – a wise one, of course, and a noble, we
  doubt not.   45
Sweet it may be and decorous, perhaps, for the country to
  die; but,
On the whole, we conclude the Romans won't do it, and I
  shan't.

III. – CLAUDE TO EUSTACE.

WILL they fight? They say so. And will the French? I
  can hardly,

---

31. oblation] An offering to the gods.
47] Claude's assumption that the Romans would not fight was shared by
Oudinot and his troops; see Farini 1854: iv, 19, Trevelyan 1919: 127.
48. Will they fight? They say so.] Claude is here referring to the demonstra-
tions of loyalty to the Republic organised by its defenders; see Farini 1854: iv,
7.

Hardly think so; and yet – He is come, they say, to Palo,
He is passed from Monterone, at Santa Severa   50
He hath laid up his guns. But the Virgin, the Daughter of
    Roma,
She hath despised thee and laughed thee to scorn, – the
    Daughter of Tiber
She hath shaken her head and built barricades against thee!
Will they fight? I believe it. Alas, 'tis ephemeral folly,
Vain and ephemeral folly, of course, compared with
    pictures,   55
Statues, and antique gems, – Indeed: and yet indeed too,
Yet methought, in broad day did I dream, – tell it not in
    St. James's,
Whisper it not in thy courts, O Christ Church! – yet did I,
    waking,
Dream of a cadence that sings, *Si tombent nos jeunes héros,*
    la
Terre en produit de nouveaux contre vous tous prêts a se battre;   60
Dreamt of great indignations and angers transcendental,
Dreamt of a sword at my side and a battle-horse
    underneath me.

49–53] An allusion to Sennacherib's assault on Jerusalem; see 2 Kings 19:21.
Cp the reference to the New Jerusalem at II.18–20 above.
49–50] Palo, Monterone and Santa Severa are towns lying between Civita
Vecchia and Rome.
54. Will they fight? I believe it.] Claude's change of mind about the willingness
of the Romans to fight echoes the opinion of most commentators that a change
of mood took place between 25 April, when the French landed, and the first
engagement on the thirtieth; see, e.g., Spada 1868: iii, 413.
57. St. James's] An area of London famous for its gentlemen's clubs.
58. Christ Church] Once the most aristocratic of Oxford colleges. Claude's language recalls 2 Samuel 1:20 on the death of Saul: 'Tell *it* not in Gath, publish
it not in the streets of Askelon; lest the daughters of the Philistines rejoice, lest
the daughters of the uncircumcised triumph.' He is worried that his mild
enthusiasm for the republican cause might leave him open to ridicule by the
'Philistines'.
59–60] Lines from the Marseillaise, the battle-hymn of the French Republic:
'If our young heroes die, new ones will spring up from the earth ready to
fight.' The ironic juxtaposition of French revolutionary rhetoric and reality
was also exploited by the Romans, who played the Marseillaise to the advancing French troops during the battle of 3 June; Trevelyan 1919: 175.

IV. – CLAUDE TO EUSTACE.

NOW supposing the French or the Neapolitan soldier
Should by some evil chance come exploring the Maison
      Serny,
(Where the family English are all to assemble for safety,)   65
Am I prepared to lay down my life for the British female?
Really, who knows? One has bowed and talked, till, little
      by little,
All the natural heat has escaped of the chivalrous spirit.
Oh, one conformed, of course; but one doesn't die for
      good manners,
Stab or shoot, or be shot, by way of a graceful attention.   70
No, if it should be at all, it should be on the barricades
      there;
Should I incarnadine ever this inky pacifical finger,
Sooner far should it be for the vapour of Italy's freedom,
Sooner far by the side of the d—d and dirty plebeians.
Ah, for a child in the street I could strike; for the full-
      blown lady –   75
Somehow, Eustace, alas, I have not felt the vocation.
Yet these people of course will expect, as of course,
      my protection,
Vernon in radiant arms stand forth for the lovely Georgina,
And to appear, I suppose, were but common civility.
      Yes, and
Truly I do not desire they should either be killed or
      offended.   80
Oh, and of course you will say, 'When the time comes,
      you will be ready.'
Ah, but before it comes, am I to presume it will be so?
What I cannot feel now, am I to suppose that I shall feel?
Am I not free to attend for the ripe and indubious instinct?
Am I forbidden to wait for the clear and lawful perception?   85
Is it the calling of man to surrender his knowledge and
      insight,
For the mere venture of what may, perhaps, be the
      virtuous action?

63. the Neapolitan soldier] Rome was also menaced by the Neapolitan army;
the exiled Pope had taken up residence in Naples, and King Ferdinand II, the
legendary 'Re Bomba', was encamped with his troops in the Alban hills south
of Rome.
64. the Maison Serny] The safe house for the English was the 'H[otel] de
Londres (Czerni)', in the Piazza di Spagna (Murray 1843).
72. incarnadine] Cp *Macbeth* II.ii.59–62.

Must we, walking our earth, discerning a little, and hoping
Some plain visible task shall yet for our hands be assigned
    us, –
Must we abandon the future for fear of omitting the
    present,　　　　　　　　　　　　　　　　　　　90
Quit our own fireside hopes at the alien call of a neighbour,
To the mere possible shadow of Deity offer the victim?
And is all this, my friend, but a weak and ignoble refining,
Wholly unworthy the head or the heart of Your Own
    Correspondent?

V. – CLAUDE TO EUSTACE.

YES, we are fighting at last, it appears. This morning, as
    usual,　　　　　　　　　　　　　　　　　　　　95
Murray, as usual, in hand, I enter the Caffé Nuovo;
Seating myself with a sense as it were of a change in the
    weather,
Not understanding, however, but thinking mostly of
    Murray,
And, for to-day is their day, of the Campidoglio Marbles,
Caffè-latte! I call to the waiter, – and *Non c'è latte*,　　100
This is the answer he makes me, and this the sign of a
    battle.
So I sit; and truly they seem to think any one else more
Worthy than me of attention. I wait for my milkless *nero*,

---

94. *Your Own Correspondent]* Claude's reluctant and ironic acknowledgement
of his position as an involuntary war correspondent.
II.v] The first version of this letter, headed 'April 30th', was sent by C. to his
friend A.P. Stanley for the gratification of the latter's 'historic soul' on 24 May
1849, i.e. less than a month after the battle it commemorates (*PR* 152). On the
battle itself see Headnote above.
95–112] Cp Carlyle's comment on the tumultuous insurrection of 9 August
1792: 'In remote streets, men are drinking breakfast-coffee; following their
affairs; with a start now and then, as some dull echo reverberates a note louder'
– *The French Revolution* II.vi, ch. 7.
96. *Caffé Nuovo]* The '*Café Novo* [sic] . . . in the Palazzo Ruspoli, in the
Corso . . . a good and handsome establishment much frequented by the Roman
nobility' – Murray 1843: 250; C. refers to it in *Corr.* i, 265, 267.
99. *the Campidoglio Marbles]* Antiquities contained in the Capitoline museum.
100. *Caffè-latte . . . Non c'è latte]* 'Coffee with milk . . . There is no milk.'
101] The first appearance of the letter's refrain; see cancelled lines given
below. Claude stresses his own active involvement in interpreting the 'signs' of
the battle which present themselves to him.
103. *nero]* Black coffee.

Free to observe undistracted all sorts and sizes of persons,
Blending civilian and soldier in strangest costume, coming
    in, and   105
Gulping in hottest haste, still standing, their coffee, –
    withdrawing
Eagerly, jangling a sword on the steps, or jogging a musket
Slung to the shoulder behind. They are fewer, moreover,
    than usual,
Much, and silenter far; and so I begin to imagine
Something is really afloat. Ere I leave, the Caffé is empty,   110
Empty too the streets, in all its length the Corso
Empty, and empty I see to my right and my left the
    Condotti.[9]

    Twelve o'clock, on the Pincian Hill, with lots of English,
Germans, Americans, French, – the Frenchmen, too, are
    protected, –
So we stand in the sun, but afraid of a probable shower;   115
So we stand and stare, and see, to the left of St. Peter's,
Smoke, from the cannon, white, – but that is at intervals
    only, –
Black, from a burning house, we suppose, by the
    Cavalleggieri;
And we believe we discern some lines of men descending
Down through the vineyard-slopes, and catch a bayonet
    gleaming.   120
Every ten minutes, however, – in this there is no
    misconception, –
Comes a great white puff from behind Michel Angelo's
    dome, and

106. in hottest haste] A Carlylean phrase; see 'The Diamond Necklace', Carlyle 1899: xxviii, 378.
111–12. Corso, Condotti] Two of Rome's principal thoroughfares.
113. the Pincian Hill] One of the seven hills of Rome, commanding a view over most of the city. C. is drawing on his own experiences at this point: 'I went up to the Pincian Hill and saw the smoke and heard the occasional big cannon and the sharp succession of skirmishers' volleys bang, bang, bang – away beyond St. Peter's' (*Corr.* i, 253).
118. Cavalleggieri] The Porta Cavalleggieri, situated in the Vatican wall.

[9] After 112: This is the sight that I meet with and this the sign of battle (*A E*)

After a space the report of a real big gun, – not the
    Frenchman's? –
That must be doing some work. And so we watch and
    conjecture.[10]
  Shortly, an Englishman comes, who says he has been to
    St. Peter's,   125
Seen the Piazza and troops, but that is all he can tell us;
So we watch and sit, and, indeed, it begins to be
    tiresome. –
All this smoke is outside; when it has come to the inside,
It will be time, perhaps, to descend and retreat to our
    houses.[11]
  Half-past one, or two. The report of small arms
    frequent,   130
Sharp and savage indeed; that cannot all be for nothing;
So we watch and wonder; but guessing is tiresome, very.
Weary of wondering, watching, and guessing, and
    gossipping idly,
Down I go, and pass through the quiet streets with the
    knots of
National Guards patrolling, and flags hanging out at the
    windows,   135
English, American, Danish, – and, after offering to help an
Irish family moving *en masse* to the Maison Serny,
After endeavouring idly to minister balm to the trembling
Quinquagenarian fears of two lone British spinsters,
Go to make sure of my dinner before the enemy enter.   140
But by this there are signs of stragglers returning; and
    voices
Talk, though you don't believe it, of guns and prisoners
    taken;
And on the walls you read the first bulletin of the
    morning. –
This is all that I saw, and all I know of the battle.

132] Mr. Jingle in Dickens's *Pickwick Papers* has the habit of ending his disconnected utterances with 'very'.

---

[10] After 124: This is the scene that we see, and this the sight of a battle (*A E*)
[11] After 129: This is meantime the sight that we see, the sight of a battle (*A E*)

VI. – CLAUDE TO EUSTACE.

VICTORY! VICTORY! – Yes! ah, yes, thou republican
    Zion,   145
Truly the kings of the earth are gathered and gone by
    together;
Doubtless they marvelled to witness such things, were
    astonished, and so forth.
Victory! Victory! Victory! – Ah, but it is, believe me,
Easier, easier far, to intone the chant of the martyr
Than to indite any paean of any victory. Death may   150
Sometimes be noble; but life, at the best, will appear an
    illusion.
While the great pain is upon us, it is great; when it is over,
Why, it is over. The smoke of the sacrifice rises to heaven,
Of a sweet savour, no doubt, to Somebody; but on the
    altar,
Lo, there is nothing remaining but ashes and dirt and ill
    odour.   155
    So it stands, you perceive; the labial muscles, that
    swelled with
Vehement evolution of yesterday Marseillaises,
Articulations sublime of defiance and scorning, to-day col–
Lapse and languidly mumble, while men and women and
    papers
Scream and re-scream to each other the chorus of Victory.
    Well, but   160
I am thankful they fought, and glad that the Frenchmen
    were beaten.

145. *Victory! Victory!]* The Roman authorities sought to make the most of their unexpected victory to boost morale; see Farini 1854: iv, 48.
145–7] Cp Psalm 48:2–4: 'The hill of Sion is a fair place, and the joy of the whole earth. . . . For lo, the kings of the earth: are gathered, and gone by together. They marvelled to see such things: they were astonished, and suddenly cast down.' As Scott points out, this is taken from the Prayer Book version rather than the slightly different Authorised one. Cp above II.19–20 and 49–53.
150. paean] A song of thanksgiving or triumph in classical antiquity.
153–4] An allusion to the refrain in the early chapters of Leviticus: 'it *is* a burnt sacrifice, an offering made by fire, of a sweet savour unto the LORD.'

VII. – Claude to Eustace.

So I have seen a man killed! An experience that, among
    others!
Yes, I suppose I have; although I can hardly be certain,
And in a court of justice could never declare I had seen it.
But a man was killed, I am told, in a place where I saw   165
Something; a man was killed, I am told, and I saw
    something.
    I was returning home from St. Peter's; Murray, as usual,
Under my arm, I remember; had crossed the St. Angelo
    bridge; and
Moving towards the Condotti, had got to the first
    barricade, when
Gradually, thinking still of St. Peter's, I became conscious   170
Of a sensation of movement opposing me, – tendency this
    way
(Such as one fancies may be in a stream when the wave of
    the tide is
Coming and not yet come, – a sort of poise and retention);
So I turned, and, before I turned, caught sight of
    stragglers
Heading a crowd, it is plain, that is coming behind that
    corner.   175
Looking up, I see windows filled with heads; the Piazza,
Into which you remember the Ponte St. Angelo enters,

II.vii] This letter alludes to the so-called 'Roman Terror', the brief outbreak
of anti–clerical violence which took place during the first few days of May
1849. For contrasting views on the reality of this 'Terror', see Trevelyan 1919:
149–51, Farini 1854: iv, 56 and Spada 1869: iii, 415, 450–66. C. did his best to
dispel the idea that such a 'Terror' existed – 'I wrote you a few lines about "the
Terror" but somehow did not send them. Assure yourself that there is nothing
to deserve that name' (*Corr.* i, 261) – but he does seem to have witnessed a few
incidents of anti–clerical violence himself. The *Roma* Notebook contains the
entry 'Il Prete' for 3 May, and on the eleventh he wrote to his mother that the
only 'awkward thing' that had happened so far had been 'the killing of four or
perhaps five priests by the mob' – *Corr.* i, 253–4. Cp Georgina Trevellyn's reference to 'republican terrors' below, II.318. The letter is dated 'the 2nd of
May' in *E*.
168. St Angelo bridge] The Ponte Sant' Angelo, the ancient *Pons Aelius* built
by Hadrian in AD 134.
175] Note the switch to the historic present; cp Carlyle's assertion that the
past tense is 'a most lying thing' because it withdraws from an event 'the hag-
gard element of Fear' – *The French Revolution* II.iii, ch. 3.

Since I passed, has thickened with curious groups; and
    now the
Crowd is coming, has turned, has crossed that last
    barricade, is
Here at my side. In the middle they drag at something.
    What is it?   180
Ha! bare swords in the air, held up! There seem to be
    voices
Pleading and hands putting back; official, perhaps; but
    the swords are
Many, and bare in the air. In the air? They descend,
    they are smiting,
Hewing, chopping – At what? In the air once more
    upstretched! And
Is it blood that's on them? Yes, certainly blood! Of
    whom, then?   185
Over whom is the cry of this furor of exaltation?
    While they are skipping and screaming, and dancing
        their caps on the points of
Swords and bayonets, I to the outskirts back, and ask a
Mercantile-seeming bystander, 'What is it?' and he,
    looking always
That way, makes me answer, 'A Priest, who was trying
    to fly to   190
The Neapolitan army,' – and thus explains the
    proceeding.
    You didn't see the dead man? No; – I began to be
    doubtful;
I was in black myself, and didn't know what mightn't
    happen; –
But a National Guard close by me, outside of the hubbub,
Broke his sword with slashing a broad hat covered with
    dust, – and   195
Passing away from the place with Murray under my arm,
    and

180–6] Cp C.'s description of the following incident which took place during
the entry of the French in July 1849: 'At this moment, some Roman bourgeois
as I fancy but perhaps a foreigner, said something either to express his sense of
the folly of it, or his sympathy with the invaders. He was surrounded, and I
saw him buffetted a good deal, and there was a sword lifted up, but I think not
bare. I was told he got off' (*Corr.* i, 265).
193] Claude begins to worry that he might be mistaken for a priest because of
his black clothes.
194. National Guard] A volunteer soldier of the Republic.

Stooping, I saw through the legs of the people the legs of a
    body.
  You are the first, do you know, to whom I have
    mentioned the matter.
Whom should I tell it to, else? – these girls? – the Heavens
    forbid it! –
Quidnuncs at Monaldini's? – idlers upon the Pincian?   200
  If I rightly remember, it happened on that afternoon
    when
Word of the nearer approach of a new Neapolitan army
First was spread. I began to bethink me of Paris
    Septembers,
Thought I could fancy the look of the old 'Ninety-two.
    On that evening
Three or four, or, it may be, five of these people were
    slaughtered.   205
Some declare they had, one of them, fired on a sentinel;
    others
Say they were only escaping; a Priest, it is currently stated,
Stabbed a National Guard on the very Piazza Colonna:
History, Rumour of Rumours, I leave it to thee to
    determine!
  But I am thankful to say the government seems to have
    strength to   210

---

200. Quidnuncs] Newsmongers (from the Latin 'quid nunc?' – 'what now?')
Monaldini's] 'Reading-Rooms. – Monaldini, in the Piazza di Spagna, supplied with the London daily newspapers, Galignani, a small English library,
and a good collection of guide-books, maps, &c., of Rome and its vicinity' –
Murray 1843: 250.
203–4] Claude's account of the Roman 'Terror' is, as he acknowledges,
indebted to the graphic description of the massacre at the Abbaye Prison in
the chapter of Carlyle's *French Revolution* entitled 'September in Paris' (III.i,
ch. 4).
208. Piazza Colonna] i.e. in the very heart of Rome.
209] Another allusion to *The French Revolution*, in which Carlyle describes
history as 'ever, more or less, the written epitomised synopsis of Rumour'
(I.ii, ch. 1). Cp also the analysis of the hardening of rumour into fact in
Easter Day 48–58: 'As circulates in some great city crowd/ A rumour
changeful, vague, importunate, and loud,/ From no determined centre, or of
fact,/ Or authorship exact,/ Which no man can deny/ Nor verify;/ So
spread the wondrous fame;/ He all the same/ Lay senseless, mouldering,
low./ He was not risen, no,/ Christ was not risen!'
210–11] Trevelyan also comments on the speed and efficiency 'with which
Mazzini's government suppressed such outbreaks of anti-clerical violence';
Trevelyan 1919: 150.

Put it down; it has vanished, at least; the place is most
    peaceful.
Through the Trastevere walking last night, at nine of the
    clock, I
Found no sort of disorder; I crossed by the Island-bridges,
So by the narrow streets to the Ponte Rotto, and onwards
Thence, by the Temple of Vesta, away to the great
    Coliseum,   215
Which at the full of the moon is an object worthy a visit.[12]

VIII. – GEORGINA TREVELLYN TO LOUISA ——.

ONLY think, dearest Louisa, what fearful scenes we have
    witnessed! –

*   *   *   *   *   *   *   *   *

George has just seen Garibaldi, dressed up in a long white
    cloak, on
Horseback, riding by, with his mounted negro behind him:
This is a man, you know, who came from America with
    him,   220
Out of the woods, I suppose, and uses a *lasso* in fighting,
Which is, I don't quite know, but a sort of noose, I
    imagine;

---

212. Trastevere] The poorest quarter of Rome on the western side of the
Tiber.
214. Ponte Rotto] Literally 'broken bridge'; the fragmentary remains of the
first stone bridge across the Tiber.
215. Temple of Vesta] '[A] circular temple near the Ponte Rotto and the
Temple of Fortuna Virilis ... now the church of Santa Maria del Sole' –
Murray 1843: 292.
217] Georgina's credulity contrasts with Claude's steadfast refusal to suc-
cumb to the glamour of rumour.
219. mounted negro] Garibaldi's 'friend and bodyguard' Aguyar.
220. America] That is, South America; Garibaldi had undergone numerous
adventures in that continent prior to returning to Italy.

---

[12] After 216:
    Do you know, I have more than half a mind after all to
    Make you believe the above is a simple ingenious fiction?
    So indeed, the truth is, it seems to myself, and really
    It would give you perhaps the truer impression to cheat you. (*A*)

This he throws on the heads of the enemy's men in a
  battle,
Pulls them into his reach, and then most cruelly kills
  them:
Mary does not believe, but we heard it from an Italian.   225
Mary allows she was wrong about Mr. Claude *being selfish*;
He was *most* useful and kind on the terrible thirtieth of
  April.
Do not write here any more; we are starting directly for
  Florence:
We should be off to-morrow, if only Papa could get
  horses;
All have been seized everywhere for the use of this
  dreadful Mazzini.   230

P.S.
      Mary has seen thus far. – I am really so angry,
        Louisa, –
Quite out of patience, my dearest! What can the man be
  intending?
I am quite tired; and Mary, who might bring him to in a
  moment,
Lets him go on as he likes, and neither will help nor
  dismiss him.

IX. – CLAUDE TO EUSTACE.

IT is most curious to see what a power a few calm words
  (in   235
Merely a brief proclamation) appear to possess on the
  people.
Order is perfect, and peace; the city is utterly tranquil;
And one cannot conceive that this easy and *nonchalant*
  crowd, that
Flows like a quiet stream through street and market-place,
  entering
Shady recesses and bays of church, *osteria*, and *caffè*,   240

225] Typical of the poem's economical delineation of character; Mary, like
Claude, 'does not believe' on the basis of hearsay and rumour.
235–6] A proclamation was issued by the Triumvirate soon after the outbreak
of anti-clerical violence; see *Corr.* i, 254.
240. osteria] Hostelry, inn.

Could in a moment be changed to a flood as of molten lava,
Boil into deadly wrath and wild homicidal delusion.
    Ah, 'tis an excellent race, – and even in old degradation,
Under a rule that enforces to flattery, lying, and cheating,
E'en under Pope and Priest, a nice and natural people.   245
Oh, could they but be allowed this chance of redemption!
    – but clearly
That is not likely to be. Meantime, notwithstanding all
    journals,
Honour for once to the tongue and the pen of the
    eloquent writer!
Honour to speech! and all honour to thee, thou noble
    Mazzini!

X. – CLAUDE TO EUSTACE.

I AM in love, meantime, you think; no doubt you would
    think so.   250
I am in love, you say; with those letters, of course, you
    would say so.
I am in love, you declare. I think not so; yet I grant you
It is a pleasure, indeed, to converse with this girl. Oh,
    rare gift,
Rare felicity, this! she can talk in a rational way, can
Speak upon subjects that really are matters of mind and
    of thinking,   255
Yet in perfection retain her simplicity; never, one
    moment,
Never, however you urge it, however you tempt her,
    consents to
Step from ideas and fancies and loving sensations to
    those vain

---

247. notwithstanding all journals] See II.26–9 above and note.
250–51] Cp Keats's letter of 29 October 1818 to his brother George, describing a woman he has recently met: 'You will, by this time, think I am in love with her, so, before I go any further, I will tell you I am not' – Milnes 1927: 137. C. was involved in a small way in the production of the first edition of Keats's letters in 1848, and actually furnished Richard Monckton Milnes, the editor, with a copy of a poem contained in this letter, although he did not possess a copy of the letter itself prior to publication. Keats's letters and poetry were discussed by C. and Matthew Arnold during 1848 and 1849; see Lowry 1932: 96–7, 100–1. See also III.vi below.

Conscious understandings that vex the minds of mankind.[13]
No, though she talk, it is music; her fingers desert not the
  keys; 'tis   260
Song, though you hear in her song the articulate vocables
  sounded,
Syllabled singly and sweetly the words of melodious
  meaning.
  I am in love, you say; I do not think so exactly.

XI. – CLAUDE TO EUSTACE.

THERE are two different kinds, I believe, of human
  attraction;
One which simply disturbs, unsettles, and makes you
  uneasy,   265
And another that poises, retains, and fixes, and holds you.
I have no doubt, for myself, in giving my voice for the
  latter.[14]

---

259. man-kind] Used advisedly; Claude is drawing a distinction, common in the nineteenth century, between male ways of thinking (ratiocinative, conscious, ultimately sterile) and female ways of thinking (intuitive, spontaneous, fruitful). Cp the cancelled lines after 259 referring to the intellectual woman as 'unsexed' and 'a Lady Macbeth of letters'.
II.xi] This letter was restored to the poem by 1859 *Corrections*; it helps to elucidate two of the poem's central metaphors, affinity and growth – see Introduction, p. 16.
264–7] Attraction was occasionally used instead of affinity by contemporary chemists to designate the force behind the combination of particular elements. Claude's 'two different kinds' of attraction correspond, respectively, to a weak affinity temporarily in force due to the proximity of the elements in question, and to an elective affinity which 'retains and fixes' them immutably.

---

[13] After 259:
  Never, however you tempt her, however you urge it, consents to
  Unsex herself, and come out as a Lady Macbeth of letters (*A*)
[14] Alt. to 264–7:
  There are four kinds, as I take it, of human magnetic affection.
  First, simple repulsion. And second simple attraction.
  Thirdly a third which fidgets and frets and makes you uneasy.
  Fourthly and lastly another which poises and fixes and holds you.
  I, on the whole, incline to prefer the fourth to the second. (*A*)

I do not wish to be moved, but growing, where I was
      growing,
There more truly to grow, to live where as yet I had
      languished.
I do not like being moved: for the will is excited; and
      action   270
Is a most dangerous thing; I tremble for something
      factitious,
Some malpractice of heart and illegitimate process;
We are so prone to these things with our terrible notions
      of duty.

XII. – CLAUDE TO EUSTACE.

AH, let me look, let me watch, let me wait, unhurried,
      unprompted!
Bid me not venture on aught that could alter or end what
      is present!   275
Say not, Time flies, and occasion, that never returns, is
      departing!
Drive me not out, ye ill angels with fiery swords, from
      my Eden,
Waiting, and watching, and looking! Let love be its own
      inspiration!
Shall not a voice, if a voice there must be, from the airs
      that environ,

270. *the will is excited]* Claude mistrusts the will because it threatens to pre-
empt the spontaneous process of growth which alone guarantees the
authenticity of action; cp III.155 below.
271. *factitious]* One of Carlyle's favourite terms, used repeatedly by Claude
(see, e.g., V.85, 164).
273. *our terrible notions of duty]* For C.'s notion of duty as something which
distorts natural impulses see 'Duty – that's to say complying' above.
276. *Time flies]* Proverbial, from Virgil's *Georgics* 3.284: 'Sed fugit interea,
fugit inreparabile tempus.'
276. *occasion]* Paul Veyriras suggests a parallel here to Goethe's invocation of
the goddess Opportunity in his *Roman Elegies* IV; Veyriras 1964: 345–6.
277. *ye ill angels with fiery swords]* An allusion to the expulsion of Adam and
Eve from Paradise: 'So he drove out the man; and he placed at the east of the
garden of Eden Cherubims, and a flaming sword which turned every way, to
keep the way of the tree of life' (Genesis 3:24). Claude's 'Eden' is the prelapsarian purity of inaction; see Introduction, p. 17.

Yea, from the conscious heavens, without our knowledge
    or effort,   280
Break into audible words? And love be its own
    inspiration?

XIII. – CLAUDE TO EUSTACE.

WHEREFORE and how I am certain, I hardly can tell;
    but it *is* so.
She doesn't like me, Eustace; I think she never will like
    me.
Is it my fault, as it is my misfortune, my ways are not
    her ways?
Is it my fault, that my habits and modes are dissimilar
    wholly?   285
'Tis not her fault, 'tis her nature, her virtue, to
    misapprehend them:
'Tis not her fault, 'tis her beautiful nature, not ever to
    know me.
Hopeless it seems, – yet I cannot, though hopeless,
    determine to leave it:
She goes, – therefore I go; she moves, – I move, not to
    lose her.

XIV. – CLAUDE TO EUSTACE.

OH, 'tisn't manly, of course, 'tisn't manly, this method
    of wooing;   290
'Tisn't the way very likely to win. For the woman, they
    tell you,
Ever prefers the audacious, the wilful, the vehement hero;
She has no heart for the timid, the sensitive soul; and for
    knowledge, –

280. without our knowledge or effort] An essential aspect of Claude's amatory
creed is the idea that true love, like divine grace, should descend unbidden.
284] Cp Isaiah 55:8: 'For my thoughts *are* not your thoughts, neither *are*
your ways my ways, saith the LORD.'
289] Cp Ruth 1:16: '. . . whither thou goest, I will go; and where thou
lodgest, I will lodge; thy people *shall be* my people, and thy God my God.'
293–4] On Claude's determination to retain his 'knowledge' in spite of the
enchantments of desire see I.xii and note.

Knowledge, O ye gods! – when did they appreciate
    knowledge?
Wherefore should they, either? I am sure I do not
    desire it.   295
   Ah, and I feel too, Eustace, she cares not a tittle about
    me!
(Care about me, indeed! and do I really expect it?)
But my manner offends; my ways are wholly repugnant;
Every word that I utter estranges, hurts, and repels her;
Every moment of bliss that I gain, in her exquisite
    presence,   300
Slowly, surely, withdraws her, removes her, and severs
    her from me.
Not that I care very much! – any way, I escape from the
    boy's own
Folly, to which I am prone, of loving where it is easy.
Not that I mind very much! Why should I? I am not in
    love, and
Am prepared, I think, if not by previous habit,   305
Yet in the spirit beforehand for this and all that is like it.
It is an easier matter for us contemplative creatures,

---

299. repels] Claude's use of this term signifies his recognition that his relationship with Mary is not based on a genuine elective affinity (see Introduction, p.
16). Contemporary chemical theory supposed that atoms of the same substance
'repel one another with a force decreasing directly as the distance of their centres from each other' (Partington 1962: iii, 767), and the implication, reiterated
later in the poem (V.63–9), is that Claude and Mary are too similar to be compatible. It is, perhaps, significant that this recognition occurs immediately after
Claude's anxieties about his lack of 'manliness', and soon after his fear that
Mary might 'unsex herself' and become 'a Lady Macbeth of letters'; the poem
seems to suggest that the conditions of modern bourgeois life erase sexual difference to an extent incompatible with genuine erotic attraction. Mary,
incidentally, concurs with Claude's judgement on the nature of their relationship, using the word 'repulsive' and cognate variants no fewer than five times
in her next two letters (II.329, 330; III.28, 30; 32).
304–12] These lines were restored by C. in 1859 *Corrections*; they constitute
one of the poem's characteristically oblique discussions of the nature of religious belief. C. provides a gloss on the terms 'things in particular' and 'things
in general' in a later cancelled passage: 'Look you, most people accepting, as
Time or Locality, Birth or/ Education suggests, some *particular* things, are
therefore/ Credited largely for faith, heaven help us, in *things in general*./ I
who sincerely believe, as I fancy, in *things in general*,/ That is, in God, you
know, am a sceptic, forsooth, as I do not/ Make-up instanter my mind to
believe in your *things in particular*.' (*A*)

Us, upon whom the pressure of action is laid so lightly:
We discontented indeed with things in particular, idle,
Sickly, complaining, by faith in the vision of things in
    general   310
Manage to hold on our way without, like others around
    us,
Seizing the nearest arm to comfort, help, and support us.
Yet, after all, my Eustace, I know but little about it.
All I can say for myself, for present alike and for past, is,
Mary Trevellyn, Eustace, is certainly worth your
    acquaintance.
You couldn't come, I suppose, as far as Florence, to see
    her?

XV. – GEORGINA TREVELLYN TO LOUISA ——.

*   *   *   To-morrow we're starting for Florence,
Truly rejoiced, you may guess, to escape from republican
    terrors;
Mr. C. and Papa to escort us; we by *vettura*
Through Siena, and Georgy to follow and join us by
    Leghorn.   320
Then —— Ah, what shall I say, my dearest? I tremble
    in thinking!
You will imagine my feelings, – the blending of hope
    and of sorrow!
How can I bear to abandon Papa and Mamma and my
    sisters?
Dearest Louisa, indeed it is very alarming; but trust me
Ever, whatever may change, to remain your loving
    Georgina.   325

---

319. vettura] Carriage; Georgina and the other women of the family are intending to travel overland to Florence, while George (and presumably Claude) are supposed to be going by sea from Rome to Leghorn (Livorno) and then on to Florence.
321–25] Georgina is, of course, referring, in characteristically conventional language, to her forthcoming marriage.

P.S. BY MARY TREVELLYN.

*   *   *   'Do I like Mr. Claude any better?'
I am to tell you, – and, 'Pray, is it Susan or I that attract
    him?'
This he has never told, but Georgina could certainly ask
    him.
All I can say for myself is, alas! that he rather repels me.
There! I think him agreeable, but also a little repulsive.   330
So be content, dear Louisa; for one satisfactory marriage
Surely will do in one year for the family you would
    establish,
Neither Susan nor I shall afford you the joy of a second.

P.S. BY GEORGINA TREVELLYN.

Mr. Claude, you must know, is behaving a little bit better;
He and Papa are great friends; but he really is too
    shilly-shally, –   335
So unlike George! Yet I hope that the matter is going on
    fairly.
I shall, however, get George, before he goes, to say
    something.
Dearest Louise, how delightful, to bring young people
    together!

Is it to Florence we follow, or are we to tarry yet longer,
    E'en amid clamour of arms, here in the city of old,   340
Seeking from clamour of arms in the Past and the Arts to be
    hidden,
    Vainly 'mid Arts and the Past seeking one life to forget?
Ah, fair shadow, scarce seen, go forth! for anon he shall
    follow, –
    He that beheld thee, anon, whither thou leadest, must go!
Go, and the wise, loving Muse, she also will follow and
    find thee!   345
    She, should she linger in Rome, were not dissevered from
    thee!

329–30] See II.299 above and note.
331. satisfactory] A stronger epithet of approbation in the nineteenth century
than now, although Mary's use of it here certainly contains more than a trace
of irony concerning her sister's expectations of marriage.
335. shilly-shally] Guilty of undue hesitation, tending to vacillate.
337] See III.271–85 below and note.

III.

YET to the wondrous St. Peter's, and yet to the solemn
    Rotonda,
  Mingling with heroes and gods, yet to the Vatican walls,
Yet may we go, and recline, while a whole mighty world
    seems above us
Gathered and fixed to all time into one roofing supreme;
Yet may we, thinking on these things, exclude what is
    meaner around us;   5
  Yet, at the worst of the worst, books and a chamber remain;
Yet may we think, and forget, and possess our souls in
    resistance. –
Ah, but away from the stir, shouting, and gossip of war,
Where, upon Apennine slope, with the chestnut the oak-trees
    immingle,
  Where amid odorous copse bridle-paths wander and wind,   10
Where under mulberry-branches the diligent rivulet sparkles,
  Or amid cotton and maize peasants their waterworks ply,
Where, over fig-tree and orange in tier upon tier still repeated,
  Garden on garden upreared, balconies step to the sky, –
Ah, that I were, far away from the crowd and the streets of
    the city,   15
Under the vine-trellis laid, O my beloved, with thee!

I. – Mary Trevellyn to Miss Roper,
– *on the way to Florence.*

WHY doesn't Mr. Claude come with us? you ask. – We
    don't know.
You should know better than we. He talked of the
    Vatican marbles;

---

1. Rotonda] See above, I.viii and note.
3–4] An allusion to the roof of the Sistine Chapel, which depicts the story of
the creation.
15–16] Scott suggests a reminiscence of the Song of Solomon 7:11–12:
'Come, my beloved, let us go forth into the field; let us lodge in the villages./
Let us get up early to the vineyards; let us see if the vine flourish, *whether* the
tender grape appear, *and* the pomegranates bud forth; there will I give thee my
loves.'
18. Vatican marbles] Museums in Rome were closed during the siege, and special permission was required to view the collections contained in them; C.
obtained his permit for the Vatican on 28 May 1849 (see *Corr.* i, 253, 257).

But I can't wholly believe that this was the actual
    reason, –
He was so ready before, when we asked him to come and
    escort us.   20
Certainly he is odd, my dear Miss Roper. To change so
Suddenly, just for a whim, was not quite fair to the
    party, –
Not quite right. I declare, I really almost am offended:
I, his great friend, as you say, have doubtless a title to
    be so.
Not that I greatly regret it, for dear Georgina distinctly   25
Wishes for nothing so much as to show her adroitness.
    But, oh, my
Pen will not write any more; – let us say nothing further
    about it.

*   *   *   *   *   *   *   *   *

Yes, my dear Miss Roper, I certainly called him repulsive;
So I think him, but cannot be sure I have used the
    expression
Quite as your pupil should; yet he does most truly repel
    me.   30
Was it to you I made use of the word? or who was it told
    you?
Yes, repulsive; observe, it is but when he talks of ideas,
That he is quite unaffected, and free, and expansive, and
    easy;
I could pronounce him simply a cold intellectual being. –
When does he make advances? – He thinks that women
    should woo him;   35
Yet, if a girl should do so, would be but alarmed and
    disgusted.
She that should love him must look for small love in
    return, – like the ivy
On the stone wall, must expect but a rigid and niggard
    support, and
E'en to get that must go searching all round with her
    humble embraces.

---

22. just for a whim] Mary's judgement of Claude's actions is based on the erroneous supposition that he had failed to accompany her and her family to Florence 'for a whim', when in fact it was the 'hints' dropped by members of the Vernon family which led to his decision to stay in Rome; see below, III.271–7.
28. repulsive] See above, II.329–30 and note.

II. – CLAUDE TO EUSTACE, – *from Rome.*

TELL me, my friend, do you think that the grain would
    sprout in the furrow,   40
Did it not truly accept as its *summum* and *ultimum bonum*
That mere common and may-be indifferent soil it is set
    in?
Would it have force to develope and open its young
    cotyledons,
Could it compare, and reflect, and examine one thing
    with another?
Would it endure to accomplish the round of its natural
    functions,   45
Were it endowed with a sense of the general scheme of
    existence?
    While from Marseilles in the steamer we voyaged to
    Civita Vecchia,
Vexed in the squally seas as we lay by Capraji and Elba,
Standing, uplifted, alone on the heaving poop of the
    vessel,
Looking around on the waste of the rushing incurious
    billows,   50
'This is Nature,' I said: 'we are born as it were from her
    waters,
Over her billows that buffet and beat us, her offspring
    uncared-for,

41. summum and ultimum bonum] From scholastic Latin: 'the complete and
highest good.'
43. develope] Claude's spelling indicates the fact that this word was still something of a neologism in English at the time of the poem's composition.
43. cotyledons] Seed-leaves.
47–59] Cp Goethe's sentiments in *Italian Journey:* 'No one who has never
seen himself surrounded on all sides by nothing but the sea can have a true
conception of the world and of his own relation to it' (Goethe 1987: 228).
47. Marseilles . . . Civita Vecchia] The standard sea route to Rome during the
early nineteenth century, taken by C. himself in April 1849 and by Oudinot
and his troops a few weeks later.
48. Capraji, Elba] Capraia and Elba are small islands lying between Corsica
and the Italian mainland.
49. poop] The deck at the stern of the ship.
52. her offspring uncared-for] Cp Froude 1849: 78: 'I think Nature, if she inter-
ests herself much about her children, must often feel that, like the miserable
Frankenstein, with her experimenting among the elements of humanity, she
has brought beings into existence who have no business here; who can do none
of her work, and endure none of her favours; whose life is only suffering; and
whose action is one long protest against the ill foresight which flung them into
consciousness.'

Casting one single regard of a painful victorious
    knowledge,
Into her billows that buffet and beat us we sink and are
    swallowed.'
This was the sense in my soul, as I swayed with the poop
    of the steamer;   55
And as unthinking I sat in the hall of the famed Ariadne,
Lo, it looked at me there from the face of a Triton in
    marble.
It is the simpler thought, and I can believe it the truer.
Let us not talk of growth; we are still in our Aqueous
    Ages.

III. – CLAUDE TO EUSTACE.

FAREWELL, Politics, utterly! What can I do? I cannot   60
Fight, you know; and to talk I am wholly ashamed. And
    although I

---

53. a painful victorious knowledge] Claude's speculations on the role of knowledge in estranging humanity from the rest of organic nature are paralleled by many similar passages in nineteenth-century poetry; see, e.g., *Childe Harold* IV, st. 126: 'Our life is a false nature – 'tis not in/ The harmony of things', and Matthew Arnold, *Empedocles on Etna*, II.345–54: 'But mind, but thought –/ If these have been the master part of us –/ Where will *they* find their parent element?/ What will receive *them*, who will call *them* home?/ But we shall be in them, and they in us,/ And we shall be the strangers of the world,/ And they will be our lords, as they are now;/ And keep us prisoners of our consciousness,/ And never let us clasp and feel the All/ But through their forms, and modes, and stifling veils.'

56. the hall of the famed Ariadne] 'The celebrated recumbent statue of Ariadne sleeping' in the Gallery of Statues in the Vatican's Museo Pio-Clementino (Murray 1843: 415); Murray also lists a Neptune and a 'Bacchus as a river god' among the exhibits.

57. Triton] A minor Greek sea-god, usually represented as half-man, half-fish; Claude uses it as an emblem of the irreducible duality of human life.

59] An allusion to the proto-evolutionary theory outlined by Robert Chambers in 1844 *Vestiges of Creation*, and parodied by Claude in a cancelled letter from the *A* manuscript (see Scott 1974: 60). Claude's point is that our present compound nature is due to our comparatively low level of evolutionary development.

60. Farewell, Politics, utterly!] C. quoted Claude in a letter of 29 October 1849 to Tom Arnold: 'I am full of admiration for Mazzini. . . . But on the whole "Farewell Politics utterly. – What can I do!" Study is more to the purpose' (Bertram 1966: 146).

60–1] Cp Luke 16:3: 'I cannot dig; to beg I am ashamed'; see also the cancelled motto from Homer's *Margites* given above, p. 76.

Gnash my teeth when I look in your French or your
    English papers,
What is the good of that? Will swearing, I wonder, mend
    matters?
Cursing and scolding repel the assailants? No, it is idle;
No, whatever befalls, I will hide, will ignore or forget it.   65
Let the tail shift for itself; I will bury my head. And
    what's the
Roman Republic to me, or I to the Roman Republic?
  Why not fight? – In the first place, I haven't so much
    as a musket.
In the next, if I had, I shouldn't know how I should use it.
In the third, just at present I'm studying ancient marbles.   70
In the fourth, I consider I owe my life to my country.
In the fifth, – I forget; but four good reasons are ample.
Meantime, pray let 'em fight, and be killed. I delight in
    devotion.
So that I 'list not, hurrah for the glorious army of martyrs!
Sanguis martyrum semen Ecclesiae; though it would seem
    this   75
Church is indeed of the purely Invisible, Kingdom-Come
    kind:
Militant here on earth! Triumphant, of course, then,
    elsewhere!
Ah, good Heaven, but I would I were out far away from
    the pother!

66–7] 'What's Hecuba to him, or he to [Hecuba],/ That he should weep for her?' (*Hamlet* II.ii.553-4). In a letter of 23 June 1849 to Matthew Arnold C. wrote 'Quid Romae faciam? What's politics to he or he to politics?' (Lowry 1932: 108)

74. *'list*] Enlist.

75. *Sanguis martyrum semen Ecclesiae*] Cp Tertullian, *Apologeticus* 50.13: 'Semen est sanguis Christianorum', 'The blood of Christians is the seed [of the church].'

76. *Kingdom-Come*] From the Lord's Prayer (Matthew 6:10): 'Thy kingdom come. Thy will be done on earth, as *it is* in heaven.'

77. *Militant, Triumphant*] The traditional distinction between the earthly church and its heavenly counterpart; Mazzini described the democratic struggle as a 'Chiesa militante per un impresa da compiersi' [Church militant for the accomplishment of a specific enterprise] in his 1849 article 'La Santa Alleanza dei popoli' (Mazzini n.d.: 132).

78. *pother*] Fuss, commotion.

79. *the olden-time inspiration*] A provocative periphrasis for the Bible; cp Carlyle's 'Hebrew old-clothes'.

IV. – CLAUDE TO EUSTACE.

NOT, as we read in the words of the olden-time
    inspiration,
Are there two several trees in the place we are set to
    abide in;   80
But on the apex most high of the Tree of Life in the
    Garden,
Budding, unfolding, and falling, decaying and flowering
    ever,
Flowering is set and decaying the transient blossom of
    Knowledge, –
Flowering alone, and decaying, the needless, unfruitful
    blossom.
    Or as the cypress-spires by the fair-flowing stream
        Hellespontine,   85
Which from the mythical tomb of the godlike Protesilaus
Rose sympathetic in grief to his lovelorn Laodamia,
Evermore growing, and, when in their growth to the
    prospect attaining,
Over the low sea-banks, of the fatal Ilian city,
Withering still at the sight which still they upgrow to
    encounter.   90
    Ah, but ye that extrude from the ocean your helpless
        faces,

80] Genesis 2:9: 'And out of the ground made the LORD God to grow every tree that is pleasant to the sight and good for food; the tree of life also in the midst of the garden, and the tree of knowledge of good and evil.'

81–3] Claude's grafting of the 'needless, unfruitful blossom' of knowledge onto the tree of life continues his earlier speculations about the compound nature of human life; cp Froude 1849: 26: 'Oh! that tree of knowledge, that death in life. Why, why are we compelled to know anything, when each step gained in knowledge is but one more nerve summoned out into consciousness of pain?'

85–90] Protesilaus was killed during the siege of Troy; legend has it that the cypress-trees planted on his grave grew until they caught sight of the city and then withered again. Claude uses this legend as an emblem for the role of knowledge in human life; it enables us to comprehend our implication in the natural cycle of growth, decay and death without allowing us to alter our situation in any way.

85. stream Hellespontine] The Hellespont separates Greece from Asia Minor.

87. lovelorn Laodamia] The wife of Protesilaus.

89. the fatal Ilian city] Troy (Ilium).

91–7] Another metaphor for the human condition; Claude represents us as rootless and drifting creatures who endure an antagonistic relation to the natural world.

Ye over stormy seas leading long and dreary processions,
Ye, too, brood of the wind, whose coming is whence we
    discern not,
Making your nest on the wave, and your bed on the
    crested billow,
Skimming rough waters, and crowding wet sands that
    the tide shall return to,   95
Cormorants, ducks, and gulls, fill ye my imagination!
Let us not talk of growth; we are still in our Aqueous
    Ages.[15]

V. – MARY TREVELLYN TO MISS ROPER,
– *from Florence.*

DEAREST MISS ROPER, – Alas, we are all at Florence
    quite safe, and
You, we hear, are shut up! indeed, it is sadly distressing!
We were most lucky, they say, to get off when we did
    from the troubles.   100
Now you are really besieged! They tell us it soon will be
    over;
Only I hope and trust without any fight in the city.
Do you see Mr. Claude? – I thought he might do
    something for you.
I am quite sure on occasion he really would wish to be
    useful.
What is he doing? I wonder; – still studying Vatican
    marbles?   105
Letters, I hope, pass through. We trust your brother is
    better.[16]

---

101. Now you are really besieged!] The siege proper began on 3 June 1849 and
lasted until 30 June; see Headnote.

---

[15] Alt. to 97:
    Let us not talk of growth; and garden and woodland fancies,
    Germs and blossoms and saps; and petal and pistil follies.
    Let us not talk of growth and vegetable Ethics;
    Crotchets vain and vain deceits; we are still in our Aqueous Ages. (*A*)
[16] Additional material in *A*:
    Oh come down to the path, come down my friend and my dear one,
    Stand not upon the heights, that are dreary and lead you to nothing.
    Come to the concourse of men, come down to your brothers and sisters.
    Be as we are and of us – is there none you can help and be helped by?

VI. – CLAUDE TO EUSTACE.

JUXTAPOSITION, in fine; and what is juxtaposition?
Look you, we travel along in the railway-carriage, or
    steamer,
And, *pour passer le temps*, till the tedious journey be ended,
Lay aside paper or book, to talk with the girl that is next
    one;   110
And, *pour passer le temps*, with the terminus all but in
    prospect,
Talk of eternal ties and marriages made in heaven.
  Ah, did we really accept with a perfect heart the
    illusion!
Ah, did we really believe that the Present indeed is the
    Only!
Or, through all transmutation, all shock and convulsion
    of passion,   115
Feel we could carry undimmed, unextinguished, the light
    of our knowledge![17]
  But for his funeral train which the bridegroom sees in
    the distance,
Would he so joyfully, think you, fall in with the marriage-
    procession?
But for that final discharge, would he dare to enlist in that
    service?

108–12] Claude's estimate of marriage recalls Keats's in the letter of 29
October 1818 referred to above (see II.250 and note). Keats describes his interest in a particular woman as 'a pastime and an amusement', and goes on to
express the hope that he will never marry: 'the mighty abstract Idea of Beauty
in all things, I have, stifles the more divided and minute domestic happiness' –
Milnes 1927: 137, 141.
111. pour passer le temps] To pass the time.
115–16] Cp I.xii above on the distorting effect of passion on knowledge.

---

[17] After 116:
  It is the virtue of Man to discern and love the ideal;
  It is the wisdom of Man to accept and live in the real;
  But if the first he discern, how then can he love the second?
  If unto this he consent can he live in the light of the other? (A)

But for that certain release, ever sign to that perilous
    contract? 120
But for that exit secure, ever bend to that treacherous
    doorway? –
Ah, but the bride, meantime, – do you think she sees it as
    he does?
  But for the steady fore-sense of a freer and larger
    existence,
Think you that man could consent to be circumscribed
    here into action?
But for assurance within of a limitless ocean divine, o'er 125
Whose great tranquil depths unconscious the wind-tost
    surface
Breaks into ripples of trouble that come and change and
    endure not, –
But that in this, of a truth, we have our being, and know
    it,
Think you we men could submit to live and move as we
    do here?
Ah, but the women, – God bless them! – they don't think
    at all about it. 130
  Yet we must eat and drink, as you say. And as limited
    beings
Scarcely can hope to attain upon earth to an Actual
    Abstract,
Leaving to God contemplation, to His hands knowledge
    confiding,

122] The mismatch between male and female perceptions of romantic love was something which C. felt keenly; see, for example, the letter of May 1852 to his fiancée Blanche Smith: 'it is true that the tie which it seems to me your heart claims is not precisely that which mine is capable of meeting it in – there is always this sad ambiguity in our human words' – *Corr.* ii, 313.
123–9] Another of the poem's cryptic discussions of the difficulties of belief.
123–4] *Othello* I.ii.24–7: 'But that I love the gentle Desdemona,/ I would not my unhoused free condition/ Put into circumscription and confine/ For the sea's worth.'
128–9] Cp Paul's words to the Athenians, Acts 17:28: 'For in him we live, and move, and have our being.'
132. Actual Abstract] A pseudo-philosophical formulation for an earthly manifestation of the divine.

Sure that in us if it perish, in Him it abideth and dies not,
Let us in His sight accomplish our petty particular
    doings, –   135
Yes, and contented sit down to the victual that He has
    provided.
Allah is great, no doubt, and Juxtaposition his prophet.
Ah, but the women, alas, they don't look at it in that way!
    Juxtaposition is great; – but, my friend, I fear me, the
    maiden
Hardly would thank or acknowledge the lover that
    sought to obtain her,   140
Not as the thing he would wish, but the thing he must
    even put up with, –
Hardly would tender her hand to the wooer that candidly
    told her
That she is but for a space, an *ad-interim* solace and
    pleasure, –
That in the end she shall yield to a perfect and absolute
    something,
Which I then for myself shall behold, and not another, –   145
Which, amid fondest endearments, meantime I forget
    not, forsake not.
Ah, ye feminine souls, so loving and so exacting,
Since we cannot escape, must we even submit to deceive
    you?
Since so cruel is truth, sincerity shocks and revolts you,
Will you have us your slaves to lie to you, flatter and
    – leave you?   150

---

137. Allah is great] 'Allahu Akbar' – 'God is great', the Muslim call to prayer.
This may have been one of the cant phrases of contemporary English high
society; Robert Blake remarks that it was one of Disraeli's 'irritating manner-
isms' to 'preface his remarks with a drawling "Allah is great" ' – Blake 1978:
80.
139–46] C.'s own wooing of his future wife was similarly honest: 'I won't say
that you are all in every way that I could imagine' – Chorley 1962: 235.
143. ad-interim] In the meantime.
145] Cp Job 19:26–7: 'And *though* after my skin *worms* destroy this *body*, yet
in my flesh shall I see God:/ Whom I shall see for myself, and mine eyes shall
behold, and not another.' This passage forms part of the Order for the Burial
of the Dead in the Book of Common Prayer.

VII. – CLAUDE TO EUSTACE.

JUXTAPOSITION is great, – but, you tell me, affinity
    greater.
Ah, my friend, there are many affinities, greater and
    lesser,
Stronger and weaker; and each, by the favour of
    juxtaposition
Potent, efficient, in force, – for a time; but none, let me
    tell you,
Save by the law of the land and the ruinous force of the
    will, ah,   155
None, I fear me, at last quite sure to be final and perfect.
Lo, as I pace in the street, from the peasant-girl to the
    princess,
Homo sum, nihil humani a me alienum puto, –
Vir sum, nihil foeminei, – and e'en to the uttermost circle,
All that is Nature's is I, and I all things that are Nature's.   160
Yes, as I walk, I behold, in a luminous, large intuition,
That I can be and become anything that I meet with or
    look at:
I am the ox in the dray, the ass with the garden-stuff
    panniers;
I am the dog in the doorway, the kitten that plays in the
    window,
On sunny slab of the ruin the furtive and fugitive lizard,   165
Swallow above me that twitters, and fly that is buzzing
    about me;
Yea, and detect, as I go, by a faint, but a faithful assurance,
E'en from the stones of the street, as from rocks or trees of
    the forest,

III.vii] This letter is written in response to one of Eustace's which did not survive revision: 'Juxtaposition! be shot! an excellent thing I assure you./ Will you
refuse your food because God puts it before you./ Ah, and your sages I think
know the name of affinity also.' On juxtaposition and affinity see Introduction,
pp. 15–16.
158–9] Slightly misquoted from Terence, *The Self-Tormentor* (*Heauton
Timorumenos*) 1.1.25: 'homo sum: humani nil a me alienum puto' – 'I am a
man; nothing human can be alien to me.' Claude changes this to 'I am male,
nothing female [can be alien to me]' in order to emphasise the indiscriminate
and instinctive nature of sexual attraction.
160–72] This feeling of universal kinship with nature has many parallels in
Romantic poetry; Scott notes similarities to Tennyson's *Ulysses* l. 19 and to
Childe Harold III, st. 72. Cp also *Natura naturans* above, ll. 41 *et seq.*
163. panniers] Baskets.

Something of kindred, a common, though latent vitality,
 greet me,
And, to escape from our strivings, mistakings,
 misgrowths, and perversions,   170
Fain could demand to return to that perfect and primitive
 silence,
Fain be enfolded and fixed, as of old, in their rigid
 embraces.

VIII. – Claude to Eustace.

AND, as I walk on my way, I behold them consorting and
 coupling;
Faithful it seemeth, and fond, very fond, very probably
 faithful;
All as I go on my way with a pleasure sincere and
 unmingled.   175
  Life is beautiful, Eustace, entrancing, enchanting to
   look at;
As are the streets of a city we pace while the carriage is
 changing,
As is a chamber filled-in with harmonious, exquisite
 pictures,
Even so beautiful earth; and could we eliminate only
This vile hungering impulse, this demon within us of
 craving,   180
Life were beatitude, living a perfect divine satisfaction.

IX. – Claude to Eustace.

Mild monastic faces in quiet collegiate cloisters:
So let me offer a single and celibatarian phrase a
Tribute to those whom perhaps you do not believe I
 can honour.

III.viii] C. wrote to his fiancée in February 1852: 'To a certain extent it seems
to me that the whole world is apt to wear a mere pictorial aspect, that it must
be by an effort that I accept anything as fact' (Bod. MS). On the significance of
the desire for a purely specular relation to life see above, II.277 and note.
182–9] The question of the value of the monastic life was brought to the fore
in the 1840s by the rigid asceticism of some of the leading members of the
Oxford Movement; see G. Faber (1954) *Oxford Apostles*, ch. 6.

But, from the tumult escaping, 'tis pleasant, of drumming
    and shouting,   185
Hither, oblivious awhile, to withdraw, of the fact and the
    falsehood,
And amid placid regards and mildly courteous greetings
Yield to the calm and composure and gentle abstraction
    that reign o'er
Mild monastic faces in quiet collegiate cloisters.
    Terrible word, Obligation! You should not, Eustace,
    you should not,   190
No, you should not have used it. But, O great Heavens,
    I repel it!
Oh, I cancel, reject, disavow, and repudiate wholly
Every debt in this kind, disclaim every claim, and
    dishonour,
Yea, my own heart's own writing, my soul's own
    signature! Ah, no!
I will be free in this; you shall not, none shall, bind me.   195
No, my friend, if you wish to be told, it was this above
    all things,
This that charmed me, ah, yes, even this, that she held
    me to nothing.
No, I could talk as I pleased; come close; fasten ties, as
    I fancied;
Bind and engage myself deep; – and lo, on the following
    morning
It was all e'en as before, like losings in games played for
    nothing.   200
Yes, when I came, with mean fears in my soul, with a
    semi-performance
At the first step breaking down in its pitiful role of
    evasion,
When to shuffle I came, to compromise, not meet,
    engagements,
Lo, with her calm eyes there she met me and knew
    nothing of it, –

185–6] Claude's attempt at latinate syntax is not particularly clear in English. The phrase 'of drumming and shouting' is adjectival, and qualifies the noun 'tumult'; 'of the fact and the falsehood' belongs with 'oblivious', and both constitute one adverbial phrase qualifying 'to withdraw'.

190–206] Claude's vehement rejection of the notion of obligation is consistent with his general desire to let love 'be its own inspiration' (II.278).

Stood unexpecting, unconscious. *She* spoke not of
          obligations,   205
Knew not of debt, – ah, no, I believe you, for excellent
          reasons.

X. – CLAUDE TO EUSTACE.

HANG this thinking, at last! what good is it? oh, and
          what evil!
Oh, what mischief and pain! like a clock in a sick man's
          chamber,
Ticking and ticking, and still through each covert of
          slumber pursuing.
     What shall I do to thee, O thou Preserver of Men? Have
          compassion;   210
Be favourable, and hear! Take from me this regal
          knowledge;
Let me, contented and mute, with the beasts of the field,
          my brothers,
Tranquilly, happily lie, – and eat grass, like
          Nebuchadnezzar!

205. Stood unexpecting, unconscious] Claude once again chooses to portray
Mary as the bearer of an instinctive wisdom beyond (or beneath) ratiocination;
see above, II.x and note.
206. I believe you] An emphatic phrase meaning something like 'You're
right!'; cp this exchange from Thackeray's *Pendennis*: 'Miss Rouncy, I gather,
was the confidante of the other?' 'Confidant? I believe you' (Thackeray 1986:
129)
207–9] Cp Byron's strictures on '[the] blight of life – the demon, Thought'
(*Childe Harold* I.860).
210–13] This desire to lose humanity's 'regal knowledge' and return to the
blissful unconsciousness of animal existence is continuous with Claude's earlier strictures on our 'painful victorious knowledge' (see above, III.ii and iv); cp
also Schopenhauer's description of animals as 'the present incarnate' and his
assertion that their 'obvious composure often puts to shame our own frequent-
ly restless and discontented condition' – Schopenhauer 1986: 45–6.
210] Cp Job 7:20: 'I have sinned. What shall I do unto thee, O thou preserver
of Men? Why hast thou set me as a mark against thee, so that I am a burden to
myself?'
212–13] The story of Nebuchadnezzar is told in the Book of Daniel; the king
'was driven from men, and did eat grass as oxen' for his iniquity and pride
(4:33).

XI. – CLAUDE TO EUSTACE.

TIBUR is beautiful, too, and the orchard slopes, and the
    Anio,
Falling, falling yet, to the ancient lyrical cadence,   215
Tibur and Anio's tide; and cool from Lucretilis ever,
With the Digentian stream, and with the Bandusian
    fountain,
Folded in Sabine recesses, the valley and villa of Horace: –
So not seeing I sung; so seeing and listening say I,
Here as I sit by the stream, as I gaze at the cell of the Sibyl,   220
Here with Albunea's home and the grove of Tiburnus
    beside me;*
Tivoli beautiful is, and musical, O Teverone,
Dashing from mountain to plain, thy parted impetuous
    waters!
Tivoli's waters and rocks; and fair under Monte Gennaro,
(Haunt even yet, I must think, as I wander and gaze, of
    the shadows,   225

*
            — domus Albuneae resonantis,
    Et praeceps Anio, et Tiburni lucus, et uda
        Mobilibus pomaria rivis.

III.xi] These lines commemorating an imaginary excursion to Horace's Sabine farm are written in imitation of a Horatian ode – hence the complex syntax and sonorous repetition of names.

214. Tibur] Modern Tivoli, a town in the Sabine hills near Horace's farm.

214. Anio] According to Murray, 'the modern Teverone' (see III.222 below): 'after forming the cascades of Tivoli it falls into the Tiber 3 miles from Rome' (Murray 1843: 477).

216. Lucretilis] 'There is no doubt that the Mons Lucretilis, which Horace has celebrated in his most beautiful ode . . . was one of the peaks of this ridge, and many writers identify it with Monte Genaro itself' – Murray 1843: 488 (see III.224 below).

217. Digentian stream] Celebrated in Horace's *Epistle* I.xviii (cited in Murray 1843: 487).

217. Bandusian fountain] *Odes* III.xiii: 'O more than crystal bright, Bandusian Spring,/ Worthy sweet wine . . .' (C.'s translation).

220. the Sibyl] Albunea, known as the Tiburtine Sibyl: 'Among the antiquities of the town the principal object is the *Temple of the Tiburtine Sybil*, a beautiful building of the best times of art, finely placed on a rock overhanging the valley of the cascades' – Murray 1843: 481.

221] C.'s loose translation of *Odes* I.vii.12–14 (the original is cited at the bottom of the letter).

Faded and pale, yet immortal, of Faunus, the Nymphs,
    and the Graces,)
Fair in itself, and yet fairer with human completing
    creations,
Folded in Sabine recesses the valley and villa of Horace: –
So not seeing I sung; so now – Nor seeing, nor hearing,
Neither by waterfall lulled, nor folded in sylvan embraces,   230
Neither by cell of the Sibyl, nor stepping the Monte
    Gennaro,
Seated on Anio's bank, nor sipping Bandusian waters,
But on Montorio's height, looking down on the tile-clad
    streets, the
Cupolas, crosses, and domes, the bushes and kitchen-
    gardens,
Which, by the grace of the Tiber, proclaim themselves
    Rome of the Romans, –   235
But on Montorio's height, looking forth to the vapoury
    mountains,
Cheating the prisoner Hope with illusions of vision and
    fancy, –
But on Montorio's height, with these weary soldiers by
    me,
Waiting till Oudinot enter, to reinstate Pope and Tourist.

XII. – MARY TREVELLYN TO MISS ROPER.

DEAR MISS ROPER, – It seems, George Vernon,
    before we left Rome, said   240
Something to Mr. Claude about what they call his
    attentions.
Susan, two nights ago, for the first time, heard this from
    Georgina.
It is *so* disagreeable and *so* annoying to think of!
If it could only be known, though we never may meet
    him again, that

---

226. *Faunus, the Nymphs, and the Graces]* Figures in classical mythology.
233. *on Montorio's height]* A hill in the Trastevere quarter (see above, II.212)
commanding a view over the city.
238. *with these weary soldiers beside me]* The besieging French troops were
encamped in a position near Montorio; Claude would, therefore, have been
close to the defenders of the Roman Republic in this position.

It was all George's doing and we were entirely
    unconscious,   245
It would extremely relieve – Your ever affectionate Mary.

P.S. (1).
  Here is your letter arrived this moment, just as I
    wanted.
So you have seen him, – indeed, – and guessed, – how
    dreadfully clever!
What did he really say? and what was your answer exactly?
Charming! – but wait for a moment, for I haven't read
    through the letter.   250

P.S. (2).
  Ah, my dearest Miss Roper, do just as you fancy about
    it.
If you think it sincerer to tell him I know of it, do so.
Though I should most extremely dislike it, I know I could
    manage.
It is the simplest thing, but surely wholly uncalled for.
Do as you please; you know I trust implicitly to you.   255
Say whatever is right and needful for ending the matter.
Only don't tell Mr. Claude, what I will tell you as a secret,
That I should like very well to show him myself I forget it.

P.S. (3).
  I am to say that the wedding is finally settled for
    Tuesday.
Ah, my dear Miss Roper, you surely, surely can manage   260
Not to let it appear that I know of that odious matter.
It would be pleasanter far for myself to treat it exactly
As if it had not occurred; and I do not think he would
    like it.
I must remember to add, that as soon as the wedding is
    over
We shall be off, I believe, in a hurry, and travel to Milan,   265
There to meet friends of Papa's, I am told, at the Croce
    di Malta;
Then I cannot say whither, but not at present to England.

---

245. *unconscious]* Unaware.
259. *the wedding]* Of George Vernon and Georgina Trevellyn.
266. *the Croce di Malta]* A hotel in the Piazza di San Sepolcro in Milan; see
Murray 1847: 142.

XIII. – CLAUDE TO EUSTACE.

YES, on Montorio's height for a last farewell of the city, –
So it appears; though then I was quite uncertain about it.
So, however it was.　And now to explain the proceeding.　　　270
　　I was to go, as I told you, I think, with the people to
　　　　Florence.
Only the day before, the foolish family Vernon
Made some uneasy remarks, as we walked to our lodging
　　　　together,
As to intentions, forsooth, and so forth. I was astounded,
Horrified quite; and obtaining just then, as it happened,
　　　　an offer　　　275
(No common favour) of seeing the great Ludovisi
　　　　collection,
Why, I made this a pretence, and wrote that they must
　　　　excuse me.
How could I go? Great Heaven! to conduct a permitted
　　　　flirtation
Under those vulgar eyes, the observed of such observers!
Well, but I now, by a series of fine diplomatic inquiries,　　　280
Find from a sort of relation, a good and sensible woman,
Who is remaining at Rome with a brother too ill for
　　　　removal,
That it was wholly unsanctioned, unknown, – not, I think,
　　　　by Georgina:
She, however, ere this, – and that is the best of the story, –
She and the Vernon, thank Heaven, are wedded and
　　　　gone – honey-mooning.　　　285
So – on Montorio's height for a last farewell of the city.
Tibur I have not seen, nor the lakes that of old I had
　　　　dreamt of;
Tibur I shall not see, nor Anio's waters, nor deep en-
Folded in Sabine recesses the valley and villa of Horace;
Tibur I shall not see; – but something better I shall see.　　　290
　　Twice I have tried before, and failed in getting the
　　　　horses;
　　Twice I have tried and failed: this time it shall not be
　　　　a failure.

III.xiii] This letter contains the long-delayed explanation of Claude's failure
to accompany the Trevellyns to Florence.
276. the great Ludovisi collection] A notoriously inaccessible collection of
antique art; C. visited it on 25 or 26 June.
279. the observed of such observers] Ophelia describes Hamlet as 'the observed
of all observers' – *Hamlet* III.i.156.

THEREFORE farewell, ye hills, and ye, ye envineyarded
    ruins!
  Therefore farewell, ye walls, palaces, pillars, and domes!
Therefore farewell, far seen, ye peaks of the mythic Albano,   295
  Seen from Montorio's height, Tibur and Aesula's hills!
Ah, could we once, ere we go, could we stand, while, to ocean
    descending,
  Sinks o'er the yellow dark plain slowly the yellow broad
    sun,
Stand, from the forest emerging at sunset, at once in the
    champaign,
  Open, but studded with trees, chestnuts umbrageous and old,   300
E'en in those fair open fields that incurve to thy beautiful
    hollow,
  Nemi, imbedded in wood, Nemi, inurned in the hill! –
Therefore farewell, ye plains, and ye hills, and the City
    Eternal!
  Therefore farewell! We depart, but to behold you again!

IV.

EASTWARD, or Northward, or West? I wander, and ask
    as I wander,
  Weary, yet eager and sure, Where shall I come to my love?
Whitherward hasten to seek her? Ye daughters of Italy, tell
    me,
  Graceful and tender and dark, is she consorting with you?
Thou that out-climbest the torrent, that tendest thy goats to
    the summit,   5
  Call to me, child of the Alp, has she been seen on the
    heights?

---

296. *Aesula's hills]* The hills around Palestrina, the site of ancient Aesula.
299. *champaign]* Open level country (Italian 'campagna').
302. *Nemi]* The principal lake of the Alban hills; it occupies 'the well-defined crater of an extinct volcano' (Murray 1843: 506–7) – hence 'inurned in the hill'.
1–10] This whole passage recalls, without direct allusion, the plaintive cry of the Song of Solomon: 'Whither is thy beloved gone, O thou fairest among women? whither is thy beloved turned aside? that we may seek him with thee' (6:1). Cp III.15–16 above.

Italy, farewell I bid thee! for, whither she leads me, I follow.
Farewell the vineyard! for I, where I but guess her, must go.
Weariness welcome, and labour, wherever it be, if at last it
   Bring me in mountain or plain into the sight of my love.   10

I. – CLAUDE TO EUSTACE, – *from Florence.*

GONE from Florence; indeed; and that is truly
        provoking; –
Gone to Milan, it seems; then I go also to Milan.
Five days now departed; but they can travel but slowly; –
I quicker far; and I know, as it happens, the house they
        will go to. –
Why, what else should I do? Stay here and look at the
        pictures,   15
Statues, and churches? Alack, I am sick of the statues and
        pictures! –
No, to Bologna, Parma, Piacenza, Lodi, and Milan,
Off we go to-night, – and the Venus go to the Devil!

II. – CLAUDE TO EUSTACE, – *from Bellaggio.*

GONE to Como, they said; and I have posted to Como.
There was a letter left, but the *cameriere* had lost it.   20
Could it have been for me? They came, however, to
        Como,
And from Como went by the boat, – perhaps to the
        Splügen, –
Or to the Stelvio, say, and the Tyrol; also it might be
By Porlezza across to Lugano, and so to the Simplon

17] Cities on the road to Milan.
18. *the Venus*] The Venus de Medici in the Uffizi in Florence.
IV.ii.] *Bellaggio*] A town on Lake Como.
19. *posted*] Travelled quickly by horse.
20. *cameriere*] Waiter or servant at an inn.
22–6] Claude's analysis of the various possibilities is founded on the assumption that the Trevellyns continued on from Como by boat. They could, in this
case, have gone in one of two directions, depending on the point at which they
alighted. They could have left the boat at Menaggio, halfway along the lake,
travelled overland to Porlezza on Lake Lugano, and continued on from there
to the Simplon Tunnel or to Lake Maggiore and the cities of Piedmont; or else
they could have stayed on the boat as far as Colico, on the northern edge of the
lake, and continued northward via the Splügen Pass into Switzerland, or the
Stelvio Pass into Austria (see Murray 1846: 258).

Possibly, or the St. Gothard, – or possibly, too, to Baveno,   25
Orta, Turin, and elsewhere. Indeed, I am greatly
   bewildered.

III. – CLAUDE TO EUSTACE, – *from Bellaggio*.

I HAVE been up the Splügen, and on the Stelvio also:
Neither of these can I find they have followed; in no one
   inn, and
This would be odd, have they written their names. I have
   been to Porlezza.
There they have not been seen, and therefore not at
   Lugano.   30
What shall I do? Go on through the Tyrol, Switzerland,
   Deutschland,
Seeking, an inverse Saul, a kingdom, to find only asses?
  There is a tide, at least in the *love* affairs of mortals,
Which, when taken at flood, leads on to the happiest
   fortune, –
Leads to the marriage-morn and the orange-flowers and
   the altar,   35
And the long lawful line of crowned joys to crowned joys
   succeeding. –

25. St. Gothard] The St. Gotthard Pass linking Italy and Switzerland.
25. Baveno] A town on Lake Maggiore.
26. Orta, Turin] Towns in Piedmont.
27–30] Claude follows through both the possible routes and finds no trace of
the Trevellyns on either. From their failure to visit Porlezza he concludes that
they cannot be at Lugano, and so does not continue his search in that direction
(30). Unknown to him, however, the Trevellyns have been at Lugano; as Mary
points out in her next letter they altered their travel plans at the last moment,
going there directly overland from Como and so (inadvertently) throwing
Claude off the scent.
32] The story of Saul, anointed king of Israel while searching for his father's
asses, is told in 1 Samuel 9.
33–4] Cp *Julius Caesar* IV.iii.217–20: 'There is a tide in the affairs of men,/
Which, taken at the flood, leads on to fortune;/ Omitted, all the voyage of their
life/ Is bound in shallows and in miseries.' C. wrote in his diary in February
1838: 'Is it not true that "there is a tide in the affairs of men" spiritually?'
(Kenny 1990: 13)

Ah, it has ebbed with me! Ye gods, and when it was
       flowing,
Pitiful fool that I was, to stand fiddle-faddling in that way!

IV. – CLAUDE TO EUSTACE, – *from Bellaggio.*

I HAVE returned and found their names in the book at
       Como.
Certain it is I was right, and yet I am also in error.   40
Added in feminine hand, I read, *By the boat to Bellaggio.* –
So to Bellaggio again, with the words of her writing, to aid
       me.
Yet at Bellaggio I find no trace, no sort of remembrance.
So I am here, and wait, and know every hour will remove
       them.

V. – CLAUDE TO EUSTACE, – *from Bellaggio.*

I HAVE but one chance left, – and that is, going to
       Florence.   45
But it is cruel to turn. The mountains seem to demand
       me, –
Peak and valley from far to beckon and motion me
       onward.
Somewhere amid their folds she passes whom fain I
       would follow;
Somewhere among those heights she haply calls me to
       seek her.
Ah, could I hear her call! could I catch the glimpse of
       her raiment!   50
Turn, however, I must, though it seem I turn to desert
       her;

38] Claude's harsh judgement on his earlier actions is echoed in a letter of 19
June 1850 from C. to J.C. Shairp: 'Let us not sit in a corner and mope, and
think ourselves clever, for our comfort, while the room is full of dancing and
cheerfulness. The sum of the whole matter is this. Whatsoever your hand find-
eth to do, do it without fiddle-faddling; for there is no experience, nor
pleasure, nor pain, nor instruction, nor anything else in the grave whither thou
goest' (*Corr.* i, 284).

For the sense of the thing is simply to hurry to Florence,
Where the certainty yet may be learnt, I suppose, from
    the Ropers.

VI. – MARY TREVELLYN, *from Lucerne*, TO MISS ROPER, *at Florence*.

DEAR MISS ROPER, – By this you are safely away, we
    are hoping,
Many a league from Rome; ere long we trust we shall
    see you.   55
How have you travelled? I wonder; – was Mr. Claude
    your companion?
As for ourselves, we went from Como straight to Lugano;
So by the Mount St. Gothard; – we meant to go by
    Porlezza,
Taking the steamer, and stopping, as you had advised, at
    Bellaggio,
Two or three days or more; but this was suddenly altered,   60
After we left the hotel, on the very way to the steamer.
So we have seen, I fear, not one of the lakes in perfection.
   Well, he is not come; and now, I suppose, he will not
    come.
What will you think, meantime? – and yet I must really
    confess it; –
What will you say? I wrote him a note. We left in a hurry,   65
Went from Milan to Como three days before we expected.
But I thought, if he came all the way to Milan, he really
Ought not to be disappointed; and so I wrote three lines to
Say I had heard he was coming, desirous of joining our
    party; –
If so, then I said, we had started for Como, and meant to   70
Cross the St. Gothard, and stay, we believed, at Lucerne,
    for the summer.
Was it wrong? and why, if it was, has it failed to bring
    him?

57–61] See above IV.27–30 and note; the route overland from Como to
Lugano is Route 92 in Murray (1846).
59–62] Mary is reflecting Murray's opinion that Bellaggio is 'a delightful spot,
commanding perhaps the most splendid views to be met with on any of the
Italian lakes' – Murray 1846: 258.
65] The letter lost by the *cameriere*; see IV.20 and note above.

Did he not think it worth while to come to Milan? He
    knew (you
Told him) the house we should go to. Or may it, perhaps,
    have miscarried?
Any way, now, I repent, and am heartily vexed that I
    wrote it.   75

THERE is a home on the shore of the Alpine sea, that
    upswelling
    High up the mountain-sides spreads in the hollow between;
Wilderness, mountain, and snow from the land of the olive
    conceal it;
    Under Pilatus's hill low by its river it lies:
Italy, utter the word, and the olive and vine will allure not, –   80
    Wilderness, forest, and snow will not the passage impede;
Italy, unto thy cities receding, the clue to recover,
    Hither, recovered the clue, shall not the traveller haste?

V.

THERE is a city, upbuilt on the quays of the turbulent Arno,
    Under Fiesole's heights, – thither are we to return?
There is a city that fringes the curve of the inflowing waters,
    Under the perilous hill fringes the beautiful bay, –
Parthenope do they call thee? – the Siren, Neapolis, seated   5
    Under Vesuvus's hill, – thither are we to recede?
Sicily, Greece, will invite, and the Orient; – or are we to
    turn to
    England, which may after all be for its children the best?

76. *the Alpine sea]* The Vierwaldstättersee or Lake of Lucerne on which the
city stands.
79. *Pilatus's hill]* Mount Pilatus overlooks the Lake of Lucerne.
1–2] The Arno runs through Florence.
5. *Parthenope]* A poetical term for Naples.
5. *the Siren, Neapolis]* Naples derives its name from the Greek word
'Neapolis'.
6. *Vesuvus's hill]* Mount Vesuvius.

I. – MARY TREVELLYN, *at Lucerne*, TO MISS ROPER, *at Florence*.

SO you are really free, and living in quiet at Florence;
That is delightful news; – you travelled slowly and safely;   10
Mr. Claude got you out; took rooms at Florence before
    you;
Wrote from Milan to say so; had left directly for Milan,
Hoping to find us soon; – *if he could, he would, you are
    certain.* –
Dear Miss Roper, your letter has made me exceedingly
    happy.
    You are quite sure, you say, he asked you about our
        intentions;   15
You had not heard as yet of Lucerne, but told him of
    Como. –
Well, perhaps he will come; – however, I will not expect it.
Though you say you are sure, – *if he can, he will, you are
    certain.*
O my dear, many thanks from your ever affectionate Mary.

II. – CLAUDE TO EUSTACE.

                                                    Florence.
Action will furnish belief, – but will that belief be the true
    one?   20
This is the point, you know. However, it doesn't much
    matter.
What one wants, I suppose, is to predetermine the action,
So as to make it entail, not a chance-belief, but the true
    one.
Out of the question, you say; *if a thing isn't wrong, we may
    do it.*

20–5] Claude is replying to Eustace's exhortations in the cancelled letter i.*A*: 'Action involves belief, Inaction such stuff as you sent me./ Act and all will be clear; the Laws of Action are God's Laws;/ What they entail to our minds, God's gift and prime revelation.' Cp Carlyle (1838) *Sartor Resartus,* Bk 2, ch. ix: 'Most true it is, as a wise man teaches us, that "Doubt of any sort cannot be removed except by Action".'

Ah! but this *wrong*, you see – but I do not know that it
    matters.   25
  Eustace, the Ropers are gone, and no one can tell me
    about them.

                            Pisa.
Pisa, they say they think; and so I follow to Pisa,
Hither and thither inquiring. I weary of making inquiries;
I am ashamed, I declare, of asking people about it. –
Who are your friends? You said you had friends who
    would certainly know them.   30

                        Florence.
But it is idle, moping, and thinking, and trying to fix her
Image more and more in, to write the old perfect
    inscription   .
Over and over again upon every page of remembrance.
  I have settled to stay at Florence to wait for your
    answer.
Who are your friends? Write quickly and tell me. I wait
    for your answer.   35

III. – MARY TREVELLYN TO MISS ROPER,
at Lucca Baths.

YOU are at Lucca Baths, you tell me, to stay for the
    summer;
Florence was quite too hot; you can't move further at
    present.
Will you not come, do you think, before the summer is
    over?
  Mr. C. got you out with very considerable trouble;
And he was useful and kind, and seemed so happy to
    serve you;   40
Didn't stay with you long, but talked very openly to you;
Made you almost his confessor, without appearing to
    know it, –

31–3] Claude begins to question the reality of the image of Mary which he has
been pursuing; cp V.57–9 and 157 below.
36. Lucca Baths] A popular spa resort in Tuscany; true to form, Claude has
now lost the Ropers as well as the Trevellyns.

What about? – and you say you didn't need his
    confessions.
O my dear Miss Roper, I dare not trust what you tell me!
    Will he come, do you think? I am really so sorry for him!   45
They didn't give him my letter at Milan, I feel pretty
    certain.
You had told him Bellaggio. We didn't go to Bellaggio;
So he would miss our track, and perhaps never come to
    Lugano,
Where we were written in full, *To Lucerne, across the St.
    Gothard.*
But he could write to you; – you would tell him where
    you were going.   50

IV. – CLAUDE TO EUSTACE.

LET me, then, bear to forget her. I will not cling to her
    falsely;
Nothing factitious or forced shall impair the old happy
    relation.
I will let myself go, forget, not try to remember;[18]
I will walk on my way, accept the chances that meet me,
Freely encounter the world, imbibe these alien airs, and   55
Never ask if new feelings and thoughts are of her or of
    others.
Is she not changing, herself? – the old image would only
    delude me.
I will be bold, too, and change, – if it must be. Yet if in
    all things,
Yet if I do but aspire evermore to the Absolute only,
I shall be doing, I think, somehow, what she will be
    doing; –   60
I shall be thine, O my child, some way, though I know not
    in what way.
Let me submit to forget her; I must; I already forget her.

46–9] For Claude's peregrinations, see above, IV.ii–iv and notes.
57–8] See above, V.31–3, and the cancelled line after 53; cp also Matthew
Arnold's *The Terrace at Berne*, the concluding poem of the 'Marguerite' series:
'Or shall I find thee still, but changed,/ But not the Marguerite of thy prime?/
With all thy being re-arranged,/ Passed through the crucible of time' (32–6).
59. *the Absolute*] One of Claude's code-words for God; cp III.144–5.

---

[18] After 53: Must not set up an idol, to live and die in its presence. (*A*)

V. – CLAUDE TO EUSTACE.

UTTERLY vain is, alas, this attempt at the Absolute,
    – wholly!
I, who believed not in her, because I would fain believe
    nothing,
Have to believe as I may, with a wilful, unmeaning
    acceptance.   65
I, who refused to enfasten the roots of my floating
    existence
In the rich earth, cling now to the hard, naked rock that
    is left me. –
Ah! she was worthy, Eustace, – and that, indeed, is my
    comfort, –
Worthy a nobler heart than a fool such as I could have
    given.

Yes, it relieves me to write, though I do not send, and the
    chance that   70

V.v] This letter was the subject of extensive revision by C. The first three sections were printed as separate letters in *AM*; the last three were restored from *A* and the present structure adopted in 1859 *Corrections*. The restored sections all deal with Claude's religious difficulties.

63–9] Claude's comments here depend on the metaphors established earlier in the poem. He finds that 'the hard, naked rock' of 'the Absolute' is a barren consolation for having passed up the opportunity to 'enfasten the roots' of his 'floating existence' with Mary; see III.ii, iv for Claude's rejection of the idea of a 'rooted' existence. Mary's use of the same figure – see above, III.37–9 – indicates a level of similarity between them incompatible with genuine affinity, which depends for its existence on antithetical qualities in the partners; see Goethe (1809) *Elective Affinities*, ch. iv and note to II.299 above.

69. a fool such as I] C. refers to Claude as his 'unfortunate fool of a hero' in a letter of November 1849 to J.C. Shairp – *Corr.* i, 278.

70–1] This notion of writing as a catharsis or purge for the overburdened mind is common in the early nineteenth century; see, e.g., Wordsworth's *Ode:*

Takes may destroy my fragments. But as men pray,
    without asking
Whether One really exist to hear or do anything for
    them, –
Simply impelled by the need of the moment to turn to
    a Being
In a conception of whom there is freedom from all
    limitation, –
So in your image I turn to an *ens rationis* of friendship.   75
Even so write in your name I know not to whom nor in
    what wise.

There was a time, methought it was but lately departed,
When, if a thing was denied me, I felt I was bound to
    attempt it;
Choice alone should take, and choice alone should
    surrender.
There was a time, indeed, when I had not retired thus
    early,   80
Languidly thus, from pursuit of a purpose I once had
    adopted.
But it is over, all that! I have slunk from the perilous field
    in
Whose wild struggle of forces the prizes of life are
    contested.
It is over, all that! I am a coward, and know it.
Courage in me could be only factitious, unnatural, useless.   85

Intimations of immortality from recollections of early childhood: 'To me alone
there came a thought of grief:/ A timely utterance gave that thought relief,/
And I again am strong' (22–4). A theory based on this notion is outlined in
John Keble's *Praelectiones Academicae* of 1833–41, translated into English by
E.K. Francis in 1912 as *Keble's Lectures on Poetry* (Keble 1912); cp also C.'s
first *Letter of Parepidemus* (*PR* 381–9).
71–5] See I.11–12 above and note.
75. ens rationis] A term from scholastic philosophy for imaginary creatures
conjured up by the faculty of invention, such as dragons and hippogriffs.

Comfort has come to [me] here in the dreary streets of the
    city,
Comfort – how do you think? – with a barrel-organ to
    bring it.
Moping along the streets, and cursing my day, as I
    wandered,
All of a sudden my ear met the sound of an English psalm
    tune.
Comfort me it did, till indeed I was very near crying.   90
Ah there is some great truth, partial very likely, but
    needful,
Lodged, I am strangely sure, in the tones of the English
    psalm tune.
Comfort it was at least; and I must take without question
Comfort however it come in the dreary streets of the city.

What with trusting myself and seeking support from
    within me,   95
Almost I could believe I had gained a religious assurance,
Found in my own poor soul a great moral basis to rest on.
Ah, but indeed I see, I feel it factitious entirely;
I refuse, reject, and put it utterly from me;
I will look straight out, see things, not try to evade them: 100
Fact shall be fact for me; and the Truth the Truth as ever,
Flexible, changeable, vague, and multiform, and
    doubtful –
Off, and depart to the void, thou subtle fanatical tempter!

I shall behold thee again (is it so?) at a new visitation,
O ill genius thou! I shall, at my life's dissolution,   105
(When the pulses are weak, and the feeble light of the
    reason

86–94] Veyriras compares Newman's complaint against 'indolent contemplation' which 'will no more sanctify a man *in fact*, than reading a poem or
listening to a chant or psalm tune' (Veyriras 1964: 134).
95–7] Claude is referring here to the 'assurance within of a limitless ocean
divine' which he had claimed to be able to feel earlier (III.125); he now rejects
this assurance as 'factitious'.
103. thou subtle fanatical tempter!] Religion is also associated with fanaticism at
I.107 above.
104–5] Scott suggests a reminiscence of *Julius Caesar* IV.iii. 275, 283: 'How ill
this taper burns! . . . Well, then, I shall see thee again.'

Flickers an unfed flame retiring slow from the socket)
Low on a sick bed laid hear one, as it were, at the
    doorway,
And looking up see thee, standing by, looking emptily at
    me.
I shall entreat thee then, though now I dare to refuse
    thee, –   110
Pale and pitiful now, but terrible then to the dying –
Well, I will see thee again: and while I can, will repel thee.

VI. – CLAUDE TO EUSTACE.

ROME is fallen, I hear, the gallant Medici taken,
Noble Manara slain, and Garibaldi has lost *il Moro*; –
Rome is fallen; and fallen, or falling, heroical Venice.   115
I, meanwhile, for the loss of a single small chit of a girl, sit
Moping and mourning here, – for her, and myself much
    smaller.
   Whither depart the souls of the brave that die in the
    battle,
Die in the lost, lost fight, for the cause that perishes with
    them?
Are they upborne from the field on the slumberous
    pinions of angels   120
Unto a far-off home, where the weary rest from their
    labour,
And the deep wounds are healed, and the bitter and
    burning moisture
Wiped from the generous eyes? or do they linger,
    unhappy,

107. socket] The hollow of a candlestick.
113. Rome is fallen] Rome finally fell to Oudinot on 30 June; see Headnote.
113. Medici] Giacomo Medici was one of Garibaldi's most trusted lieutenants; he commanded a 'legion' during the siege but was not in fact either captured or killed by the French – see Trevelyan 1919: 222.
114. Noble Manara] Luciano Manara, the commander of the regiment of Lombard Bersaglieri which participated in the defence of the Republic. He was killed during the final desperate stages of the siege.
114. il Moro] See note to II.219; he too was killed on the last day of the siege.
115. heroical Venice] The Venetian Republic was proclaimed on 22 March 1848; the city was subsequently besieged by the Austrians, and eventually capitulated in August 1849 (see Headnote to *Dipsychus*).
116. chit] A slightly pejorative term for a young girl. Claude contrasts his own abandonment of the struggle with the heroic resistance of the Italians in a cause they know is lost.
120. pinions] Wings.

Pining, and haunting the grave of their by-gone hope and
    endeavour?
  All declamation, alas! though I talk, I care not for
    Rome, nor   125
Italy; feebly and faintly, and but with the lips, can lament
    the
Wreck of the Lombard youth and the victory of the
    oppressor.
Whither depart the brave? – God knows; I certainly do
    not.

VII. – MARY TREVELLYN TO MISS ROPER.

HE has not come as yet; and now I must not expect it.
You have written, you say, to friends at Florence, to see
    him,   130
If he perhaps should return; – but that is surely unlikely.
Has he not written to you? – he did not know your
    direction.
Oh, how strange never once to have told him where you
    were going!
Yet if he only wrote to Florence, that would have reached
    you.
If what you say he said was true, why has he not done so?   135
Is he gone back to Rome, do you think, to his Vatican
    marbles? –
O my dear Miss Roper, forgive me! do not be angry! –
You have written to Florence; – your friends would
    certainly find him.
Might you not write to him? – but yet it is so little likely!
I shall expect nothing more. – Ever yours, your
    affectionate Mary.   140

---

127. the Lombard youth] Manara and the Bersaglieri.

VIII. – CLAUDE TO EUSTACE.

I CANNOT stay at Florence, not even to wait for a letter.
Galleries only oppress me. Remembrance of hope I had
　　cherished
(Almost more than as hope, when I passed through
　　Florence the first time)
Lies like a sword in my soul. I am more a coward than
　　ever,
Chicken-hearted, past thought. The *caffès* and waiters
　　distress me.　　　　　　　　　　　　　　　　145
All is unkind, and, alas, I am ready for any one's kindness.
Oh, I knew it of old, and knew it, I thought, to perfection,
If there is any one thing in the world to preclude all
　　kindness,
It is the need of it, – it is this sad self-defeating
　　dependence.
Why is this, Eustace? Myself, were I stronger, I think I
　　could tell you.　　　　　　　　　　　　　　　150
But it is odd when it comes. So plumb I the deeps of
　　depression,
Daily in deeper, and find no support, no will, no purpose.
All my old strengths are gone. And yet I shall have to do
　　something.
Ah, the key of our life, that passes all wards, opens all
　　locks,
Is not *I will*, but *I must*. I must, – I must, – and I do it.　　155

After all do I know that I really cared so about her?
Do whatever I will, I cannot call up her image.
For when I close my eyes, I see very likely St. Peter's,
Or the Pantheon facade, or Michael Angelo's figures,
Or at a wish, when I please, the Alban hills and the
　　Forum, –　　　　　　　　　　　　　　　　　160
But that face, those eyes, – ah no, never anything like
　　them;

V.viii] The second part of this letter was restored (from *A*) in 1859 *Corrections*;
prior to this the first and third parts were separate letters.
154–5] This capitulation to Necessity is paralleled in *Dipsychus* 2.5.87–95.

Only, try as I will, a sort of featureless outline,
And a pale blank orb, which no recollection will add to.
After all perhaps there was something factitious about it;
I have had pain, it is true; have wept; and so have the
    actors.[19]   165

At the last moment I have your letter, for which I was
    waiting.
I have taken my place, and see no good in inquiries.
Do nothing more, good Eustace, I pray you. It will only
    vex me.
Take no measures. Indeed, should we meet, I could not
    be certain;
All might be changed, you know. Or perhaps there was
    nothing to be changed.   170
It is a curious history, this; and yet I foresaw it;
I could have told it before. The Fates, it is clear, are
    against us;
For it is certain enough that I met with the people you
    mention;
They were at Florence the day I returned there, and
    spoke to me even;
Staid a week, saw me often; departed, and whither I
    know not.   175
Great is Fate, and is best. I believe in Providence, partly.

165] This cryptic statement seems to refer to Claude's division of himself into a
real self and a 'shadow' or actor who participates in society's charades; cp I.83–6
and the cancelled l. 165 below. There might also be an allusion to Claude's con-
tinual representation of himself as Hamlet; cp *Hamlet* II.ii.543–601.
167. I have taken my place] 'I have booked my passage.'
171–2] Cp Matthew Arnold's 'To Marguerite – Continued': 'Who ordered
that their longing fire/ Should be, as soon as kindled, cooled?/ Who renders
vain their deep desire?/ A God, a God their severance ruled!' (19–22).
176–9] Claude's half-hearted endorsement of providence contrasts with the
sentiments of the more radical Philip Hewson at the end of C.'s earlier poem
The Bothie (1848): 'I am sorry to say your Providence puzzles me sadly;/
Children of Circumstance are we to be? you answer, On no wise!/ Where does
Circumstance end, and Providence where begins it?/ What are we to resist,
and what are we to be friend with?' (IX.47–50).

---

[19] Alt.: 'It may be acting, in fine; I have suffered; as also do actors'. (*A*)

What is ordained is right, and all that happens is ordered.
Ah, no, that isn't it. But yet I retain my conclusion:
I will go where I am led, and will not dictate to the
    chances.
Do nothing more, I beg. If you love me, forbear
    interfering.   180

IX. – CLAUDE TO EUSTACE.

SHALL we come out of it all, some day, as one does
    from a tunnel?
Will it be all at once, without our doing or asking,
We shall behold clear day, the trees and meadows
    about us,
And the faces of friends, and the eyes we loved looking
    at us?
Who knows? Who can say? It will not do to suppose it.   185

X. – CLAUDE TO EUSTACE, – *from Rome*.

ROME will not suit me, Eustace; the priests and soldiers
    possess it;
Priests and soldiers; – and, ah! which is worst, the priest
    or the soldier?
    Politics farewell, however! For what could I do? with
    inquiring,
Talking, collating the journals, go fever my brain about
    things o'er
Which I can have no control. No, happen whatever may
    happen,   190

V.ix] Claude's railway tunnel is a modern and agnostic version of Plato's cave;
cp V.x.
186. priest and soldiers] The defeat of the Roman Republic led to the restoration of the Pope's temporal power.

Time, I suppose, will subsist; the earth will revolve on its
    axis;
People will travel; the stranger will wander as now in the
    city;
Rome will be here, and the Pope the *custode* of Vatican
    marbles.
    I have no heart, however, for any marble or fresco;
I have essayed it in vain; 'tis vain as yet to essay it: 195
But I may haply resume some day my studies in this kind.
Not as the Scripture says, is, I think, the fact. Ere our
    death-day,
Faith, I think, does pass, and Love; but Knowledge
    abideth.[20]
Let us seek Knowledge; – the rest must come and go as
    it happens.
Knowledge is hard to seek, and harder yet to adhere to.   200
Knowledge is painful often; and yet when we know, we
    are happy.

---

191. the earth will revolve on its axis] Cp Byron, *Don Juan* II, 25–8: 'Well –
well, the world must turn upon its axis,/ And all mankind turn with it, heads
or tails,/ And live and die, make love and pay our taxes,/ And as the veering
wind shifts, shift our sails.' C. was fond of this image as a way of describing the
return to normality after the turbulence and excitement of a revolutionary
period; cp the following letter of May 1848 from Paris to A.P. Stanley describing the 'bourgeoisification' of the Revolution: 'Bring forth, ye millionaires, the
three-months-hidden carriages; rub clean, ye new nobles, the dusty emblazon-
ries; ride forth, ye cavalier-escorted amazons, in unerring flirtation, to your
Bois de Boulogne: the world begins once more to move on its axis and draw on
its kid gloves' (*Corr.* i, 210).
193. custode] Keeper.
197. the Scripture] I Corinthians 13:12–13: 'For now we see through a glass,
.darkly; but then face to face: now I know in part; but then shall I know even as
also I am known./ And now abideth faith, hope, charity, these three; but the
greatest of these *is* charity.' Like most modern translators, Claude translates
the Greek word *agappe* not as charity but as love. This rewriting of Paul's epistle signifies the end of Claude's attempt to arrive at a direct intuition of the
divine.
199–201] Claude's endorsement of 'Knowledge' contrasts with his earlier
desire to lose it – see III.x, and the cancelled lines after 198 given above.

---

[20] After 198:

    Art is delusion perhaps; but a stupid and sterile knowledge,
    There is my fetish, my friend; my recentest shape of an Idol;
    Beaten and broken-to-be I suppose like the others. (*Canc. in A*)

Seek it, and leave mere Faith and Love to come with
    the chances.
As for Hope, – to-morrow I hope to be starting for Naples.
Rome will not do, I see, for many very good reasons.
   Eastward, then, I suppose, with the coming of winter,
    to Egypt.   205

XI. – Mary Trevellyn to Miss Roper.

YOU have heard nothing; of course, I know you can have
    heard nothing.
Ah, well, more than once I have broken my purpose, and
    sometimes,
Only too often, have looked for the little lake-steamer to
    bring him.
But it is only fancy, – I do not really expect it.
Oh, and you see I know exactly how he would take it: 210
Finding the chances prevail against meeting again, he
    would banish
Forthwith every thought of the poor little possible hope,
    which
I myself could not help, perhaps, thinking only too much
    of;
He would resign himself, and go. I see it exactly.
So I also submit, although in a different manner.   215
   Can you really not come? We go very shortly to
    England.

So go forth to the world, to the good report and the evil!
   Go, little book! thy tale, is it not evil and good?
Go, and if strangers revile, pass quietly by without answer.
   Go, and if curious friends ask of thy rearing and age,   220

---

218. *Go, little book!]* Cp Southey's 'L'Envoy' to *The Lay of the Laureate*: 'Go, little book, from this my solitude!/ I cast thee on the waters, go thy ways!/ And if, as I believe, thy vein be good,/ The world will find thee after many days.' Quoted by Byron in *Don Juan* I, 1769–72. C. refers to the closing lines as 'L'Envoi' in *A*.

Say, I am flitting around from brain unto brain of
   Feeble and restless youths born to inglorious days;
But, *so finish the word,* I was writ in a Roman chamber,
   When from Janiculan heights thundered the cannon of
      France.[21]

222] C. claims that his poem has been written collectively by the 'feeble and restless youths' of his 'inglorious generation'.
224. Janiculan heights] The Monte Gianicolo, from which the French bombarded the city during the siege.

---

[21] An alternative 'Envoi' reads:
   So to the critical speech go forth and the critical silence
      Go; and if scrupulous souls ask of thy moral and end,
   What, if exclaim they, and wherefore, and how do we leave thee adjudging
      Peace to the selfish and vain, grief to the beautiful soul,
   Nay, but rewrite, rearrange, bring it all in the ending to comfort,
      Call things at least by their names; this is a good, this a bad;
   Say, – Am I God to make dead or alive, to repair the injustice,
      Balance the pains, and undo all the vext ravel of life,
   Am I the judge, say, Am I, of all the Earth to assign things
      One name or other and give sentence to this or to that?
   Ah no! I am not so: or such. I am but a poor foolish mirror
      Helpless to judge or to act, faithful alone to reflect.
   Ah, could a poor dumb glass, could a silvered plate make answer,
      Ah, if a mirror could speak, angry perhaps it would say,
   There! thou world! look, there! is the vile dirty face that you show me –
      Nay, but provoke not to speech, Silence beseemeth it best. (*A*)

Dipsychus and The Spirit

Publication: 1865 *Letters and Remains of A.H.C.*

Text and MSS: There are four stages in the poem's evolution: 1. *The 1850 (Venice) Notebook*. This contains early sketches for several scenes. The main characters are referred to throughout as Faustulus and Mephistopheles rather than as Dipsychus and The Spirit. 2. *MS1 'First Revision'*. This consists of two notebooks; the first, headed 'Dipsychus and The Spirit. Pt I', contains the current scenes 1.6 and 1.7; the second, headed 'Dipsychus and The Spirit. Pt II' contains the current scenes 2.2, 2.3, 2.4, 2.5, 2.6, 2.7 and the Epilogue. There are a number of pages cut away at the start of the first of these books. The characters are named Faustulus and Mephistopheles at first, but change to Dipsychus and The Spirit towards the end. 3. *MS1 'Second Revision'*. This is a single notebook containing the Prologue and the current scenes 1.1, 1.2, 1.3, 1.4, 2.1 and 1.5. Here the characters are named Dipsychus and The Spirit throughout. 4. *MS2 'Third Revision'*. This consists of a rewriting and drastic reduction of scenes 1.1, 1.2, 1.4 and 1.5. It is labelled by Mrs A.H. Clough Jr 'Latest copy (incomplete), B'.

Editorial decisions concerning copy-text and the ordering of scenes depend on the interpretation of this textual evidence. The First and Second Revisions were labelled 'MS1' by the Oxford editors because they do not duplicate one another's scenes and appear to form a complete draft of the poem. This label is, however, somewhat misleading. The First Revision was almost certainly written by the time C. departed for the USA towards the end of 1852; the Second Revision, in contrast, cannot have been written before late 1854 at the very earliest (see 1.3.172 and note). A better way of looking at the evidence is to see both the Second and Third Revisions as alternative supplements to the First Revision. In these circumstances, the question of copy-text becomes one of choosing a partner for the First Revision. The Third Revision is unquestionably the later of the two, and so would appear to take precedence as embodying the author's final intention. There is, however, clear evidence of bowdlerisation in the Third Revision; its adoption would, for example, require the omission of much of 1.2 and the whole of 1.3. Mulhauser (1974) attempts to get round this problem by conflating the Second and Third Revisions, but this produces a hybrid which misrepresents the history of the text. In the light of these problems, it seems to me preferable to follow the much fuller Second Revision throughout, and this is the procedure I have adopted.

This interpretation of the relation between the various MSS of the poem also helps to clarify the difficult question of the ordering of scenes. The Oxford editors abandon the division of the poem into two parts on the grounds that C. was unclear about the position of certain scenes, notably 'In a Gondola' (1.5). This appears after the first scene of Part 2 in the Second Revision (and also in Mrs C.'s version of the poem), but after the current 1.4 in the Third Revision. It is, however, possible to make sense of C.'s intentions with regard to this and other problematic scenes if we read the Second Revision as a supplement to the First. After scenes 1–4 of the Second Revision C. writes 'End of Act I'; there then follows a scene headed 'Pt 2. The Interior Arcade of the Doge's Palace' (i.e. the current 2.1); and after this comes the 'In a Gondola' scene. This could, as the Oxford editors suggest, mean that C. had changed his mind about where the first part of the poem was to end; it might also mean that he had decided to divide his poem into 'Acts' as well as 'Parts'. The instructions make more sense, however, if they are read in conjunction with the First Revision. 'End of Act I' can plausibly be taken to mean 'go to end of Pt I', i.e. consult the First Revision for the remainder of Part 1; similarly, 'Pt. 2. The Interior Arcade of the Doge's Palace' could mean that C. wanted to place this scene before the existing scenes of Part 2 in the First Revision. This hypothesis also solves the problem concerning the position of the 'In a Gondola' scene. It is clear that the seven pages cut away from the start of the First Revision (see above) cannot have contained a first draft of scenes 1–5, as has been suggested; there is simply not enough room for such a quantity of material. In view of this, and of the fact that lines from 'In a Gondola' are visible on the cut-away sheets, it seems reasonable to suggest that the first book of the First Revision originally contained, not scenes 1.1–7, but scenes 1.5–7, and that scenes 1.1–4 were contained in a (lost or destroyed) separate Notebook. The position of the 'In a Gondola' scene can then be explained on the assumption that C. originally intended to use the existing version of this scene in the First Revision, but later changed his mind and rewrote it in the book containing the rest of the Second Revision. This assumption is supported by the position of 'In a Gondola' in the later Third Revision, where it appears after a truncated version of the first four scenes.

The order I have adopted below seems to me, then, the one most consistent with the textual evidence of all four sources. It is also supported by literary and structural evidence. 1.4 ends with the lines 'For mind you, if you don't do this, you still/ Have got to tell me what it is you will'; 1.5 opens with the words '*Per ora* [For now]. To the Grand Canal./ And after that as fancy shall'. There is a similar link between the end of the scene and the start of the next one; Dipsychus and The Spirit go to 'The Parthenone', a cafe, and it is there that the 'insult' takes place. This would be the most likely location for such an occurrence; the cafés in Venice were strictly divided into 'Austrian' and 'Italian' after the restoration of Austrian rule, and Dipsychus might inadvertently have strayed into the wrong one. It is true that the time-scheme is not coherent (see 1.5.272 and note), but there is no alternative order which could make it so. The placing of the 'Lido' scene at the end of the first part – disputed only by Oxford – emphasises the structural role of *Easter Day* in the piece; it appears at the beginning and end of Part 1, and again at the beginning of Part 2.

The fragmentary 'sequel' to this poem, *Dipsychus Continued*, which C. began in America in 1852–3 but never completed, is not included in the present collection; for a discussion of the circumstances of its composition see Chorley 1962: 264–5.

Biographical and historical information. The idea of 'dipsychia' or double-mindedness began to appear in C.'s letters and diaries during his first year at Oxford: 'just now I am rather troubled by certain beginnings of double-mindedness and want of faith' (*Corr.* i, 62; cp Kenny 1990: 22, 43–4). He seems to have derived the term from one of John Henry Newman's sermons on 'Sincerity and Hypocrisy': '[Hypocrites] have two ends which they pursue, religion *and* the world; and hence St. James calls them "double-minded" ' (Newman 1868: v, 229; see James 1:8 and 4:8). The term also occurs in Richard Hurrell Froude's 'Private Journal', a key document for the Oxford Movement which C. and his Mathematics tutor W.G. Ward read together; see Froude 1838: i, 62. The basic conflict explored in *Dipsychus and The Spirit* was, then, in C.'s mind well before the visit to Venice in 1850 which occasioned the poem. This visit seems to have coincided with a period of great personal stress for the poet; in 1851 he wrote to Tom Arnold, '*I* could have gone cracked at times last year with one thing or another, I think' (*Corr.* ii, 290). Under these circumstances his choice of destination was not a propitious one. Like Rome, which C. had visited the previous year, Venice was a standing reminder of the failure of the Revolutions of 1848 and the ideals which had inspired them; the 'Republic of St. Mark', declared in August 1848, had lasted just over a year before succumbing to Austrian bombardment and being absorbed once again into the Hapsburg Empire. Unlike *Amours*, however, *Dipsychus* makes little reference to this background of political struggle; the only hint of the tension caused by the presence of an occupying army comes during Dipsychus's altercation with one of the Imperial Army's Croatian troops (see 1.6 below).

Literary background. The most obvious literary precursor for the poem is Goethe's *Faust*; the poem centres on a bargain with a tempter, and for most of MS1 the characters are called 'Faustulus' (little Faust) and Mephistopheles. In a letter of 13 April 1852, however, C. wrote to his fiancée, 'Faust I have never read properly myself' (Veyriras 1964: 369), and attempts to establish substantial links between the two poems have proved inconclusive. C. seems, rather, to have used the Faust-theme as the starting point for his own exploration of the notion of 'double-mindedness'; in the *Roma* Notebook he wrote '[why] is it Palinurus and Somnus: Faust & Mephisto even are not quite expressive to us, we want to be told that they mean contradictory elements of our own unity - ?' (f. 40). There is no evidence that the various English translations and adaptations of *Faust* had any influence on C.'s poem; Veyriras mentions the fact that part of George Soane (1825) *Faustus: A Romantic Drama* is set in Venice, but Soane's Regency frolic is a long way from C.'s anguished meditation.

Venice has played a significant part in the English literary imagination since the Renaissance, chiefly through *Othello* and *The Merchant of Venice*, but most nineteenth-century visitors would have had to agree with Ruskin: 'My Venice, like Turner's, had been chiefly created for us by Byron' (Ruskin 1899: ii, 82). Byron's legendary personal exploits reinforced Venice's well-established reputation for sexual licence of all kinds, especially prostitution, while his poetry

highlighted the magical and dream-like qualities of the city. This Byronic
Venice casts a long shadow over *Dipsychus*, throwing the hero's enervated fear
of action in general, and of sex in particular, into sharper relief (see 1.7.3–4,
2.2.5–8 and 2.3.104–6 and note). It is also likely that C. profited from Ruskin's
vision of Venice (see esp. 1.1 below and notes); the drafting of the Second
Revision came after the publication of the second and third volumes of *The
Stones of Venice* in 1853. On the subject of the literary representation of Venice,
see Tony Tanner (1992) *Venice Desired*, Oxford, Blackwell.

Prologue

'I hope it is in good plain verse,' said my uncle; 'none of your
hurry-scurry anapaests, as you call them, in lines which sober
people are reading for plain heroics. Nothing is more disagreeable
than to say a line over two, or, it may be, three or four times, and
at last not be sure that there are not three or four ways of reading,   5
each as good and as much intended as another. *Simplex duntaxat et
unum.* But you young people think Horace and your uncles old
fools.'

   'Certainly, my dear sir,' said I; 'that is, I mean, Horace and my
uncle are perfectly right. Still, there is an instructed ear and an   10
uninstructed. A rude taste for identical recurrences would exact
sing-song from "Paradise Lost", and grumble because "Il
Penseroso" doesn't run like a nursery rhyme.'

   'Well, well,' said my uncle, '*sunt certi denique fines*, no doubt. So
commence, my young Piso, while Aristarchus is tolerably wakeful,   15
and do not waste by your logic the fund you will want for your
poetry.'

---

2. *anapaests]* Feet of two short or unstressed syllables followed by one long or
stressed syllable.
3. *heroics]* Rhyming couplets, usually iambic pentameter; the classical metre of
English verse.
6–7. *Simplex duntaxat et unum]* From Horace's *Ars Poetica* (*Epistles* II.iii.23):
'So make what you like, *provided the thing is a unified whole.*'
14. *Sunt certi denique fines]* 'In short, there are definite limits'; Horace, *Satires*
1.1.106.
15. *Piso, Aristarchus]* Piso, the addressee of Horace's *Ars Poetica*, is believed to
have been an aspiring poet. Aristarchus was a proverbial name for a critic in
classical antiquity; the name is used in the *Ars Poetica* (*Epistles* II.iii.350).

Part 1

SCENE 1: VENICE - THE PIAZZA. 9 pm.

Dipsychus: The scene is different and the Place, the air
    Tastes of the nearer north; the people too
    Not perfect southern levity: wherefore then
    Should those old verses come into my mind
    I made last year at Naples[?] O poor fool   5
    Still nesting on thyself. – A thing ill worked,
    A moment's thought committed on the moment
    To doubtful words and rugged verse. And yet
    What we have written like a brother sticks
    And we like parents hug it. Is it vanity   10
    That makes it such a solace? Is it self love
    In watches of the night and when the soul
    Is sick and begs for medicine to recur
    To what had been its medicine in old days
    And repeat-over poems of one's own[?]   15
    Why should not other peoples' do as well?
    'Tis a bad habit; better far forget [them].

[The Spirit]: O Good heaven: pooh pooh
    Why go and make a d—d to do

Scene 1: Venice - the Piazza, 9 pm] The Piazza San Marco, the main square in Venice. With this scene as a whole compare the chapter on St Mark's in Ruskin (1853) *The Stones of Venice*. After describing the splendours of the cathedral's external aspect, Ruskin turns to consider its influence on the Venetian populace: 'And what effect has this splendour on those who pass beneath it? You may walk from sunrise to sunset, to and fro, before the gateway of St Mark's, and you will not see an eye lifted to it, nor a countenance brightened by it. [. . .] Round the whole square in front of the church there is almost a continuous line of cafes, where the idle Venetians of the middle classes lounge, and read empty journals; in its centre the Austrian bands play during the time of vespers, their martial music jarring with the organ notes, – the march drowning the miserere, and the sullen crowd thickening round them, – a crowd, which, if it had its will, would stiletto every soldier that pipes to it. And in the recesses of the porches, all day long, knots of men of the lowest classes, unemployed and listless, lie basking in the sun like lizards; and unregarded children, – every heavy glance of their young eyes full of desperation and stony depravity, and their throats hoarse with cursing, – gamble, and fight, and snarl, and sleep, hour after hour, clashing their bruised centesimi upon the marble ledges of the church porch. And the images of Christ and His angels look down upon it continually' (Ruskin 1903: 10, 84–5).

11–15] On this 'therapeutic' theory of poetry see *Amours* V.70–1 and note.

> As if such were a sin!   20
> If you've a fancy, spout: begin!

D: Through the great sinful streets of Naples as I past
       With fiercer heat than flamed above my head:
       My heart was hot within; the fire burnt; and at last
       My brain was lightened when my tongue had said   25
           Christ is not risen.

S: Christ is not risen? O indeed!
       I didn't know that was your creed.

D: So it went. Too lengthy to repeat –
       'Christ is not risen.'   30
       Interpret it I cannot; I but wrote it:
       At Naples, truly, as the preface tells,
       Last year; it came upon me, in the street
       And did me good at once. At Naples then,
       At Venice now. Ah and I think at Venice   35
       Christ is not risen either.

S: Nay.
       Twas well enough once in a way.
       Having once done it, as we know,
       Some eighteen hundred years ago,
       How should he now at Venice here?   40
       Where people true enough appear
       To appreciate more and understand

22–6] A quotation from C.'s own *Easter Day* – see below, p. 256. On the function of *Easter Day* in *Dipsychus* see Introduction, p. 21. Dipsychus's quotation of it at this point seems to be prompted by the apparent indifference of the Venetians to the message of resurrection proclaimed by the cathedral – see below 1.75–6. Cp Ruskin's description of the contrast between cathedral and city: 'Daily, as the white cupolas rose like wreaths of sea-foam in the dawn, while the shadowy campanile and frowning palace were still withdrawn into the night, they rose with the Easter Voice of Triumph, – "Christ is risen;" and daily, as they looked down upon the tumult of the people, deepening and eddying in the wide square that opened from their feet to the sea, they uttered above them the sentence of warning, – "Christ shall come" ' (Ruskin 1903: 10, 139–40).

31] Dipsychus is perplexed about the meaning of his own poem, claiming that it was written to provide 'relief' rather than to promote a particular point of view.

Their ices and their Austrian band
And dark-eyed girls than what occurred
So long ago to the Eternal Word;   45
Look at them there –

D: The whole great square they fill
From the red flaunting streamers on the staffs
And that barbaric portal of St Mark's
To where unnoticed at the darker end
I sit upon my step. One great gay crowd;   50
The Campanile to the silent stars
Goes up, above – its apex lost in heaven.
While these do – what? –

S: Enjoy the minute
And the substantial blessings in it:
Music and ice and evening air   55
And company enough to spare,
And all the sweets in perfect plenty
Of the old dolce far niente
More wise, I say it without danger
Than mawkish meditative stranger   60
Who chooses which is scarcely fit
Upon a dirty step to sit;
Up, to the cafe, take a chair
And join the crowd of idlers there
Aye! what a crowd, and what a noise   65
With all those screaming half-breeched boys.
Partout boys dogs and women wander
And see that fellow singing yonder.
Singing ye gods and dancing too
Tooraloo tooraloo tooraloo loo   70
Fiddle di diddle di diddle di da

---

43. their Austrian band] The occupying Austrian army gave band-concerts in St Mark's Square; the Venetians later boycotted these as a form of protest, but this particular form of resistance does not seem to have been in operation at the time of C.'s visit.

48. that barbaric portal of St Mark's] The idea seems to have been commonplace; Ruskin describes a modern English archivolt, and then adds: 'Let [the reader] remember that the men who design such work as that call St Mark's a barbarous monstrosity, and let him judge between us' – Ruskin 1903: 10, 117.

51. Campanile] Bell-tower.

58. dolce far niente] Sweet idleness.

67. Partout] Everywhere.

> *Figaro sù Figaro giù*
> *Figaro quà Figaro là,*
> How he likes doing it! ha ha!

D: While these do what? Ah heaven! too true at Venice   75
        Christ is not risen either –

S: If you want to pray
> I'll step aside a little way;
> I go, but will not far be gone:
> You may be wanting me anon;
> Our lonely pious altitudes   80
> Are followed soon by prettier moods
> We know how easily devotion
> Slips into earthlier emotion.

SCENE 2: THE PUBLIC GARDEN

D: Assuredly a lively scene:
        And ah, how pleasant something green
        – With circling heavens one perfect rose,
        Each smoother patch of water glows
        Hence to where o'er the full tide's face,   5
        We see the Palace and the Place
        And the White Dome. Beauteous but hot.
        Where in the meantime is the spot,
        My favourite, where by masses blue
        And white cloud folds I follow true   10
        The great Alps rounding grandly o'er
        Huge arc, to the Dalmatian shore?

S: This rather stupid place to-day,
> 'Tis true, is most extremely gay,
> And rightly - the Assunzione   15
> Was always a *grand' funzione*.

72–3. Figaro sù, Figaro giù &c] Part of the famous aria 'Largo al factotum'
from Rossini's *Barber of Seville*.
Scene 2. The Public Garden] Murray 1847: 362: 'The *Giardino Publico* [sic], at
the end of the Riva de' Schiavoni, was founded by the French.' On Venice's
reputation as a place for illicit sexual encounters, see Headnote.
6–7] The Palace is the Palazzo Ducale (The Doge's Palace); the Place is the
Piazzetta; and the White Dome belongs to the church of Santa Maria della
Salute – see Ruskin 1903: 10, 6.
15. the Assunzione] The Feast of the Assumption takes place on 15 August.
16. grand' funzione] Big event.

D: What is this persecuting voice that haunts me
         What, whence, of whom? How am I to discover!
         Myself or not myself? My own bad thoughts?
         Or some external agency at work   20
         To lead me who knows whither –

S: What lots of boats before us plying
            What lots of pretty girls too, hieing
            Hither and thither; coming, going;
            And with what satisfaction showing,   25
            To our male eyes unveiled and bare
            The exuberant blackness of their hair,
            Dark eyes, rich tints, and sundry graces
            Of classic pure Italian faces[.]

D: Off off – Oh heaven, depart, depart, depart   30
         Oh heaven. [The] toad that whispered in Eve's ear
         Whispered no dream so dangerous as this[.]

S: A perfect show of girls I see it is.
            Ah what a charming leg; ye deities!
            In that attraction as one fancies   35
            Italy's not so rich as France is
            In Paris –

D: Cease, cease, cease,
    I will not hear this – Go –

S: Eh?
    What do those pretty verses say?

        Ah comme je regrette   40
           Mon bras si dodu
        Ma jambe bien faite
            Et le temps perdu
            Et le temps perdu[.]

    'Tis here, I see, the practice too   45

17–21] One of the central (and unresolved) questions of the poem.
31–2] An allusion to the episode in Bk iv of *Paradise Lost* when Ithuriel and Zephon discover Satan '[squat] like a toad, close at the ear of Eve;/ Assaying by his devilish art to reach/ The organs of her fancy, and with them forge/ Illusions as he list, phantasms and dreams' (*PL* iv.800–3). On the significance of the motif of the Fall here and elsewhere in C.'s work see Introduction, pp. 10–11.
40–4] A slight misquotation of the refrain from Béranger's bawdy song 'Ma Grand'Mère': 'Combien je regrette/ Mon bras si dodu,/ Ma jambe bien faite,/ Et le temps perdu!' [How much I miss/ My well-rounded arm,/ My well-made leg,/ And the time gone by!]

For damsels eager to be lovered
To go about with arms uncovered.
And doubtless there's a special charm
In a full round voluptuous arm,
At Paris I was saying –

D: Ah me, me   50
Clear stars above, thou roseate westward sky
Take up my being into yours: assume
My sense to know you only: fill my brain
In your essential purity: or great Alps
That wrapping round your heads in solemn clouds   55
Seem sternly to sweep past our vanities
Lead me with you – take me away, preserve me:
Ah if it must be, look then, foolish eyes
Listen fond ears, but oh poor mind stand fast[.]

S: At Paris at the Opera, –   60
          In the *coulisses* – but ah, aha!
          There was a glance:– I saw you spy it
          So! shall we follow suit and try it?
          Pooh! what a goose you are! quick, quick
          This hesitation makes me sick.   65
          You simpleton! what's your alarm?
          She'd merely thank you for your arm.

D: Sweet thing! ah well! but yet I am not sure.
          Ah no. I think she did not mean it. No.

S: Plainly, unless I much mistake   70
          She likes a something in your make:
          She turned her head, another glance:
          She really gives you every chance.

D: Ah, pretty thing – well well. Yet should I go
          Alas, I cannot say! What should I do?   75

54–7] This attempt to transform the Alps into the guardians of Dipsychus's moral being obviously owes a good deal to Wordsworth's treatment of the mountains of his native Lake District; cp *Tintern Abbey* ll. 93–111 and 5.256–61 below.

57. take me away, preserve me] Cp Job 7:20: 'I have sinned. What shall I do unto thee, O thou preserver of men?' (Also alluded to in *Amours* III.210.)

61. In the coulisses] In the wings (of the theatre).

63] C. originally seems to have intended to end Scene 2 at this point, using Scene 3 for much more explicit reflections on the nature of the temptation offered by the prostitute; see note to 3.117 below for a sample of the alternative and cancelled material.

S: What should you do? Well that is funny!
        I think you are supplied with money.

D: No no; it may not be. I could, I would
    And yet I would not cannot. To what end?

S: Trust her for teaching – go but you,   .   80
        She'll quickly show you what to do.
        Well well! It's too late now – they're gone
        Some wiser youth is coming on.
        Really I could be in a passion
        To see you treat in that odd fashion   85
        As [sweet a little thing as e'er]
        I saw since first I learnt to stare.

D: Ah me –
    O hateful hateful hateful! to the Hotel!

SCENE 3: THE QUAYS

D: O hateful, hateful, hateful! To the Hotel.

S: Pooh, what the devil! what's the harm?
        I only bid you take her arm.

D: And I half yielded! O unthinking I!
    O weak weak fool! O God how quietly   5
    Out of our better into our worst selves
    Out of a true world which our reason knew
    Into a false world which our fancy makes
    We pass and never know – O weak weak fool.

S: Well, if you don't wish, why, you don't.   10
        Leave it! but that's just what you won't.
        Come now! how many times per diem
        Are you not hankering to try 'em?

D: O moon and stars forgive! And thou clear heaven
    Look pureness back into me. O great God,   15
    Why, why in wisdom and in grace's name
    And in the name of saints and saintly thoughts
    Of mothers and of sisters and chaste wives,

86] Line supplied from alternative material.
3.12. per diem] Per day.
15–24] Dipsychus finds it impossible to reconcile the reality of his sexual
desire to the images of women furnished by Victorian domestic piety.

And angel woman-faces we have seen,
And angel woman-spirits we have guessed,   20
And innocent sweet children, and pure love,
Why did I ever one brief moment's space
To this insidious lewdness lend chaste ears
Or parley with this filthy Belial?
O were it that vile questioner that loves   25
To put his fingers into right and wrong
And before proof knows nothing – or the fear
Of being behind the world – which is, the wicked.

S: O yes, you dream of sin and shame
            Trust me – it leaves one much the same.   30
            – 'Tisn't Elysium any more
            Than what comes after or before:
            But heavens! as innocent a thing
            As picking strawberries in spring. –
            You think I'm anxious to allure you.   35
            My object is much more to cure you
            With the high amatory-poetic
            My temper's no way sympathetic;
            To play your pretty woman's fool
            I hold but fit for boys from school.   40
            Come now: it's mainly your temptation
            To think the thing a revelation
            A mystic mouthful that will give
            Knowledge and death,– none know and live;
            I tell you plainly, that it brings   45
            Some ease, but the emptiness of things
            (That one old sermon Earth still preaches
            Until we practice what she teaches)
            Is the sole lesson you'll learn by it
            Still you undoubtedly should try it.   50
            'Try all things' bad and good, no matter

---

24. *Belial*] A biblical adjective meaning worthless, reckless or lawless, usually used in personifying phrases like 'children of Belial' or 'son of Belial'; see, e.g., Deut 13:13, Judges 19:22.

25–8] Dipsychus suggests two possible reasons for his momentary lapse: the desire for experience, and the fear of not knowing what everybody else knows.

29–62] Dipsychus sees sex as a Fall into experience; speaking from the other side, The Spirit reassures him that it is not 'a revelation' but an innocent and natural part of life. On the importance of these figures in C.'s poetry see Introduction.

31. *Elysium*] Heaven in classical mythology.

You can't till then hold fast the latter.
If not, this itch will stick and vex you
Your livelong days till death unsex you,
Hide in your bones for aught I know   55
And with you to the next world go:
Briefly – you cannot rest, I'm certain,
Until your hand has drawn the curtain:
Once known the little lies behind it
You'll go your way, and never mind it.   60
Ill's only cure is, never doubt it,
To do and think no more about it. –

D: Strange talk. Strange words. – Ah me. I cannot say.
Could I believe it even of us men
That once the young exuberance drawn off   65
The liquor would run clear; that once appeased
The vile inquisitive wish, brute appetite fed,
The very void that ebbing flood had left
From purer sources would be now refilled;
That to rank weeds of rainy spring mowed off   70
Would a green wholesome aftermath succeed
That the empty garnished tenement of the soul
Would not behold the seven replace the one:
Could I indeed as of some men I might
Think this of maidens also. But I know;   75
Not as the male is, is the female, Eve
Was moulded not as Adam.

S: Stuff!
The women like it; that's enough.

D: Could I believe, as of a man I might,
So a good girl from weary workday hours   80
And from the long monotony of toil
Might safely purchase these wild intervals,
And from that banquet rise refreshed, and wake
And shake her locks and as before go forth

61–2] The philosophy of *solvitur ambulando* questioned by C. throughout his
work.
70–1] Playing on the etymology of the word aftermath, from O.E. 'after
maeth' meaning a second mowing of grass in the same season.
73. the seven replace the one] The seven deadly sins rushing in to fill the void
left by the satisfaction of one (lust).
82. these wild intervals] C. was originally going to write 'intervals of joy', but
could not bring himself to finish the last word.

<pre>
       Invigorated, unvitiate to the task   85
       But no it is not so.

S: That may be true
            It is uncommon, though some do.
            In married life you sometimes find
            Proceedings something of the kind.   90

D: No no, apart from pressures of the world
       And yearning sensibilities of soul,
       The swallowed dram entails the drunkard's curse
       Of burnings ever new; and the coy girl
       Turns to the flagrant woman of the street   95
       Ogling for hirers, horrible to see.

S: That is the high moral way of talking
            I'm well aware about street-walking.

D: Hungering but without appetite; athirst
       From impotence; no humblest feeling left   100
       Of all that once too rank exuberance.
       No kindly longing, no sly coyness now
       Not a poor petal hanging to that stalk
       Where thousands once were redolent and rich.
       Look, she would fain allure; but she is cold   105
       The ripe lips paled, the frolick pulses stilled,
       The quick eye dead, the once fair flushing cheek
       Flaccid under its paint; the once heaving bosom –
       Ask not! for oh, the sweet bloom of desire
       In hot fruition's pawey fingers turns   110
       To dullness and the deadly spreading spot
       Of rottenness inevitably soon
       That while we hold, we hate – Sweet Peace! no more!

S: Fiddle di diddle, fal lal lal!
            By candlelight they are *pas mal*;   115
</pre>

---

104. *redolent*] Fragrant.
106. *frolick*] Frolicsome (archaic).
110. *pawey*] Foul, obscene (archaic).
115. *pas mal*] Not bad.

> Better and worse of course there are;
> Star differs (with the price) from star.

D: Could I believe that any child of Eve
     Were formed and fashioned, raised and reared for nought
     But to be swilled with animal delight   120
     And yield five minutes' pleasure to the male,
     Could I think cherry lips and chubby cheeks
     That seem to exist express for such fond play,
     Hold in suppression nought to come; o'ershell
     No lurking virtuality of more –   125

S: It was a lover and his lass
          With a hey and a ho, and a hey nonino
     Betwixt the acres of the rye
          With a hey and a ho, and a hey nonino
     These pretty country folks would lie   130
          In the spring time, the pretty spring time.

D: And could I think I owed it not to her
     In virtue of our manhood's stronger sight,
     Even against entreaty to forbear –

S: O Joseph and Don Quixote! This   135
     A chivalry of chasteness is,
     That turns to nothing all, that story
     Has made out of your ancient glory!
     Still I must urge, that though 'tis sad,
     'Tis sure, once gone, for good or bad   140
     The prize whose loss we are deploring
     Is physically past restoring:
     C'en est fait. Nor can God's own self
     As Coleridge on the dusty shelf

117] After these lines are the following (cancelled in Second Revision): 'I found it hard I must confess/ To a small Frenchman to say yes/ Who told me, in a steamer talking,/ That one can pick up in one's walking/ In the Strand Street in London town/ Something quite nice for half a crown,/ But – in the dark what comes amiss?/ Except bad breath and syphilis.'

125. virtuality] Essential nature, potentiality.

134. Even] Possibly 'ever'.

135. Joseph and Don Quixote] The Story of Joseph and Potiphar's wife is in Genesis 39; Don Quixote is, of course, the famously self-deluding knight in Cervantes's novel.

143. C'en est fait] It's done.

Says in his wicked Omniana   145
Renew to Ina frail or Ana
Her once rent hymenis membrana.
So that it needs consideration
By what more moral occupation
To support this vast population[.]   150

D: Could I believe that purity were not
Lodged somewhere precious pearl, e'en underneath
The hardest coarsest outside: could I think
That any heart in woman's bosom set
By tenderness o'ermastering mean desire,   155
Faithfulness, love, were unredeemable
Or could I think it sufferable in me
For my poor pleasure's sake to superadd
One possible finger's pressure to the weight
That turns, and grinds as in a fierce machine   160
This hapless kind, these pariahs of the sex –

S: Well; people talk – their sentimentality.
Meantime, as by some sad fatality
Mortality is still mortality,
Nor has corruption, spite of facility,   165
And doctrines of perfectibility,
Yet put on incorruptibility,
As women are and the world goes
They're not so badly off – who knows?
They die, as we do in the end;   170
They marry; or they – *superintend*:

145. wicked Omniana] 'The torch of love may be blown out wholly, but not that of Hymen. Whom the flame and its cheering light and genial warmth no longer bless, him the smoke stifles; for the spark is inextinguishable, save by death: – "Nigro circumvelatus amictu/ Maeret Hymen, fumantque atrae sine lumine taedae" ' (*Omniana* no. 263).

146. Ina frail or Ana] Characteristic endings of Italian female names (e.g. Cristina, Giovanna); cp the reference to foreign women as 'Inas and Trinas' in Carlyle's translation of Goethe's *Wilhelm Meister's Travels* (Carlyle 1899: ii, 240).

147. hymenis membrana] The hymen or membrane inside the vagina, the rupturing of which signifies the loss of virginity.

161. pariahs] Outcasts.

> Or Sidney Herberts sometimes rise,
> And send them out to colonize.

D: Or could I think that it had been for nought,
That from my boyhood until now – in spite   175
Of most misguiding theories – at the moment
Somewhat has ever stepped in to arrest
My ingress at that fatal-closing door,
That many and many a time my foolish foot
O'erspreading the dim sill spite of itself   180
And spite of me instinctively fell back.

S: Like Balaam's ass in spite of thwacking
Against the wall his master backing;
Because of something hazy stalking
Just in the way they should be walking;   185
Soon after too he took to talking[.]

D: Backed and refused my bidding – Could I think,
In spite of carnal understanding's sneers
All this fortuitous only – all a chance –

S: Ah, just what I was going to say;   190
An angel met you in the way
Cry mercy of his heavenly highness,
I took him for that cunning shyness.

D: Shyness. 'Tis but another word for shame;
And that for Sacred Instinct. Off ill thoughts!   195
'Tis holy ground your foot has stepped upon.

---

172. Sidney Herberts] Sidney, first Baron Herbert of Lea (1810–61), was secretary at war in Lord Aberdeen's administration during the Crimean conflict, and later colonial secretary under Palmerston. He was a close friend of Florence Nightingale, C.'s wife's cousin, and these lines represent a clear allusion to his request to her to lead an 'expedition' of British nurses to the military hospital at Scutari in October 1854: 'There is but one person in England that I know of [he wrote] who would be capable of organising and superintending such a scheme' – Stanmore 1906: i, 339. This allusion means that the Second Revision cannot have been composed before the end of 1854; see textual note above.

182–6] The story of Balaam's ass, which was instructed by God to disobey its master 'in spite of thwacking', is told in Numbers 22:20–34; the ass 'takes to talking' in vv. 28 and 30.

192–3] Cp *Othello* IV.ii.90–2: 'I cry you mercy,/ I took you for that cunning whore of Venice,/ That married with Othello.'

S: Ho, Virtue quotha! trust who knows;
          There's not a girl that by us goes
          But mightn't have you if she chose;
          No doubt but you would give her trouble;   200
          But then you'd pay her for it double.
          By Jove – if I were but a lass,
          I'd soon see what I'd bring to pass.

D: O welcome then the sweet domestic bonds,
          The matrimonial sanctities; the hopes   205
          And cares of wedded life; parental thoughts,
          The prattle of young children, the good word
          Of fellow men, the sanction of the law,
          And permanence and habit, that transmute
          Grossness itself to crystal. O why why   210
          Why ever let this speculating brain
          Rest upon other objects than on this?

S: Well well – if you must stick perforce
          Unto the ancient holy course;
          And map your life out on the plan   215
          Of the connubial puritan;
          For God's sake carry out your creed,
          Go home, and marry – and be d—d;
          I'll help you.

D: You!

S: O never scout me;
          I know you'll ne'er propose without me.   220

D: I have talked o'er much. The Spirit passes from me.
          O folly folly – what have I done? Ah me!

S: You'd like another turn, I see.
          Yes yes, a little quiet turn.
          By all means let us live and learn.   225
          Here's many a lady still waylaying,
          And sundry gentlemen purveying.
          And if 'twere only just to see
          The room of an Italian *fille*,
          'Twere worth the trouble and the money.   230
          You'll like to find – I found it funny –

218] Note that 'd—d' is supposed to rhyme with 'creed'.
219. scout] To dismiss or reject with disdain.

The chamber *où vous faites votre affaire*
Stand nicely fitted up for prayer;
While dim you trace along one end
The sacred supper's length extend,   235
The calm Madonna o'er your head
Smiles, *col bambino*, on the bed
Where – but your chaste ears I must spare –
Where – as we said – *vous faites votre affaire*.
They'll suit you, these Venetian pets,   240
So natural, not the least coquettes,
Really at times one quite forgets –
Well would you like perhaps to arrive at
A pretty creature's home in private?
We can look in, just say goodnight,   245
And if you like to stay, all right
Just as you fancy – is it well?

D: O folly folly folly! To the Hotel[.]

SCENE 4: THE HOTEL

D: O hateful, hateful – let me shudder it off.
       Thank God, thank God we are here – that's well at least.

S: Well, well. I may have been a little strong;
       Of course I wouldn't have you do what's wrong.
       But we who've lived out in the world, you know,   5
       Don't see these little things precisely so.
       You feel yourself, to shrink and yet be fain,
       And still to move and still draw back again,
       Is a proceeding wholly without end.
       So if you really hate the street, my friend,   10
       Why, one must try the drawing room, one fancies:
       Say, will you run to concert and to dances
       And with my help go into good society?

---

232. *où vous faites votre affaire*] 'Where you do your business'; it is characteristic of The Spirit to hide behind decorous French euphemisms.
237. *col bambino*] 'With the infant [Jesus]'; the picture referred to is a Madonna and child. The Spirit is stressing the contrast between the outward manifestations of Christianity and the total failure to adhere to any of its moral standards; cp scene 1 above. The emphasis on Venetian venality might also owe something to the memory of Shakespeare's Venetian plays, especially *Othello* (see note to 3.192–3 above): 'In Venice they do let God see the pranks/ They dare not show their husbands' (III.iii.206–7).

The world don't love, 'tis true, this peevish piety:
E'en they with whom it thinks to be securest,   15
Your most religious, delicatest, purest,
Discern, and show as well bred people can,
Their feeling that you are not quite a man.
Still the thing has its place; and with sagacity
Much might be done by one of your capacity.   20
A virtuous attachment formed judiciously
Would come, one sees, uncommonly propitiously:
Turn you but your affections the right way,
And what mayn't happen none of us can say:
For in despite of devils and of mothers   25
Your good young men make catches too like others.
Oh yes! into society we go:
At worst 'twill teach you much you ought to know.

D: To herd with people one can feel no care for,
To drain the heart with empty complaisance,   30
To warp the unfashioned diction on the lips
And twist one's mouth to counterfeit; enforce
The laggard cheeks to falsehood; base-alloy
The ingenuous golden frankness of the past;
To calculate, to plot; be rough and smooth   35
Forward and silent, deferential, cool,
Not by one's humour, which is the true truth,
But on consideration.

S: That is, act
Upon dispassionate judgement of the fact
Look all the data fairly in the face,   40
And rule your conduct simply by the case.

D: On vile consideration. At the best
With pallid hotbed courtesies to forestall

21–2] Cp Thackeray's *Pendennis*: 'The major surveyed the state of things with
a sigh. "If it were but a temporary liaison," the excellent man said, "one could
bear it. A young fellow must sow his wild oats, and that sort of thing. But a
virtuous attachment is the deuce. It comes of the d—d romantic notions boys
get from being brought up by women" ' (Thackeray 1986: 125).
29. *To herd*] To mix unthinkingly with; cp Tennyson, 'Locksley Hall': 'I, to
herd with narrow foreheads, vacant of our glorious gains,/ Like a beast with
lower pleasures, like a beast with lower pains!' (175-6)
30. *complaisance*] Desire to please.
33–4. *base-alloy*] i.e. mix the 'gold' of frankness with a baser element.
43–4] The courtesies are 'pallid' because they are artificially forced in the
'hothouse' of society, unlike the 'vernal spontaneities' of authentic feeling.

One's native vernal spontaneities
And waste the priceless moments of the man   45
In softening down grimace to grace. Whether these things
Be right I do not know; I only know 'tis
To lose one's youth too early. Oh not yet
Not yet I make this sacrifice!

S: *Du tout!*
    To give up nature's just what wouldn't do.   50
    By all means keep your sweet ingenuous graces,
    And bring them in, at proper times and places.
    For work, for play, for business, talk, and love,
    I own as wisdom truly from above
    That scripture of the Serpent and the dove.   55
    Nor's aught so perfect for the world's affairs
    As the old parable of wheat and tares;
    What we all love is good touched up with evil,
    Religion's self must have a spice of devil.

D: Let it be enough   60
That in our needful mixture with the world,
On each new morning with the rising sun
Our rising heart, fresh from the seas of sleep,
Scarce o'er the level lifts his purer orb
Ere lost and mingled with polluting smoke   65
A noonday coppery disk. Lo scarce come forth
Some vagrant miscreant meets and with a look
Transmutes me his; and for a whole sick day
Lepers me.

48–9] C.'s habitual fear of sacrificing a possibly perfect future to a manifestly imperfect present; cp *Amours* II.81–94.

49. Du tout!] Not at all!

53–5] Matthew 10:16: 'Behold, I send you forth as sheep in the midst of wolves; be ye, therefore, wise as serpents, and harmless as doves.' That is to say (according to The Spirit) adapt your behaviour to the occasion.

56–7] Matthew 13:24–30; Jesus explains the parable as follows: 'He that soweth the good seed is the Son of man;/ The field is the world; the good seed are the children of the kingdom; but the tares are the children of the wicked *one*;/ The enemy that sowed them is the devil; the harvest is the end of the world; and the reapers are the angels' (Matthew 13:37–9). The Spirit seems to interpret the parable as meaning that good and bad seed are equally necessary for 'the world's affairs', whatever the situation may be in heaven.

60] Somewhat elliptical; Dipsychus seems to be extrapolating the logic of The Spirit's argument. The sense is '[You say I should] Let it be enough', etc.

S: Just the one thing, I assure you,
           From which good company can't but secure you.   70
           About the individuals t'an't so clear,
           But who can doubt the general atmosphere?

D: Ay truly, who at first? But in a while –

S: O dear this o'er-discernment makes me smile.
           You don't pretend to tell me you can see   75
           Without one touch of melting sympathy
           Those lovely, stately flowers that fill with bloom
           The brilliant season's gay *parterre*-like room
           Moving serene yet swiftly through the dances
           Those graceful forms and perfect countenances;   80
           Whose every fold and line in all their dresses
           Something refined and exquisite expresses;
           To see them smile and hear them talk so sweetly
           In me destroys all grosser thoughts completely.
           I really seem without exaggeration   85
           To experience the True Regeneration;
           One's own dress too, one's manners, what one's doing
           And saying all assist to one's renewing,
           I love to see in these their fitting places
           The bows, and forms and all you call grimaces,   90
           I heartily could wish we'd kept some more of them
           However much they talk about the bore of them
           Fact is, your awkward parvenus are shy at it,
           Afraid to look like waiters if they try at it.
           'Tis sad to what democracy is leading;   95
           Give me your Eighteenth Century for high breeding.
           Though I can put up gladly with the present,
           And quite can think our modern parties pleasant,
           One shouldn't analyse the thing too nearly;
           The main effect is admirable clearly.   100
           Good manners, said our great aunts, next to piety;
           And so, my friend, hurrah for good society.
           For mind you, if you don't do this, you still
           Have got to tell me what it is you will.

79–80] The dance often serves in C.'s work as a symbol for unthinking adherence to the demands of society; cp 'Why should I say . . .?' above, p. 40.
85–6. True Regeneration] A parody of the language of evangelical Protestantism; the 'true regeneration' is the feeling of inward redemption through faith in Christ.
93. parvenus] Social climbers or *arrivistes*.
95–6] Cp Byron, *Don Juan* XIII.751–2: 'Society is smooth'd to that excess,/ That manners hardly differ more than dress.'

SCENE 5: IN A GONDOLA

D: *Per ora.* To the Grand Canal.
          And after that as fancy shall.

          Afloat; we move. Delicious[.] Ah,
          What else is like the gondola?
          This level floor of liquid glass   5
          Begins beneath us swift to pass.
          It goes as though it went alone
          By some impulsion of its own.
          How light it moves, how softly[.] Ah,
          Were all things like the gondola?   10

          How light it moves; how softly[.] Ah,
          Could life as does our gondola
          Unvexed with quarrels aims and cares
          And moral duties and affairs
          Unswaying noiseless swift and strong   15
          For ever thus thus glide along,
          How light we move, how softly! Ah,
          Were life but as the gondola[.]

          With no more motion than should bear
          A freshness to the languid air;   20
          With no more effort than exprest
          The need and naturalness of rest,
          Which we beneath a grateful shade
          Should take on peaceful pillows laid;–
          How light we move, how softly! – Ah,   25
          Were all things like the gondola!

          In one unbroken passage borne
          To closing night from opening morn!
          Uplift at whiles slow eyes to mark

Scene 5:In a Gondola] This scene is the most difficult to place, although it seems clear that C. intended it to be in the first half of the poem; see textual note above. The scene is thematically but not stylistically continuous with those before and after it; Dipsychus and The Spirit adopt the same attitudes as before, but the debate moves into a lyrical register. Gondola scenes were a *topos* of Venetian travel-writing in the early nineteenth century; see, e.g., 'The Gondola' in Samuel Rogers (1830) *Italy, a poem*, Browning's 'In a Gondola' and the last chapter of the first volume of *The Stones of Venice.*
1. Per ora] For now.

Some palace front, some passing bark   30
Through windows catch the varying shore
And hear the soft turns of the oar –
How light we move, how softly! Ah,
Were all things like the gondola!

Yes, it is beautiful ever, let foolish men rail at it never;   35
Life it is beautiful truly, my brothers, I grant it you duly,
Wise are ye others that choose it, and happy are all that
    can use it;
Life it is beautiful wholly, and could we eliminate only
This interfering, enslaving, o'ermastering demon of
    craving
This wicked tempter inside us to ruin still eager to guide
    us,   40
Life were beatitude, action a possible pure satisfaction.

Ah but it will not, it may not, its nature and law is to stay
    not,
This semi-vision enchanting with but actuality wanting,
And as a picture or book at, this life that is lovely to look
    at
When that it comes as we go on to th' eating and drinking
    and so on   45
Is not beatitude, Action in no way a pure satisfaction[.]

S: Hexameters by all that's odious
        Beshod with rhyme to run melodious[.]

D: All as I go on my way I behold them consorting and
    coupling
Faithful it seemeth and fond, very fond, very possibly
    faithful,
All as I go on my way with a pleasure sincere and
    unmingled.   50
Life it is beautiful truly, my brothers, I grant it you duly.
But for perfection attaining is one method only, abstaining;
Let us abstain, for we should so, if only we thought that
    we could so.

S: This world is bad enough, may be;   55
           We little comprehend it;
        But in one fact can all agree,
           God won't, and we can't mend it.

35–41] On this desire for a purely specular relation to life see *Amours* III.viii.

                    Being common sense it can't be sin
                        To take it as we find it,   60
                    The pleasure to take pleasure in,
                        The pain, try not to mind it.

D: Better it were, thou sayest, to consent,
      Feast while we may, and live ere life be spent;
      Close up clear eyes, and call the unstable sure   65
      The unlovely lovely and the filthy pure,
      In self belyings self deceivings roll
      And lose in Action, Passion, Talk the soul.

      Ah better far to mark off so much air
      And call it heaven, place bliss and glory there   70
      Fix perfect homes in the unsubstantial sky
      And say what is not shall be by and by,
      What here exists not, must exist elsewhere.
      Play then not tricks upon thy self, O man;
      Let fact be fact, and life the thing it can.   75

S: These juicy meats, this flashing wine
          Are all an unreal mere appearance;
      Only – for my inside in fine
          They show a singular coherence.

      This lovely creature's glowing charms   80
          Are gross illusion, I don't doubt that,
      But folded in each other's arms
          We didn't somehow think about that:

      O yes, my pensive youth, abstain:
          And any empty sick sensation   85
      Any fierce hunger, any pain
          You'll know is mere imagination.

      Trust me, I've read your German sage
          To far more purpose e'er than you did
      You find it in his wisest page   90
          Whom God deludes is well deluded.

---

59. *common sense*] The Spirit's guiding principle; see below, 2.3.160–90.
61–2] Pleasure and pain were held to be the sole springs of human action by materialist philosophers, especially the Benthamites; The Spirit is therefore indicating his adherence to their 'godless' views.
91] From Goethe's 'Rhymed Distichs': 'Wen Gott betrügt ist wohl betrogen' – 'Whom God deceives, is well deceived'. Used as the title for 'Is it true, ye gods' (above, p. 47) by Mrs C. in *1869*.

St Giorgio and the Redemptore!
This Gothic is a worn-out story;
No building, trivial, gay, or solemn
Can spare the shapely Grecian column;   95
'Tis not these centuries four for nought
Our European world of thought
Has made familiar to its home
The classic mind of Greece and Rome:
In all new work that dare look forth   100
To more than antiquarian worth
Palladio's pediments and bases
Or something such will find their places:
Maturer optics don't delight
In childish dim religious light: 105
In evanescent vague effects
That shirk not face one's intellects
They love not fancies fast betrayed
And artful tricks of light and shade
But pure form nakedly displayed,   110
And all things absolutely made.

The Doge's palace, though, from hence,
In spite of Ruskin's d—d pretence,

92–111] Characteristically, The Spirit attempts to tempt Dipsychus out of his
reverie by returning to the reality around him.

92. St Giorgio and the Redemptore!] San Giorgio Maggiore and *Il Santissimo
Redentore* are neo-classical churches built by Palladio (1518–80). They had
traditionally been considered among the architectural treasures of Venice, but
Ruskin, the propagandist of Gothic, thought otherwise; of San Giorgio
Maggiore he wrote: 'It is impossible to conceive a design more gross, more
barbarous, more childish in conception, more servile in plagiarism, more
insipid in result, more contemptible under every point of rational regard' –
Ruskin 1903: 11, 381. The Spirit's diatribe in favour of Palladio and his school
can, then, be seen as a counterblast to Ruskin and the whole Gothic revival.

104–11] The Spirit argues that Gothic was adequate for a less mature period
of European culture, one in which the credulous minds of worshippers could
be impressed by 'tricks of light and shade' that 'shirk, not face, one's intellects', but that it cannot co-exist with the clear light of knowledge and reason.
Cp the description of common sense as the 'siccum lumen' of the mind at
2.3.164–72 below, and *Epi-Strauss-ium* below, p. 229. The phrase 'dim religious light' occurs in Milton's poem *Il Penseroso* (l. 160).

113. Ruskin's d—d pretence] i.e. pretentiousness; for Ruskin's views on the
Doge's Palace, see Ruskin 1903: X, ch. viii. The Spirit is disconcerted to find
himself in agreement with his enemy on the question of the architectural mer-
its of the Doge's Palace.

The tide now level with the quay,
Is certainly a thing to see.   115
We'll turn to the Rialto soon,
One's told to see it by the moon.

D: Where are the great whom thou would'st wish should
       praise thee?
    Where are the pure whom thou would'st choose should
       love thee?
    Where are the brave to stand supreme above thee   120
    Whose high commands would cheer, whose chiding raise
       thee?
       Seek, seeker, in thyself; submit to find
       In the stones bread and life in the blank mind.

    Written in London, standing in the Park,
    An evening in last June, just before dark.   125

S: As I sat at the cafe, I thought to myself,
    They may talk as they please about what they call pelf,
    They may jeer if they like about eating and drinking
    But help it I cannot, I cannot help thinking
        How pleasant it is to have money, high ho   130
        How pleasant it is to have money.

I sit at my table *en grand seigneur,*
And when I have done, toss a crust to the poor:
Not only the pleasure, one self, of good living,
But also the pleasure of now and then giving.   135
        So pleasant it is to have money, high-o
        So pleasant it is to have money.

The horses are brought, and the horses they stay,
I haven't quite settled on riding today,
The servants they wait, and they mustn't look sour   140

---

116. Rialto] The largest and most important of the bridges across the Grand
Canal.
123. In the stones bread] From the Sermon on the Mount: 'Or what man is
there of you, whom if his son ask bread, will he give him a stone?' (Matthew
7:9).
126–91] A version of The Spirit's song was printed separately in *1862* under
the title 'Spectator ab extra'; Coleridge described this as Wordsworth's 'proper
title' in his *Table Talk* (Coleridge 1835: ii, 72).
127. pelf] Money; note The Spirit's use of rakish slang, e.g. 'town' for London
(168) and 'cad' for a person of no importance (146).
132. en grand seigneur] Playing the part of a grandee.

Though we change our intention ten times in an hour
 So pleasant it is to have money, high ho
 So pleasant it is to have money.

I drive through the streets and I care not a damn
The people they stare and they know who I am   145
And if I should chance to run over a cad
I can pay for the damage, if ever so bad
 So pleasant it is to have money, high ho
 So pleasant it is to have money.

We stroll to our box, and look down on the pit,   150
If it weren't rather low should be tempted to spit:
We loll and we talk until people look up
And when it's half over we go out and sup.
 So pleasant it is to have money, high ho
 So pleasant it is to have money.   155

The best of the rooms and the best of the fare
And as for all others the devil may care
It isn't our fault, if they dare not afford
To sup like a prince and be drunk as a lord.
 So pleasant it is to have money, high ho   160
 So pleasant it is to have money.

We sit at our table and tipple champagne,
Ere one bottle goes, comes another again,
The waiters they skip and they scuttle about,
And the landlord attends us so civilly out   165
 So pleasant it is to have money, high ho
 So pleasant it is to have money.

It was but last winter I came up to town,
But I'm getting already a little renown
I enter good houses without much ado,   170
Am beginning to see the nobility too
 So pleasant it is to have money, high ho
 So pleasant it is to have money.

Oh dear what a pity they ever should lose it,
For they are the gentry that know how to use it,   175
[So] grand and so graceful, such manners, such dinners,
But yet in the end it is we shall be winners
 So pleasant it is to have money, high ho
 So pleasant it is to have money.

So I sat at my table *en grand seigneur*,   180
And when I had done, threw a crust to the poor,

Not only the pleasure one self of good living
But also the pleasure of now and then giving
    So pleasant it is to have money, high ho
    So pleasant it is to have money.   185

They may talk [as they] please about what they call pelf,
Declare one ought never to think of one self,
Say that pleasures of thought surpass eating and drinking;
My pleasure of thought is the pleasure of thinking
    How pleasant it is to have money, high ho   190
    How pleasant it is to have money.

    Written in Venice, somewhere about two;
    'Twas not a crust I gave him, but a sous
    And now it's time I think, my men
    We try the Grand Canal again[.]   195

A gondola here and a gondola there
'Tis the pleasantest fashion of taking the air
To right and to left; stop, turn, and go yonder;
And let us repeat o'er the tide as we wander
    How pleasant it is to have money, high ho   200
    How pleasant it is to have money.

D: How light we go, how soft we skim
    And all in moonlight seem to swim.
    The south side rises o'er our bark
    A wall impenetrably dark;   205
    The north is seen profusely bright;
    The water – is it shade or light?
    Say gentle moon, which conquers now,
    The flood, those bulky hulls, or thou?
    How light we go, how softly! Ah,   210
    Were life but as the gondola!

    How light we go, how soft we skim
    And all in moonlight seem to swim.
    In moonlight is it now or shade?
    In planes of clear division made   215
    By angles sharp of palace walls
    The clear light and the shadow falls:
    O sight of glory, sight of wonder,
    Seen, a pictorial portent under

193. sous] A French coin; a generic term for a coin of little value.
202] Dipsychus returns to his original lyric, apparently unmoved by all The
Spirit's arguments in favour of the pleasures of this world.

O great Rialto, the clear round   220
Of thy vast solid arch profound.
How light we go, how softly – Ah,
Life should be as the gondola!

How light we go, how softly –

S: Nay,
Enough I think of that to-day.   225
I'm deadly weary of your tune,
And half-*ennuyé* with the moon;
The shadows lie, the glories fall,
And are but moonshine after all;
It goes against my conscience really   230
To let myself feel so ideally:
Make me repose no power of man shall
In things so deuced unsubstantial
Come – to the Piazzetta steer,
'Tis nine by this, or very near.   235
These airy blisses, skiey joys
Of vague romantic girls and boys,
Which melt the heart (and the brain soften)
When not affected, as too often
They are, remind me I protest   240
Of nothing better at the best
Than Timon's feast to his ancient lovers,
Warm water under silver covers;
Lap dogs, I think I hear him say,
And lap who will, so I'm away.   245

D: How light we go, how soft we skim,
And all in open moonlight swim:

---

227. half-ennuyé] Half-bored.
229. moonshine] Cp Carlyle's dismissal of Coleridge's 'moonshine' philosophy
in his 1851 *Life of John Sterling*, Part 1, chs 8 and 9.
233. deuced] A polite expletive.
234. Piazzetta] The small square next to St Mark's between the Doge's Palace
and the Procuratie Nuove.
242–4] Timon of Athens invites his 'ancient lovers' – i.e. his fair-weather
friends – to a banquet at which he gives them covered dishes filled with nothing but warm water. His ironic benediction ends with the words 'Uncover,
dogs, and lap' – *Timon of Athens* III.vi.82. The Spirit's (rather laboured) point
is that the 'airy blisses' indulged in by Dipsychus represent similarly insub-
stantial nourishment in spite of their fine appearance.

Bright clouds against, reclined I mark
That white dome now projected dark:
And by o'er brilliant lamps displayed   250
The Doge's columns and arcade;
Over smooth waters mildly come
The distant laughter and the hum.
How light we go, how softly! – ah,
Life should be as the gondola!   255

S;   By Jove we've had enough of you,
       Quote us a little Wordsworth, do;
       Those lines which are so true, they say:
       'A something far more deeply' eh
       'Interfused' what is it, they tell us?   260
       Which and the sunset are bedfellows?

D: How light we go, how soft we skim,
       And all in open moonlight swim.
       Oh gondolier, slow, slow, more slow!
       We go; but wherefore thus should go?   265
       Ah, let not muscles all too strong
       Beguile betray thee to our wrong!
       On to the landing, onward – Nay,
       Sweet dream a little longer stay!
       On to the landing. Here. And ah   270
       Life is not as the gondola.

S: *Tre ore.* So. The Parthenone,
       Is it? you haunt for your *limone*.

249. The white dome] Santa Maria della Salute; see note to 1.2.7 above.
256–61] The Spirit is alluding to (and debunking) Wordsworth's 'Lines
Composed a Few Miles above Tintern Abbey': 'And I have felt/ A presence
that disturbs me with the joy/ Of elevated thoughts; a sense sublime/ Of
something far more deeply interfused,/ Whose dwelling is the light of setting
suns,/ And the round ocean and the living air,/ And the blue sky, and in the
mind of man:/ A motion and a spirit, that impels/ All thinking things, all
objects of all thought,/ And rolls through all things' (93–102).
272. Tre ore] Three hours. The time-sequence in *Dipsychus* is unclear, to say the
least, and further confused by the use of two different time-schemes. The Spirit
says ''Tis nine by this or very near' above (1.5.235), and the scene is clearly set at
night, yet he now states that it is 'tre ore'. This discrepancy might be due to the
peculiarities of the Italian time-keeping system. As Goethe points out (Goethe
1987: 61) the Italians did not at this time have fixed clocks, but calculated the
time according to the sunset. Thus, in August, three rings of the bell – *tre ore* –
would have signified three hours after sunset, ie. around eleven o'clock.
272. The Parthenone] Presumably a well-known cafe.
273. limone] Lemon drink.

Let me induce you to join me
In *gramolata persici*.   275

SCENE 6

S: Insulted. By the living Lord!
He laid his hand upon his sword.
Fort did he say? a German brute,
With neither heart nor brains to shoot.

D: What does he mean? he's wrong, I had done nothing.   5
'Twas a mistake – more his I am sure than mine.
He is quite wrong – I feel it. Come let us go.

S: Go up to him. You must, that's flat.
Be threaten'd by a beast like that!

D: He's violent. What [can I] do against him.   10
I neither wish to be killed or to kill.
What's more, I never yet have touched a sword
Nor fired, but twice, a pistol in my life.

S: O never mind, 'twon't come to fighting
Only some verbal small requiting;   15
Or give your card – we'll do't by writing:
He'll not stick to it – soldiers too
Are cowards just like me or you.
What! not a single word to throw at
This snarling dog of a d—d Croat [?]   20

D: My heaven! why should I care? He does not hurt me.
If he is wrong, it is the worse for him.
I certainly did nothing – I shall go.

S: Did nothing! I should think not; no,

---

275. gramolata persici] A drink made with crushed ice.
Scene 6] The large Austrian military presence in Venice and the atmosphere of
suspicion which persisted after the fall of the Republic meant that duels, or at
least challenges, were still fairly common occurrences; even John Ruskin, for
example, was challenged during his visit to Venice of 1851–2 (Clegg 1981: 94).
The scene contrasts Dipsychus's determination to live according to the precepts of Christianity with The Spirit's altogether more worldly and pragmatic
attitude.
3. Fort] 'Get out'; see below, 6.225–6.
20. Croat] The main detachment of Austrian troops in Venice was Kinsky's
Croat regiment, stationed on the Zattere; see Trevelyan 1923: 86, 90–1.

Nor ever will, I dare be sworn: 25
But oh my friend, well bred, well born
You to behave so in these quarrels
Makes me half doubtful of your morals.
<   > It were all one,
You had been some shopkeeper's son   30
Whose childhood ne'er was shown aught better
Than bills of creditor and debtor.

D: By heaven it falls from off me like the rain
From the oil-coat. I seem in spirit to see
How he and I at some great day shall meet   35
Before some awful judgement-seat of truth;
And I could deem that I behold him there
Come praying for the pardon I give now,
Did not I think these matters too too small
For any record on the leaves of time.   40

S: Oh Lord! and walking with your sister
If some foul brute stept up and kissed her
You'd leave that also I dare say
On account for the judgement day[.]

D: Oh these skin-bites, these airy words   45
Which at the moment seem to pierce us through
And one hour after are acknowledged nought
These pricks of pride these petty personal hurts
O thou great Watcher of this noisy World
What are they in thy sight? or what in his   50
Who finds some End of Action in his life.
What e'en in his whose sole permitted course
Is to pursue his peaceful byway walk
And live his brief life purely in Thy sight
And righteously towards his brother-men.   55

S: And whether, so you're just and fair,
Other folks are so, you don't care;
You who profess more love than others
For your poor sinful human brothers.
But this anon we'll come, my friend, to   60
My previous question first attend to.

D: For grosser evils their gross remedies
The law affords us, let us be content
For finer wounds the law would, if it could,

29–32] Typical anti-mercantile prejudice; cp *Amours* I.vi.

D: Find medicine too – it cannot: let us bear;   65
For sufferance is the badge of all men's tribes.

S: <   >

D: For these no code of delicatest enactment
No court of honour's subtlest precedents
No rules, no judges, can ensure defence.
A wretched witling with his hour of prate   70
Destroys my nascent thoughts: the infectious eyes
Of some poor misbegotten waif of clay
Breed scurvy in my peace. Say shall I draw
This sword you love, to save myself from these,
Because a man is vulgar cut him down,   75
And shoot a witling for an inept joke[?]

S: Because we can't do all we would
Does it follow to do nothing's good
No way to help the law's rough sense
By equities of self defence [?]   80

D: Draw the line where you will it will exclude
Much it should comprehend. I draw it here[.]

S: Well, for yourself it may be nice
To serve vulgarity and vice
Must sisters too and wives and mothers   85
Fare like their patient sons and brothers[?]

D: He that loves sister mother more than me[. . .]

S: But the injustice – the gross wrong
To whom on earth does it belong
If not to you, to whom 'twas done,   90
Who see it plain as any sun,
To make the base and foul offender
Acknowledge and atonement render;
At least before the termination of it
Prove your own lofty reprobation of it.   95
Though gentleness I know was born in you
Surely you have a little scorn in you[?]

D: Heaven! to pollute one's fingers to pick up
The fallen coin of honour from the dirt

66] There is a blank space in the MS here for a reply by The Spirit.
87] Cp Matthew 10:37: 'He that loveth father or mother more than me is not worthy of me: and he that loveth son or daughter more than me is not worthy of me'; cp 13.66 below.

Pure silver though it be let it rather lie. 100
To take up any offence, where't may be said
That temper, vanity, I know not what
Had led me on –
To enter the base crowd and bare one's flanks
To all ill voices of a blustering world 105
To have so much as e'en half-felt of one
That ever one was angered for oneself -
Beyond suspicion Caesar's wife should be.
Beyond suspicion this bright honour shall.
Did he say scorn – I have some scorn, thank God. 110

S: Certainly – only if it's so
Let us leave Italy and go
Post-haste, to attend, you're ripe and rank for't
The Great Peace-Meeting up at Frankfort[.]

Joy to the Croat. Take our lives, 115
Sweet friends and please respect our wives.
Myself, a trifle quite, you slaughter
But pray be decent with my daughter.

Joy to the Croat. Some fine day
He'll see the error of his way, 120
No doubt, and will repent and pray.
At any rate he'll open his eyes,
If not before, at the last Assize:
Not, if I rightly understood you,
That even then you'd punish, would you? 125

Nay, let the hapless soul escape.
Mere murder, robbery, and rape,
In whate'er station, age or sex

108–9] Julius Caesar left his wife Pompeia after a scandalous incident (in spite
of her apparent innocence) saying ' "I wished my wife to be not so much as
suspected" ' – from C.'s translation of Plutarch's 'Life' of Caesar in Clough
1925: ii, 537. An allusion to this incident also appears in Byron's Venetian
play *Marino Faliero* (1820) I.ii.168–70, which deals with the outraged reaction
of a Doge of Venice to a slur on his wife's honour. The theme of honour and
justice versus mercy and forgiveness, examined in the 'Insulted!' scene, also
plays an important part in Shakespeare's Venetian plays *Othello* and *The
Merchant of Venice*.
114. The Great Peace-Meeting up at Frankfort] Probably a reference to the
constituent assembly which met in Frankfurt in May 1848 in the aftermath of
the German and Austrian uprisings of that year.
123. the last Assize] The Day of Judgment.

Your sacred spirit scarce can vex.
De minimis non curat lex. 130

To the Peace Congress – Ring the bell.
Horses to Frankfort – and to hell.

D: I am not quite in union with myself
On this strange matter. I must needs confess
Instinct turns instinct in and out; and thought 135
Wheels round on thought. To bleed for others' wrongs
In vindication of a Cause, to draw
The sword of the Lord and Gideon – O that seems
The flower and top of life. But fight because
Some poor misconstruing trifler haps to say 140
I lie, when I do not lie, or is rude
To some vain fashionable thing, some poor
Curl-paper of a doll, that's set by chance
To dangle a dull hour on my vext arm
Why should I – call you this a Cause? I can't. 145
Oh he is wrong, no doubt. He misbehaves.
But is it worth so much as speaking loud?
And things more merely personal to myself
Of all earth's things do least affect myself.

S: Sweet eloquence – at next may meeting 150
How it would tell in the repeating!
I recognise – and kiss the rod
The Methodistic voice of God
I catch contrite that angel whine
That snuffle human yet divine; 155
The doctrine own, and no mistaker,
Of the bland Philanthropic Quaker.
O come blest age from bloodshed cease
Bewildered brothers, dwell at peace
This holy effluence from above 160
Shall fill your wildest hearts with love,
Shall bring the light of inward day

130] 'The law does not concern itself with trifles.'
138] Judges 7:18–22; Gideon was called to fight for the Lord in spite of his reluctance.
150. May meeting] The meeting of Evangelical groups of all denominations held in London's Exeter Hall every year for most of the nineteenth century.
153] The Spirit is accusing Dipsychus of the kind of ostentatious piety which he thinks characteristic of Methodists and Quakers.

To Caffre fierce and sly Malay
Soften hard pirates with a kiss
And melt barbarian isles with bliss   165
Leaving, in lieu of war and robbing
Only a little mild stock-jobbing
O doubtless – let the simple heart
Mind her own business, do her part
Her wrongs repel, maintain her honour   170
O fiend and savage out upon her!
Press, pulpit from each other borrow
The terms of scandal, shame and sorrow,
Vulgarity shrieks out in fear of it
And Piety turns sick to hear of it.   175
The downright things twixt you and me,
The wrongs we really feel and see,
The hurts that actually try one,
Like common plain good deeds close by one,
Decidedly have no existence   180
They are at such a little distance.
But to protect the lovely figures
Of your half ourang-outang niggers,
To preach the doctrine of the cross
To worshippers in house of joss,   185
To take steps for the quick conversion
Of Turk Armenian Jew and Persian
Or send up missions per balloon
To those poor heathens in the moon:
Oh that –
       But I'm afraid I storm   190
I'm quite ashamed to be so warm.

D: It may be I am somewhat a poltroon.
      I never fought at school. Whether it be
      Some native poorness in my spirit's blood

---

163. Caffre fierce and sly Malay] 'Caffre' (more usually Kaffir) is a pejorative term for a black African; the attribution of cunning to Malaysians and other inhabitants of Indo-China was a commonplace of nineteenth-century ethnology.
167. stock-jobbing] Stock-broking.
183. half ourang-outang niggers] The Spirit is, of course, giving vent to his prejudices at this point, and the opinions he expresses should not necessarily be identified with those of the poet.
185. house of joss] That is to say, temples where incense (joss-sticks) are burned.
192. poltroon] Pusillanimous, lacking in spirit.

Or that the holy doctrine of our faith   195
In too exclusive fervency possessed
My heart with feelings, with ideas my brain[.]

S: Yes, you would argue that it goes
   Against the Bible I suppose.
   But our revered religion – yes   200
   Our common faith seems, I confess,
   On these points to propose to address
   The people more than you or me,
   At best the vulgar bourgeoisie[.]
   The sacred writers don't keep count,   205
   But still the Sermon on the Mount
   Must have been spoken, by what's stated
   To hearers by the thousand rated.
   I cuff some fellow. Mild and meek
   He should turn round the other cheek   210
   For him it may be right and good
   We are not all of gentle blood
   Really or as such understood.

D: There are two kindreds upon earth I know
  The oppressors and the oppressed. But as for me   215
  If I must choose to inflict wrong, or accept
  May my last end, and life too, be with these.
  Yes – whatsoe'er the reason, want of blood,
  Lymphatic humours, or my childhood's faith,
  So is the thing and be it well or ill   220
  I have no choice – I am a man of peace
  And the old Adam of the gentleman
  Dares seldom in my bosom stir against
  The good plebeian Christian seated there.

S: Forgive me, if I name my doubt,   225
   Whether you know *fort* means Get out.

SCENE 7: THE LIDO

S: What now? the Lido shall it be?
   That none may say we didn't see

209–10] C.'s earlier version was slightly racier: 'Kick a cad's bottom; mild and
meek/ He'll turn we trust the other cheek' (*Venice* notebook).
219. Lymphatic humours] An allusion to the belief that a person's temperament
was determined by the 'humours' in their blood; by C.'s time this had become
largely metaphorical.

The ground which Byron used to ride on
And do I don't know what beside on.
Ho, *barca* – here, and this light gale   5
Will let us run it with a sail.

D: I dreamt a dream – till morning light
A bell rang in my head all night
Tinkling and tinkling first, and then
Tolling; and tinkling; tolling again   10
So brisk and gay, and then so slow
O joy! and terror: Mirth, and woe.
Ting ting, there is no God, ting, ting:
Dong, there is no God; dong
There is no God: dong; dong.   15

Ting ting, there is no God, ting ting
Come dance and play, and merrily sing
Ting ting a ding. Ting ting a ding.
O pretty girl, who trippest along
Come to my bed, it isn't wrong.   20
Uncork the bottle; sing the song:
Ting ting a ting: – Dong; dong.
Wine has dregs; the song an end
A silly girl is a poor friend
And age and weakness who shall mend?   25
Dong; there is no God; Dong[.]

Ting ting a ding. Come dance and sing!
Staid Englishmen, who toil and slave
From your first breeching to your grave
And seldom spend and always save,   30
And do your duty all your life
By your young family and wife;
Come, be't not said you ne'er had known
What earth can furnish you alone;
The Italian, Frenchman, German even   35
Have given up all thoughts of heaven;
And still you linger – oh you fool,

3–4] 'The shore of the Littorale towards the Adriatic constitutes the *Lido*, now associated with the name of Byron, as the spot where he used to take his rides, and where he designed to have been buried' (Murray 1847: 366). See also 7.190 below.
5. barca] 'Boat' – metonymic expression for boatman.
7] Dipsychus's song might owe something to Tennyson's *In Memoriam* cvi: 'Ring out the old, ring in the new' etc.

Because of what you learnt at school;
You should have gone at least to college,
And got a little ampler knowledge.　　　　　　40
Ah well and yet: dong, dong dong;
Do if you like as now you do
If work's a cheat, so's pleasure too
And nothing's new and nothing's true
Dong, there is no God[.] [D]ong.　　　　　　45

O Rosalie, my precious maid
I think thou thinkest love is true;
And on thy fragrant bosom laid
I almost could believe it too.
O in our nook unknown unseen　　　　　　50
We'll hold our fancy like a screen
Us and the dreadful fact between.
And it shall yet be long, aye, long,
The quiet notes of our low song
Shall keep us from that sad dong dong.　　　　　　55
Hark hark hark; O voice of fear:
It reaches us here, even here
Dong, there is no God; dong.

Ring ding, ring ding, tara tara,
To battle, to battle, haste, haste　　　　　　60
To battle, to battle, aha, aha,
On on, to the conqueror's feast.
From west and east and south and north,
Ye men of valour and of worth,
Ye mighty men of arms – come forth.　　　　　　65
And work your will, for that is just;
And in your impulse put your trust;
Beneath your feet the fools are dust.
Alas, alas! O grief and wrong
The good are weak, the wicked strong,　　　　　　70
And oh my God, how long, how long,
Dong; there is no God; dong.

44] Cp Emerson's essay 'Montaigne; or, the Skeptic': 'Life's well enough; but we shall be glad to get out of it, and they will all be glad to have us. Why should we fret and drudge? Our meat will taste tomorrow as it did yesterday, and we may at last have had enough of it. "Ah," said my languid gentleman at Oxford, "there's nothing new or true – and no matter" ' (Poirier 1990: 314). C. became Emerson's friend, and his guide to Oxford, during the latter's visit to England in 1848.

Ring ting; to bow before the strong,
There is a rapture too in this;
Speak outraged maiden in thy wrong   75
Did terror bring no secret bliss?
Were boys' shy lips worth half a song
Compared to the hot soldier's kiss?
Work for thy master; work, thou slave
He is not merciful, but brave.   80
Be't joy to serve who free and proud
Scorns thee and all the ignoble crowd;
Take that; 'tis all thou art allowed,
Except the snaky hope that they
May some time serve who rule to-day   85
When, by hell-demons, shan't they pay?
O wickedness, O shame and grief!
And heavy load and no relief!
Oh God, oh God, and which is worst
To be the curser or the curst,   90
The Victim or the Murderer? Dong
Dong; there is no God; dong.

Ring ding ring ding; tara, tara,
Away, and hush that preaching, fagh!
Ye vulgar dreamers about peace   95
Who offer noblest hearts to heal
The tenderest hurts honour can feel
Paid magistrates and the Police.
O piddling merchant justice go,
Exacter rules than yours we know,   100
Resentment's rule, and that high law
Of whoso best the sword can draw
Ah well and yet – dong, dong, dong
Go on, my friends as now you do
Lawyers are villains, soldiers too;   105
And nothing's new and nothing's true.
Dong; there is no God; dong.

O Rosalie, my lovely maid
I think thou thinkest love is true
And on thy faithful bosom laid   110
I almost could believe it too
The villainies, the wrongs; the alarms

85] Cp Milton's sonnet on his blindness: 'They also serve who only stand and waite.'

Forget we in each other's arms
No justice here; no God above;
But where we are, is there not love[?]   115
What? what? thou also go'st? For how
Should dead truth live in lover's vow[?]
What thou, thou also lost? dong
Dong; there is no God; dong.–
I had a dream from eve to light   120
A bell went sounding all the night
Gay mirth; black woe; thin joys; huge pain.
I tried to stop it but in vain;
It ran right on, and never broke:
Only when day began to stream   125
Through the white curtains to my bed
And like an angel at my head
Light stood and touched me, I awoke
And looked, and said, 'It is a dream'.

S: Ah! – Not so bad. You've read, I see,   130
        Your Béranger, and thought of me
        But really, you owe some apology
        For harping thus upon theology.
        I am not a judge, I own; in short
        Religion may not be my forte.   135
        The Church of England I belong to,
        But think Dissenters not far wrong too;
        They're vulgar dogs; but for his *creed*
        I hold that no man will be d—d.
        My Establishment I much respect,   140
        Her ordinances don't neglect.
        Attend at Church on Sunday once,
        And in the Prayer-book am no dunce;
        Baptise my babies; nay, my wife
        Would be churched too once in her life.   145
        She's taken I regret to state
        Rather a Puseyite turn of late.
        To set the thing quite right I went

---

131. Béranger] It is Béranger's general Epicureanism rather than any specific poem which seems to be referred to here; cancelled lines suggest Voltaire as an alternative inspiration.
137. Dissenters] Protestants outside the Church of England.
147. Puseyite] E.B. Pusey (1800–82) was one of the leaders of the Oxford Movement. The followers of the Movement were widely known as Puseyites, especially after Newman's defection to the Roman Catholic Church in 1845.

At Easter to the Sacrament.
'Tis proper once a year or so   150
To do the civil thing and show
But come and listen in your turn
And you shall hear and mark and learn.

There is no God, the wicked saith
    And truly it's a blessing   155
For what he might have done with us
    It's better only guessing.

There is no God, a youngster thinks
    Or really, if there may be
He surely didn't mean a man   160
    Always to be a baby.

There is no God, or if there is,
    The tradesman thinks, 'twere funny
If he should take it ill in me
    To make a little money.   165

Whether there be, the rich man says
    It matters very little
For I and mine, thank somebody,
    Are not in want of victual.

Some others also to themselves   170
    Who scarce so much as doubt it
Think there is none, when they are well
    And do not think about it.

But country folks who live beneath
    The shadow of the steeple   175
The parson and the parson's wife
    And mostly married people

Youths green and happy in first love
    So thankful for illusion
And men caught out in what the world   180
    Calls guilt, in first confusion

And almost every one when age
    Disease or sorrows strike him
Inclines to think there is a God,
    Or something very like him.   185

169. victual] Food.

But *eccoci*! with our *barchetta*
Here at the Sant' Elisabetta.

D: Vineyards and maize that's pleasant for sore eyes

S;   And on the island's other side
        The place where Murray's faithful Guide   190
        Informs us Byron used to ride[.]

D: These trellised vines! enchanting! Sandhills ho!
    The sea; at last the sea; the real broad sea
    Beautiful, and a glorious breeze upon it.

S: Look back; one catches at this station   195
        Lagoon and sea in combination.

D: On her still lake the city sits
    Where bark and boat about her flits,
    Nor dreams, her soft siesta taking
    Of Adriatic billows breaking   200
    I do, and see and hear them – Come! To the sea!

S: The wind I think is the *sirocco*.
        Yonder, I take it, is Malmocco.
        Thank you! it never was my passion
        To skip o'er sand-hills in that fashion.   205

D: O a grand surge; we'll bathe; quick, quick; undress.
    Quick quick; in, in,
    We'll take the crested billows by their backs
    And shake them. Quick in in
    And I will taste again the old joy   210
    I gloried in so, when a boy.

S: Well. But it's not so pleasant for the feet;
        We should have brought some towels and a sheet.

D: In, in. I go. Ye great winds blow
    And break, thou curly wave upon my breast.   215

S: Hm. I'm undressing. Doubtless all is well.
        I only wish these thistles were at hell.
        By heaven; I'll stop, before that bad yet worse is,
        And take care of our watches and our purses.

186. *eccoci!*] Here we are!
186. *barchetta*] Little boat.
187. *Sant' Elisabetta*] The Piazza Santa Maria Elisabetta, the landing-place on the Lido.
189–91] See 7.3–4 above and note.
202. *sirocco*] A hot southern wind.
203. *Malmocco*] Malamocco; a port on the Lido south of Venice.

D: Ah ha. come come; great waters, roll!   220
      Accept me, take me, body and soul! –

S: <   >

D: Aha!

S: Come, no more of that stuff
              I'm sure you've stayed in long enough.

D: That's done me good. It grieves me though
      I never came here long ago.   225

S: Pleasant perhaps. However, no offence,
              Animal spirits are not common sense.
              You think perhaps I have outworn them,
              Certainly I have learnt to scorn them;
              They're good enough as an assistance,   230
              But in themselves a poor existence.
              But you – with this one bathe no doubt
              Have solved all questions out and out.
              'Tis Easter Day, and on the Lido
              Lo, Christ the Lord is risen indeed, O!   235

Part 2

SCENE 1: INTERIOR ARCADE OF THE DOGE'S PALACE

D: Thunder and rain! O dear, O dear!
              But see, a noble shelter here,
              This grand arcade where our Venetian
              Has formed of Gothic and of Grecian
              A combination strange, but striking,   5
              And singularly to my liking.
              Let moderns reap where ancients sowed –
              I at least make it my abode[.]

234–5] On the significance of *Easter Day* in the poem, see Introduction, p. 21
1–8] These lines were originally attributed to the Spirit, but reassigned to
Dipsychus by Clough when correcting the MS.
3–6] The mixture of Greek (Byzantine) and Gothic elements in the Doge's
Palace is emphasised by Ruskin (1903: ii, 278–9).

S: And now let's hear your famous ode:
            'Through the great sinful' – how d'ye go on?   10
            For Principles of Art and so on
            I care perhaps about three curses,
            But hold myself a judge of verses.

D: 'My brain was lightened when my tongue had said,
                  "Christ is not risen" '   15

S: Christ is not risen. Very odd.
            You'll tell us next 'there is no God'
            I thought twas in the Bible plain,
            On the third day he rose again.

                    ****

            Well. Now it's anything but clear,   20
            What is the tone that's taken here;
            What is your logic? What's your theology?
            Is it or is it not neology?
            That's a great fault. You're this and that,
            And here and there, and nothing flat.   25
            Yet writing's golden word what is it
            But the three syllables, 'explicit'[?]
            Say if you cannot help it, less,
            But what you do put, put express.
            I fear that rule won't meet your feeling;   30
            You think half-showing, half-concealing,
            Is God's own method of revealing.

---

9. your famous ode] Easter Day. It had become 'famous' among C.'s friends; see, for example, Richard Monckton Milnes's letter asking to see it in *Corr.* ii, 323.

16–19] These lines and 38–41 below are repeated in the first scene in MS2, and omitted from their current position in Mulhauser (1974) to avoid repetition. Because of this duplication, Kenny suggests that this scene should be regarded as 'alternative or additional material' for I.i (Kenny 1988: 146).

19] The asterisks indicate that Dipsychus is reciting more of the *Easter Day* ode at this point.

23. neology] Neologism was a critical movement founded in Germany in the second half of the eighteenth century by J.S. Semler and J.D. Michaelis; it aimed at an interpretation of the Bible based on grammatical and philological principles rather than on Christian doctrine. The Spirit is, of course, using the term in a very loose sense here.

31–2] Cp the Tractarian notion of 'reserve' in the communication of religious knowledge: 'there appears in GOD's manifestations of Himself to mankind, in conjunction with an exceeding desire to communicate that knowledge, a tendency to conceal, and throw a veil over it, as if it were injurious to us, unless we were of a certain disposition to receive it.' See Williams 1840: iv, 3.

D: To please my own poor mind! to find repose,
       To physic the sick soul; to furnish vent
       To diseased humours in the moral frame.   35

S: A sort of seton, I suppose,
           A moral bleeding at the nose:
           Hm; and the tone too after all
           Something of the ironical?
           Sarcastic, say. Or were it fitter   40
           To style it the religious bitter?

D: Interpret it. I cannot; I but wrote it.

S: Perhaps; but no sane man can doubt it
           There is a strong Strauss-smell about it.
           Heavens! at your years your time to fritter   45
           Upon a critical hair-splitter!
           Take larger views (and quit your Germans)
           From the Analogy and Sermons;
           I fancied – you must doubtless know,
           Butler had proved an age ago,   50
           That in religious as profane things,
           'Twas useless trying to explain things;
           Men's business-wits, the only sane things,

33–35] On the notion of poetry as 'relief' for the sick mind, see *Amours*
V.70–1 and note.
36. seton] A thread passed through the skin as a means of obtaining drainage
for an infection.
44. a strong Strauss-smell] In his *Life of Jesus*, published in 1835, D.F. Strauss
applied the 'mythological' method of analysis to the Christian gospels and concluded that their historical content was negligible; see below, *Epi-Strauss-ium*
and notes.
48. the Analogy and Sermons] Bishop Butler's *The Analogy of Religion* (1736)
and *Fifteen Sermons Preached at the Rolls Chapel* (1726) are works of Christian
apology; they were compulsory reading for Oxford undergraduates in C.'s
time. The Spirit's ironic summary of the *Analogy* in lines 49–66 closely
resembles C.'s outline of it in his 'Lecture on the Development of English
Literature': '[The] great argument of the 'Analogy' . . . nakedly stated, would
seem to run, that we have no right to claim a religion according to our own
fancies, that as the world of ordinary facts is full of difficulties, so also it is to
be expected will be religion also' (*PR* 349). Butler's arguments had been
almost entirely superseded by critical developments in Germany; The Spirit's
advice to Dipsychus to 'quit your Germans' and return to Butler is, then, a
betrayal of his own ignorance of German Higher Criticism, and bears more
than a passing resemblance to the advice given to C. by Edward Hawkins, the
Provost of Oriel, when he was contemplating resigning his Tutorship; see
Corr. i, 191, 192–8, 219–22.

These and compliance are the main things.
God, Revelation, and the rest of it,   55
Bad at the best, we make the best of it.
Not quite the things we chose to think;
But neither is the World rose pink.
Yet *it* is fact as plain as day;
So may the rest be; who can say?   60
This life we see is wondrous odd
And so we argue may be God.
Like a good subject and wise man
Believe whatever things you can,
Take your religion as 'twas found you,   65
And say no more of it — confound you. –
And now I think the rain has ended
And the less said, the sooner mended.

SCENE 2: THE ACADEMY

D: A modern daub it was perchance;
        I know not; but I dare be sure
        From Titian's hues no connoisseur
        Had turned one condescending glance

        Where Byron, somewhat drest up, draws   5
        His sword, impatient long, and speaks
        Unto a tribe of motley Greeks
        His pledge word unto their brave cause.

        Not far, assumed to mystic bliss
        Behold the ecstatic Virgin rise.   10
        Ah wherefore vainly to fond eyes
        That melt to burning tears for this[?]

        Yet if we must live, as would seem
        These peremptory heats to claim, –
        Ah not for profit, not for fame,   15
        And not for pleasure's giddy dream,

3] The centrepiece of the Accademia delle Belle Arti in Venice was Titian's
'Assumption'; see lines 9–10.
5–8] The picture of Byron pledging his word to the Greek cause has not been
identified, although modern pictures were habitually exhibited alongside Old
Masters in the Accademia. The contrast between the two pictures – one
inspiring religious devotion, the other glorifying forthright action – is, of
course, emblematic of Dipsychus's dilemma throughout the poem.

And not for piping empty reeds
And not for colouring idle dust, –
If live we positively must
God's name be blest for noble deeds.   20

Verses! well they are made, so let them go.
No more, if I can help. This is one way
The procreant heat and fervour of our youth
Escapes, in puff and smoke, and shapeless words
Of mere ejaculation, nothing worth;   25
Unless to make maturer years content
To slave in base compliance to the World.

I have scarce spoken yet to this strange follower
Whom I picked up, ye great gods, tell me where!
And when! for I remember such, long years   30
And yet he seems new come. I commune with myself,
He speaks, I hear him, and resume to myself;
Whate'er I think, he adds his comments to;
Which yet not interrupts me. Scarce I know
If ever once directly I addressed him.   35
Let me essay it now: for I have strength.
Yet what he wants and what he fain would have,
O I know all too surely. [N]ot in vain
Although unnoticed has he dogged my ear.
Come, we'll be definite, explicit, plain.   40
I can resist, I know. And 'twill be well
To have used for colloquy this manlier mood
Which is to last, ye chances, say how long.
How shall I call him? Mephistopheles?

S: I come I come.

D: So quick! so eager. [H]a!   45
Like an eaves-dropping menial on my thought,
With something of an exultation too, methinks,
Out peeping in that springy, jaunty gait;
I doubt about it; shall I do it? – Oh! Oh!
Shame on me, come. – Should I, my follower,   50
Should I conceive, (not that at all I do,
'Tis curiosity that prompts my speech)
But should I form, a thing to be supposed,

21–7] Yet another statement of the 'therapeutic' theory of poetry.
34–5] Dipsychus has in fact addressed The Spirit directly before this; see
above, 1.3.219.
44] At this stage in the manuscript Dipsychus and The Spirit are still referred
to as Faustulus and Mephistopheles.

A wish to bargain for your merchandise,
Say what were your demands; what were your terms[?]   55
What should I do, what should I cease to do?
What incense on what altars must I burn
And what abandon, what unlearn or learn[?]
Religion goes, I take it.

S: Oh,
You'll go to church of course, you know.   60
Or at the least will take a pew
To send your wife or servants to.
Trust me, I make a point of that;
No infidelity, that's flat.

D: Religion is not in a pew, say some;   65
Cucullus, *you* hold, *facit* monachum.

S: Why, as to feelings of devotion, –
I interdict all vague emotion;
But if you will, for once and all
Compound with ancient Juvenal,   70
Orandum est, one perfect prayer
For savoir-vivre, savoir-faire.
Theology – don't recommend you,
Unless, turned lawyer, Heaven should send you
In your profession's way the case   75
Of Baptism and Prevenient Grace,
But that's not likely: I'm inclined,
All circumstances borne in mind,

66. *Cucullus . . . facit monachum*] An inversion of the proverb 'cucullus non facit monachum', 'the hood does not make the monk' – cited in Erasmus, *Adagia* (1523) and by Shakespeare in *Twelfth Night* (1.5.53–4) and *Measure for Measure* (5.1.261).
70–2] The original quotation is from Juvenal (60 AD – *c.* 130 AD): 'Orandum est ut sit mens sana in corpore sano' – 'Your prayer must be that you may have a sound mind in a sound body'. This is changed by The Spirit to a plea for savoir-vivre (knowing how to live) and savoir-faire (knowing what to do).
76] An allusion to 'the Gorham affair', an acrimonious theological dispute between the High-Church Bishop of Exeter and one of his evangelical clergymen which was eventually decided by the Judicial Committee of the Privy Council (in Gorham's favour) in 1850. The dispute turned on the question of baptismal regeneration, i.e. 'whether sacramental grace is given instrumentally, by and at the moment of the act of baptism, or in consequence of an act of prevenient grace rendering the receiver worthy – that is to say, whether sacramental grace in baptism is given absolutely or conditionally' (Strachey 1918: 47).

To think (to keep you in due borders)
You'd better enter holy orders[.]   80

D: On that, my friend, you'd better not insist.

S: Well well. 'Tis but a good thing missed.
The item's optional, no doubt:
But how to get your bread without?
You'll marry. I shall find the lady.   85
Make your proposal, and be steady.

D: Marry, ill spirit! and at your sole choice?

S: De rigueur! can't give you a voice.
What matter? Oh! trust one who knows you,
You'll make an admirable sposo.   90
Un' bella donn' un' gran' riposo.
As said the soldier in our carriage,
Although he didn't mean in marriage:
As to the rest I shall not quarrel,
Your being, as it seems, *so* moral.   95
Though, – orders laid upon the shelf,
In merest justice to myself,
But that I hate the pro and con of it,
I should have made a sine-qua-non of it.
Come, my dear boy, I will not bind you;   100
But scruples must be cast behind you
All mawkish talking I dislike
But when the iron *is* hot strike
Good God! to think of youthful bliss
Restricted to a sneaking kiss. –   105

D: Enough. – But action, look to that well, mind me
See that some not unworthy work you find me.
If man I be, then give the man expression.

S: Of course you'll enter a profession.
If not the church, why then the law.   110
By Jove we'll teach you how to draw!
Once in the way that you should go

---

88. *De rigueur!]* Of course!
90. *sposo]* Husband (Italian).
91. *Un' bella donn' un' gran' riposo]* 'A beautiful woman is a great comfort.'
99. *sine-qua-non]* *Conditio sine qua non* is a term in logic meaning an essential or minimum condition for the establishment of a particular position.
111. *how to draw!]* i.e. how to make one's way in the world, to get ahead.

You'll do your business well, I know.
Besides, the best of the concern is
I'm hand in glove with the attorneys   115
With them and me to help, don't doubt
But in due season you'll come out
Leave Kelly, Cockburn in the lurch –
And yet, do think about the Church.
By all that's rich 'twould do me good   120
To fig you out in robe and hood.
Wouldn't I give up wine and wench,
To mount you fairly on the bench!

D: 'Tis well, ill spirit. I admire your wit
      As for your wisdom, I shall think of it.   125
      And now farewell.

SCENE 3

D: The law! 'twere honester, if 'twere genteel,
      To say the dung-cart. What? shall I go about
      And like the walking shoeblack roam the flags
      With heedful eyes down bent and like a glass
      In a sea-captain's hand sweeping all round   5
      To see whose boots are dirtiest. O the luck
      To stoop and clean a pair.
      Religion: – if indeed it be in vain
      To expect to find in this more modern time
      That which the old world styled in old world phrase 10
      Walking with God – It seems His newer will
      We should not think of him at all, but trudge it,
      And of the world He has assigned us make
      What best we can. – Then love; I scarce can think
      That these bemaddening discords of the mind   15

---

118. Kelly, Cockburn] Legal authorities.

Scene 3] Dipsychus here sums up his predicament, which is in fact the central problem of most of C.'s poetry; how is it possible to manage the transition from innocence to experience so as to avoid the possibility of fatal and irreversible error? His analysis employs most of C.'s habitual metaphors; see Introduction.

1–7] Veyriras points out that Thomas Arnold detested the law as a profession, describing it as possessed of 'the spirit of Mephistopheles' (Veyriras 1964: 390).

3. flags] Paving stones.

To pure melodious sequence could be changed
And all the vext conundrums of our life
Solved to all time, by this old Pastoral
Of a new Adam and a second Eve
Set in a Garden which no serpent seeks. 20
And yet I hold heart can beat true to heart:
And to hew down the tree which bears this fruit
To do a thing which cuts me off from hope,
To falsify the movement of love's mind,
To seat some alien trifler on the throne 25
A queen may come to claim; that were ill done.
What! to the close hand of the clutching Jew
Hand up that rich reversion! and for what?
This would be hard, did I indeed believe
'Twould ever fall. – But love the large repose 30
Restorative not to mere outside needs
Skin deep, but thoroughly to the total man,
Exists I will believe but so so rare
So doubtful, so exceptional; hard to guess
When guessed, so often counterfeit; in brief 35
A thing not possibly to be conceived
An item in the reckonings of the wise.

Action, that staggers me – For I had hoped.
Midst weakness, indolence, frivolity,
Irresolution still had hoped; and this 40
Seems sacrificing hope. Better to wait.
The wise men wait; it is the foolish haste
And ere the scenes are in their slides would play
And while the instruments are tuning, dance.
I see Napoleon on the heights, intent 45
To arrest that one brief unit of loose time
Which hands high Victory's thread; his Marshals fret,
His soldiers clamour low: the very guns

19–20] Dipsychus's problem is that he must leave 'the garden of the infinite choices', the prelapsarian state of innocence, and he imagines that true love might be a way of achieving this without having to undergo the trauma of the Fall – see Introduction.

27. clutching Jew] Jews were virtually synonymous with money-lenders for English people of C.'s generation. The characterisation might also possibly owe something to the background presence of *The Merchant of Venice* in C.'s Venetian drama.

35–7] Like Claude, Dipsychus realises that true love or elective affinity is practically unattainable, and so scales down his expectations.

43] A theatrical metaphor; the 'slides' are the runners into which the background scenes for the play are inserted.

Seem going off of themselves; the cannon strain
Like hell-dogs in the leash. But he[,] he waits.   50
And lesser chances and inferior hopes
Meantime go pouring past. Men gnash their teeth,
The very faithful have begun to doubt,
But they molest not the calm eye that seeks
Midst all this huddling silver little worth   55
The one thin piece, that comes, pure gold. He waits.
Oh me, when the great deed e'en now has broke
Like a man's hand the horizon's level line
So soon to fill the zenith with rich clouds
Oh, in this narrow interspace, this moment,   60
This list and selvage of a glorious time
To despair of the great and sell to the mean!
O thou of little faith, what hast thou done?
Yet if the occasion coming should find *us*
Undexterous incapable? – in light things   65
Prove thou the arms thou long'st to glorify,
Nor fear to work up from the lowest ranks
Whence come great Nature's captains. And high deeds
Haunt not the fringy edges of the fight
But the pell-mell of men. Oh what and if   70
E'en now by lingering here I let them slip,
Like an unpractised spyer through a glass
Still pointing to the blank; too high: – And yet
In dead details to smother vital ends,
Which should give life to them. – in the deft trick   75
Of prentice-handling to forget great art,
To base mechanical adroitness yield
The Inspiration and the Hope a slave
Oh and to blast that Innocence which, though
Here it may seem a dull unopening bud   80
May yet bloom freely in celestial clime.
Were it not better done then to keep off,

---

61. *list and selvage]* A Shakespearian-sounding phrase of no specific provenance; both words mean a border or edge.
63. *O thou of little faith]* 'O ye of little faith' is one of Jesus's characteristic
admonitions; see Matthew 6:30, 14:31, 16:8 and Luke 12:28.
76. *prentice-handling]* The skills learnt by an apprentice. Dipsychus is here
rehearsing another of C.'s perennial problems; do duty and habit increase
one's ability to act by heightening technique and awareness, or do they stifle
the actions which might otherwise have occurred spontaneously?

And see not share the strife; stand out the waltz
Which fools whirl dizzy in[?] Is it possible?
Contamination taints the idler first.   85
And without base compliance, e'en that same
Which buys bold hearts free course, Earth lends not these
Their pent and miserable standing-room.
Life loves no lookers-on at his great game,
And with boy's malice still delights to turn   90
The tide of sport upon the sitters-by
And set observers scampering with their notes.
Oh it is great to do and know not what,
Nor let it e'er be known. The dashing stream
Stays not to pick his steps among the rocks,   95
Or let his water breaks be chronicled.
And though the hunter looks before he leap
'Tis instinct rather than a shaped-out thought
That lifts him his bold way. Then instinct hail,
And farewell hesitation. If I stay,   100
I am not innocent nor if I go,
E'en should I fall, beyond redemption lost.

Ah if I had a course like a full stream,
If life were as the field of chase. No, no.
The age of instinct has, it seems, gone by   105
And will not be forced back. And to live now
I must sluice out myself into canals
And lose all force in ducts. The modern Hotspur
Shrills not his trumpet of To Horse, To Horse,
But consults columns in a railway guide;   110
A demigod of figures; an Achilles
Of computation –

83–4] Another use of the dance as a figure for the formalised ritual of social behaviour.
104–6] Dipsychus, having made the decision to trust his instincts, even at the risk of the fall (99–102), now realises that he has no instincts left to trust; the 'full stream' of the self's desires has been harnessed into a network of canals. Cp Byron, 'Venice. An Ode': 'Still, still, for ever/ Better, though each man's life-blood were a river,/ That it should flow, and overflow, than creep/ Through thousand lazy channels in our veins,/ Damm'd like the dull canal with locks and chains' (148–52).
108–10] Harry Hotspur, firebrand son of the Earl of Northumberland, appears in *Henry IV*, Part 1; the words 'To horse! to horse!' appear not in this play, however, but in Byron's play *The Deformed Transformed* (I.i.548).
111. Achilles] The bravest of the Greek warriors in Homer's *Iliad*.

A verier Mercury express come down
To *do* the world with swift arithmetic.
Well one could bear with that; were the end ours,   115
One's choice and the correlative of the soul.
To drudge were then sweet service. But indeed
The earth moves slowly, if it move at all
And by the general, not the single force.
At the [huge] members of the vast machine   120
In all those crowded rooms of industry
No individual soul has loftier leave
Than fiddling with a piston or a valve.
Well, one could bear that also: one could drudge
And do one's petty part, and be content   125
In base manipulation, solaced still
By thinking of the leagued fraternity,
And of co-operation, and the effect
Of the great engine. If indeed it work
And is not a mere treadmill! Which it may be.   130
Who can confirm it is not? We ask Action,
And dream of arms and conflict; and string up
All self devotion's muscles; and are set
To fold up papers. To what end? We know not.
Other folks do so: it is always done;   135
And it perhaps is right. And we are paid for it.
For nothing else we can be. He that eats
Must serve; and serve as other servants do:
And don the lacquey's livery of the house.
O could I shoot my thought up to the sky   140
A column of pure shape, for all to observe.
But, I must slave, a meagre coral worm
To build beneath the tide with excrement
What one day will be island or be reef
And will feed men or wreck them. Well well well   145
Adieu ye twisted thinkings. It must be.

Action is what one must get, it is clear
And one could dream it better than one finds
In its kind personal, in its motive not;
Not selfish as it now is, nor as now   150
Maiming the individual. If we had that
It would cure all indeed.

---

113. *Mercury]* The messenger of the Gods in Roman mythology.
142–5] A similar notion of poetry as a waste product of the mind is outlined in
C.'s first *Letter of Parepidemus* (1853), reprinted in *PR* 381–9.

Yes, if we could have that; but I suppose
We shall not have it, and therefore I submit.

From within: Submit, submit.   155
'Tis common sense and human wit
Can claim no higher name than it
Submit, submit.

Devotion and Ideas and Love
And beauty claim their place above.   160
But Saint and Sage and Poet's dreams
Divide the light in coloured streams
Which this alone gives all combined
The siccum lumen of the mind;
Called common sense; and no high wit   165
Gives better counsel than does it,
Submit, submit[.]

To see things simply as they are
Here, at our elbows, transcends far
Trying to spy out at midday   170
Some 'bright particular star' which may,
Or not, be visible at night
But clearly is not in daylight.
No inspiration vague outweighs
The plain good common sense that says   175
Submit, submit[.]

'Tis common sense and human wit
Can ask no higher name than it
Submit submit[.]

O did you think you were alone?   180
That I was so unfeeling grown
As not with joy to leave behind

---

164. siccum lumen] From the Latin version of the saying attributed to the early
Greek philosopher Heraclitus (*c* 500 BC) 'Lumen siccum optima anima' – 'the
dry light is the wisest soul'. The phrase 'lumen siccum' is used by Bacon on a
number of occasions; see, e.g., *The Advancement of Learning* 1.3. The equation
of common sense with enlightenment is also present in The Spirit's strictures
on Gothic architecture; see above, 1.5.92–111.
171. 'bright particular star'] *All's Well That Ends Well* I.i.84.
181–5] Luke 15:4: 'What man of you, having an hundred sheep, if he lose one
of them, doth not leave the ninety and nine in the wilderness, and go after that
which is lost, until he find it?' This is typical of The Spirit's inversion of
Scripture.

My ninety nine in hope to find
(How sweet the words my sense express!)
My lost sheep in the wilderness?   185

SCENE 4

D: There have been times, not many but enough
     To quiet all repinings of the heart,
     There have been times in which my [tranquil] soul,
     No longer nebulous, sparse, errant, seemed
     Upon its axis solidly to move,   5
     Centred and fast; no mere chaotic blank
     For random rays to traverse unretained
     But rounding luminous its fair ellipse
     Around its central sun; aye yet again
     As in more faint sensations I detect   10
     With it too round an inner mightier orb[;]
     May be with that too, this I dare not say,
     Around yet more[,] more central[,] more supreme[,]
     Whate'er, how numerous soe'er be which,
     I am, and feel myself where'er I wind   15
     What vagrant chance soe'er I seem to [obey]
     Communicably theirs. – O happy hours
     O compensation ample for long days
     Of what impatient tongues call wretchedness
     O beautiful, beneath the magic moon   20
     To walk the watery way of palaces:
     O beautiful o'ervaulted with gemmed blue
     This spacious court: with colour and with gold

Scene 4] In this scene Dipsychus tries the Wordsworthian solution of hoping that 'spots of time' will provide him with compensation for the bleak and unproductive periods of his life.

9–17] This passage is obscure but not unintelligible. After having compared his soul at certain moments to the earth orbiting the sun, Dipsychus goes on to suggest that both earth and sun might be orbiting 'an inner mightier orb', and then, more tentatively, that this system too might be circling 'yet more[,] more central[,] more supreme' celestial bodies. The point is that the moments of 'compensation' are not purely personal, but carry with them a feeling of universal harmony and order which hints at the existence of a supreme being at the centre of everything. The vagueness and tortuousness of this passage highlight Dipsychus's uncertainty about the legitimacy of this claim – 'this I dare not say' – and help us to understand why such moments do not constitute an adequate reason for refusing to submit to the world.

22–31] An enraptured description of St Mark's Square.

With cupolas, and pinnacles and points
And crosses multiplex and tips and balls,   25
(Wherewith the bright stars unreproving mix
Nor scorn by hasty eyes to be confused)
Fantastically perfect this low pile
Of oriental glory; these long ranges
Of Classic chiselling, this gay flickering crowd,   30
And the calm campanile. Beautiful.
O beautiful, and that seemed more profound,
This morning by the pillar when I sat
Under the great arcade, at the review;
And took, and held and ordered on my brain   35
The faces, and the voices, and the whole mass
O' the motley facts of existence flowing by.
O perfect, if 'twere all. But it is not.
Hints haunt me ever of a More beyond:
I am rebuked by a sense of the [incomplete],   40
Of a completion over-soon assumed,
Of adding up too soon. What we call sin
I could believe a painful opening out
Of paths for ampler virtue. The bare field
Scant with lean ears of harvest long had mocked   45
The vext laborious farmer. Came at length
The deep plough in the lazy undersoil
Down-driving: with a cry earth's fibres crack,
And a few months and lo, the golden leas,
And autumn's crowded shocks and loaded wains.   50
Let us look back on life. Was any change
Any now blest expansion, but at first
A pang, remorse-like, shot to the inmost seats
Of moral being? To do anything,
Distinct on any one thing to decide,   55
To leave the habitual and the old, and quit
The easy chair of use and wont, seems crime
To the weak soul forgetful how at first
Sitting down seemed so too. Oh, oh these qualms,
And oh these calls. And oh this woman's heart,   60
Fain to be forced, incredulous of choice,

28–9 *this low pile/ Of oriental glory]* The Doge's Palace.
34. *the review]* The military review by the occupying Austrian army.
38–44] The transition here is slightly abrupt, and requires a knowledge of C.'s
habitual patterns of thought. It is the possibility of 'More' which prevents
Dipsychus from resting content with contemplation of the beauty of this
world. This 'More' imposes on him an imperative to act, even if the action he
performs at first seems like a sin or fall from grace.

And waiting a necessity for God.
Yet I could think indeed the perfect call
Should force the perfect answer. If the Voice
Ought to receive its echo from the soul,   65
Wherefore this silence? If it *should* rouse my being,
Why this reluctance? Have not I thought o'ermuch
Of other men and of the ways of the world?
But what they are, or have been matters not,
To thine own self be true, the wise man says.   70
Are then my fears myself? O double self!
And I untrue to both. O there are hours
When love and faith and dear domestic ties,
And converse with old friends and pleasant walks,
Familiar faces, and familiar books,   75
Study and art, upliftings into prayer,
And admiration of the noblest things
Seems all ignoble only. All is mean,
And nought as I would have it. Then at others
My mind is on her nest; my heart at home   80
In all around; my soul secure in place
And the vext needle perfect to her poles[.]
Aimless and hopeless in my life I seem
To thread the winding byways of the town
Bewildered, baffled, hurried hence and thence,   85
All at cross-purpose ever with myself
Unknowing whence from whither. Then in a moment,
At a step, I crown the Campanile's top
And view all mapped below. Islands, lagoon,
An hundred steeples and a million roofs   90
The fruitful champaign, and the cloud capt Alps
And the broad Adriatic. Be it enough,
If I lose this how terrible. No, no
I am contented and will not complain.
To the old paths, my soul! O be it so!   95
I bear the workday burden of dull life
About these footsore flags of a weary world
Heaven knows how long it has not been: at once

71–2] A central if rather enigmatic outburst. Dipsychus begins to worry that
his fears and hesitations before experience might not be a defence mechanism
which safeguards the purity of his essential self, but a part of that essential self.
It is in this sense that he is 'double'. He is divided between the drive towards
action and the avoidance of it, and is 'untrue to both' selves in his failure to
indulge either of them fully.
91. champaign] Countryside.

Lo I am in the Spirit on the Lord's day
With John in Patmos. Is it not enough[?]   100
[One day in seven?] and if this should go
If this pure solace should desert my mind
What were all else? I dare not risk this loss.
To the old paths, my soul[.]

S: O yes.
To moon about religion; to inhume   105
Your ripened age in solitary walks,
For self discussion; to debate in letters
Vext points with earnest friends; past other men
To cherish natural instincts, yet to fear them
And less than any use them. O no doubt   110
In a corner sit and mope and be consoled
With thinking one is clever, while the room
Rings through with animation and the dance.
[Then talk] of old examples; to pervert
Ancient real facts to modern unreal dreams;   115
And build up baseless fabrics of romance
And heroism upon historic sand.
To burn forsooth for Action, yet despise
Forsooth, its accidence and alphabet[;]
Cry out for service, and at once rebel   120
At the application of its plainest rules
This, you call life, my friend, reality
Doing your duty unto God and man,
I know not what. Stay at Venice, if you will,
Sit musing in its churches hour on hour,   125
Cross-kneed upon a bench; climb up at whiles
The neighbouring tower, and [kill] the lingering day
With old comparisons. When night succeeds
Evading, yet a little seeking, what
You would and would not, turn your doubtful eyes   130
On moon and stars to help morality.

---

100. John in Patmos] The place where St John is supposed to have composed
the Book of Revelation; see Rev. 1:9. Dipsychus's identification with John represents a momentary return of belief in the possibility of genuine revelation.
105. inhume] Bury (as opposed to exhume).
110–13] A neat inversion of the dance-metaphor; here it is the solitary non-
participant who is criticised, not the dancers.

Once in a fortnight say, by lucky chance
Of happier-tempered coffee, gain (great Heaven)
A pious rapture; is it not enough? –
O that will keep you safe. Yet don't be sure   135
Emotions are so slippery. Aye keep close
And burrow in your bedroom, pace up and down
A long half hour; with talking to yourself
Make waiters wonder; sleep a bit; write verse,
Burn in disgust, then ill-restore, and leave   140
Half-made, in pencil scrawl illegible.
Sink ere the end, most like, the hapless prey
Of some chance chambermaid, more sly than fair,
And in vain call for me. O well I know
You will not find, when I am not to help,   145
E'en so much face as hires a gondola.
Beware.

D: 'Tis well; thou cursed spirit, go thy way –
I am in higher hands than yours. 'Tis well.
Who taught you menaces? Who told you, pray,   150
Because I asked you questions and made show
Of hearing what you answered, therefore,

S: Oh
As if I didn't know.

D: Come come my friend
I may have wavered, but I have thought better,
We'll say no more of it.

S: O I dare say.   155
But as you like, 'tis your own loss. Once more,
Beware. –

D alone: Must it be then? So quick upon my thought
That follow the fulfilment and the deed.
I counted not on this. I counted ever   160
To hold and turn it over in my hands
Much longer. Much. I took it up indeed
For speculation rather; to gain thought
New data. O, and now, to be goaded on

132–4] The Spirit suggests that the redemptive moods eulogised by
Dipsychus might be simply physiological reactions; cp 'Is it true, ye gods'
above, p. 47.
139–41] An accurate description of the state of much of C.'s verse, including
Dipsychus itself.

By menaces, entangled amongst tricks.   165
That I won't suffer. Yet it is the law;
'Tis this makes action always. But for this
We ne'er should act at all. – And act we must.
Why quarrel with the fashion of a fact
Which, one way, must be; one time, why not now?   170

S: Submit, submit[.]
For tell me then, in earth's great laws
Have you found any saving clause,
Exemption special granted you
From doing what the rest must do   175
Of Common Sense who made you quit,
And told you, you'd no need of it
Nor to submit[?]

To move on angels' wings were sweet;
But who would therefore scorn his feet[?]   180
It cannot walk up to the sky
It therefore will lie down and die
Rich meats it don't obtain at call
It therefore will not eat at all.
Poor babe! and yet a babe of wit.   185
But common sense? not much of it
Or 'twould submit.

Submit, submit.
As your good father did before you
And as the mother who first bore you!   190
O yes! a child of heavenly birth!
But yet it *was* pupped too on earth.
Keep your new birth for that far day
When in the grave your bones you lay
All with your kindred and connection   195
In hopes of happy resurrection.
But how meantime to live is fit
Ask common sense: and what says it?
Submit submit.

'Tis Common Sense and human wit   200
Can find no higher name than it.
Submit submit.

O I am with you, my sweet friend
Yea, always, even to the end.

SCENE 5

D: 'Tis gone, the fierce inordinate desire
      The burning thirst for Action. Utterly.
      Gone like a ship that passes in the night
      On the high seas; gone, yet will come again
      Gone, yet expresses something that exists.   5
      Is it a thing ordained then, is it a clue
      For my life's conduct, is it a law for me
      That opportunity shall breed distrust
      Not passing until that pass. Chance and Resolve
      Like two loose comets wandering wide in space   10
      Crossing each other's orbits time on time
      Meet never. Void Indifference and Doubt
      Let through the present boon, which ne'er turns back
      To await the after sure-arriving Wish.
      How shall I then explain it to myself   15
      That in blank thought my purpose lives[?]
      The uncharged cannon mocking still the spark
      When come, which *ere* come it had loudly claimed.
      Am I to let it be so still? For truly
      The need exists I know, the wish but sleeps   20
      (Sleeps, and anon will wake and cry for food)
      And to put by these unreturning gifts
      Because the feeling is not with me now
      Which will I know be with me presently,
      Seems folly more than merest babyhood's.   25

203–4] Cp the closing words of Matthew's gospel: 'lo, I am with you alway,
even unto the end of the world.'
7–12] Cp C.'s bizarre 'Conversations of the Earth with the Universe': 'the
Earth went on to say, very extravagantly as it seems, In fact whenever I do
fancy anything about myself, it always appears that from that moment what I
think true ceases to be true any longer whatever it might have been before.'
Cited in Greenberger 1970: 192.

But must I then do violence to myself,
And push-on Nature, force desire (that's ill)
Because of knowledge? Which is great, but works
By rules of large exception; to tell which
Nought is less fallible than mere caprice.   30
To use knowledge well we must learn of ignorance
To apply the rule forget the rule. Ah but
I am compromised, you think: oh but indeed
I shan't do it more for that. No! nor refuse
To vindicate a scarce contested right   35
And certify vain independentness.
But what need is there[?] I am happy now
I feel no lack – What cause is there for haste
Am I not happy, is that not enough?

S: O yes, O yes! and thought no doubt   40
'T had locked the very devil out
He he! he he! and didn't know
Through what small places we can go?
How do, my pretty dear? What drying
Its pretty eyes! Has it been crying?   45

D: Depart!

S: O yes! you thought you had escaped no doubt
This worldly fiend that follows you about
This compound of convention and impiety
This mongrel of uncleanness and propriety.   50
What else were bad enough? but let me say
I too have my *grandes manières* in my way.
Could speak high sentiment as well as you
And out-blank-verse you without much ado
Have my religion also in my kind   55

26–32] Another dense passage requiring a certain amount of explication. Dipsychus persuades himself that the absence of the desire to act at any given moment does not constitute a good reason for not acting, since he knows he is constitutionally incapable of making 'chance' and 'resolve' coincide. As a result, he decides to force himself into action in the knowledge that he will regain the desire for it at a later stage. This decision to subordinate 'nature' or instinct to knowledge, however, represents the kind of obedience to preconceived rules which he has been attempting to resist throughout. He concludes, therefore, that knowledge of this kind can only be used if we manage to forget the rules at the very instant of applying them, and in this way restore at least the semblance of spontaneity and authenticity.

52. grandes manières] Grand manners.

For dreaming – unfit, because not designed.
What! you know not that I too can be serious
Can speak big words, and use the tone imperious;
Can speak – not honeyedly of love and beauty,
But sternly of a something much like Duty?   60
Oh, do you look surprised? were never told
Perhaps that all that glitters is not gold[?]
The Devil oft the Holy Scriptures uses,
But God can act the Devil when he chooses.
Farewell. But, *verbum sapienti satis*,   65
I do not make this revelation gratis.
Farewell; beware!

D: Ill spirits can quote holy books I knew,
      What will they *not* say? what not dare to do?

S: Beware beware[.]   70

D: What loitering still? Still, O foul spirit, there?
      Go hence I tell thee, go! I *will* beware.

(Alone)

It must be then. I feel it in my soul;
The iron enters sundering flesh and bone,
And sharper than the two edged sword of God.   75
I come into deep waters – help, O help!
The floods run over me.

Therefore farewell! a long and last farewell,
Ye pious sweet simplicities of life,
Good books, good friends, and holy moods, and all   80
That lent rough life sweet Sunday-seeming rests,
Making earth heavenlike – Welcome wicked world
The hardening heart, the calculating brain
Narrowing its doors to thought, the lying lips,

---

62. all that glitters is not gold] 'All that glisters is not gold' – *Merchant of Venice* II.vii.65.
65. verbum sapienti satis] 'A word to the wise is enough' – proverbial.
75. the two edged sword of God] Hebrews 4:12: 'For the word of God *is* quick, and powerful, and sharper than any twoedged sword, piercing even to the dividing asunder of soul and spirit, and of the joints and marrow, and *is* a discerner of the thoughts and intents of the heart.' This text was cited by John Henry Newman in the Sermon in which he used the term 'double-minded'; see Newman 1868: v, 226.

The calm-dissembling eyes; the greedy flesh,   85
The World, the Devil. – Welcome, welcome, welcome.

(From within)

This stern Necessity of things
On every side our being rings
Our sallying eager actions fall
Vainly against that iron wall.   90
Where once her finger points the way
The wise think only to obey
Take life as she has ordered it
And come whatever may, submit
Submit submit.   95

Who takes implicitly her will
For these her vassal-chances still
Bring store of joys, successes, pleasures.
But whoso ponders, weighs and measures
She calls her torturers up to goad   100
With spur and scourges on the road;
He does at last with pain whate'er
He spurned at first. Of such beware
Beware beware. –

D: O God. O God. The great floods of the fiend   105
    Flow over me. I come into deep waters
    Where no ground is –

S: Don't be the least afraid.
    There's not the slightest reason for alarm.
    I only meant by a perhaps rough shake
    To rouse you from a dreamy unhealthy sleep.   110
    Up, then. Up, and be going. The large world
    The thronged life waits us. –
                    Come, my pretty boy,

85–6. the greedy flesh,/ The world, the Devil] Cp Donne, Holy Sonnet no 3:
'Impute me righteous, thus purg'd of evill,/ For thus I leave the world, the
flesh, and devill.'

87–95] There are several parallels to this sentiment in Romantic and post-
Romantic poetry; cp Goethe's paean to Necessity 'Human Limits', Byron's
lines in *The Deformed Transformed* – 'You must obey what all obey, the rule/
Of fixed Necessity: against her edict/ Rebellion prospers not' (I.ii.31–33) –
and the sentiments expressed in the second of Matthew Arnold's sonnets
addressed to his 'Republican Friend' C.: 'Seeing this vale, this earth, whereon
we dream,/ Is on all sides o'ershadowed by the high/ Uno'erleaped
Mountains of Necessity,/ Sparing us narrower margin than we deem' (5–8).

You have been making mows to the blank sky
Quite long enough for good. We'll put you up;
Into the higher form. 'Tis time you learn   115
The Second Reverence, for things around.
Up then; and go amongst them; don't be timid;
Look at them quietly a bit: by and by
Respect will come and healthy appetite.
So let us go.
            How now, not yet awake.   120
Oh, you will sleep yet, will you; O you shirk
You try and slink away; you cannot, eh?
Nay now, what folly's this? Why will you fool yourself?
Why will you walk about thus with your eyes shut?
Treating for facts the self made hues that float   125
On tight pressed pupils, which you know are not facts.
To use the undistorted light of the sun
Is not a crime; to look straight out upon
The big plain things that stare one in the face
Does not contaminate; to see pollutes not   130
What one must feel if one won't see; what *is*,
And will be too, however we blink, and must
One way or other make itself observed.
Free walking's better than being led about; and
What will the blind man do, I wonder, if   135
Some one should cut the string of his dog. Just think,
What could you do, if I should go away?
        O, you have paths of your own before you, have you?
What shall it take to? literature no doubt?
Novels, reviews? or poems! if you please!   140
The strong fresh gale of life will feel no doubt
The influx of your mouthful of soft air.
Well, make the most of that small stock of knowledge
You've condescended to receive from me
That's your best chance. Oh you despise that, oh.   145
Prate then of passions you have known in dreams
Of huge experience gathered by the eye,
Be large of aspiration; pure in hope,

---

113. *mows*] Grimaces.
115–16] An allusion to Carlyle's translation of Goethe's novel *Wilhelm Meister's Travels: or, The Renunciants*: 'Then comes the second: Reverence for what is under us. . . . [We] are to regard the Earth with attention and cheerfulness: from the bounty of the Earth we are nourished: the Earth affords unutterable joys; but disproportionate sorrows she also brings us' (Carlyle 1899: ii, ch. x).

Sweet in fond longings, but in all things vague.
Breathe out your dreamy scepticism, relieved   150
By snatches of old songs; People will like that, doubtless.
Or will you write about Philosophy
For a waste far off *may-be* overlooking
The fruitful *is*, close by[?] Live in metaphysic,
With transcendental logic fill your stomach,   155
Schematise joy, effigiate meat and drink,
Or let me see, a mighty Work, a Volume,
The Complemental of the inferior Kant,
The Critic of Pure Practic; based upon
The Antinomies of the Moral Sense; for look you,   160
We cannot act without assuming *x*
And at the same time *y* its contradictory.
Ergo, to act. People will buy that, doubtless.
Or you'll perhaps teach youth (I do not question
Some downward turn you may find, some evasion   165
Of the broad highway's glaring white ascent)
Teach youth – in a small way; that is, always
So as to have much time left for yourself.
This you can't sacrifice, your leisure's precious.
Heartily you will not take to anything: 170
Will parents like that, think you? he writes poems,
He's odd opinions – hm – and's not in orders
For that you won't be. Well, old college fame,
The charity of some freethinking merchant,
Or friendly intercession brings a first pupil;   175
And not a second. Oh or if it should
Whatever happen, don't I see you still
Living no life at all[?] Even as now
An o'ergrown baby, sucking at the dugs
Of Instinct, dry long since. Come come you are old enough   180
For spoon meat surely.

153–63] The Spirit parodies the terms of German 'transcendental' philosophy, which had become popular due to the active proselytising of Coleridge
and Carlyle. Kant was the founder and best-known exponent of this philosophy, and The Spirit accuses Dipsychus of wanting to write a practical
complement to the *Critique of Pure Reason*, the work in which Kant had
attempted to analyse the basic forms of perception and cognition. He seems to
be unaware that Kant himself had already performed this feat in his *Critique of
Practical Reason*.
156. effigiate] Form into a specific shape.
160. antinomies] Discrepant though apparently logical conclusions from the
same premises.

               Will you go on thus
Until death end you? if indeed it does.
For what it does, none knows. Yet as for you
You'll hardly have the courage to die outright
You'll somehow halve even it. Methinks I see you   185
Through everlasting limbos of void time,
Twirling and twiddling ineffectively,
And indeterminately swaying about.
Come come, spoon meat at any rate.
                       Well, well
I will not persecute you more, my friend.   190
Only do think, as I observed before;
What *can* you do, if I should go away?

D: Is the hour here then – is the minute come,
      The irretrievable instant of stern time[?]
      O for a few few grains in the running glass   195
      Or for some power to hold them. Oh for a few
      Of all that went so wastefully before.
      It must be then; e'en now.

S: It must. It must.
      'Tis Common Sense! and human wit
      Can claim no higher name than it   200
      Submit submit.

      Necessity! and who shall dare
      Bring to *her* feet excuse or prayer
      Beware, beware
      We must, we must   205
      Howe'er we turn and pause and tremble
      Howe'er we shrink, deceive, dissemble
      Whate'er our doubting, grief, disgust
      The hand is on us, and we must,
      We must, we must   210
      'Tis Common Sense! and human wit
      Can find no better name than it
      Submit, submit!

193–8] Cp Marlowe's *Doctor Faustus*: 'Ah Faustus,/ Now thou hast but one
bare hour to live,/ And then thou must be damned perpetually./ Stand still,
ye ever-moving spheres of heaven,/ That time may cease and midnight never
come' (V.ii.143–7).

Fear not, my lamb, whate'er men say
I am the Shepherd; and the Way. 215

SCENE 6

D: I had a vision – was it in my sleep[?]
And if it were, what then[?] But sleep or wake
I saw a great light open o'er my head
And sleep or wake uplifted to that light
Out of that light proceeding heard a voice 5
Uttering high words, which, whether sleep or wake,
In me were fixed, and in me must abide.

When the enemy is near thee
Call on us
In our [hands] we will upbear thee 10
He shall neither scathe nor scare thee
Call on us[.]

Call when all good friends have left thee
All good sights and sounds bereft thee
Call; when hope and heart are sinking 15
And the brain is sick with thinking
Help O help[.]

Call and following close behind thee
There shall haste and there shall find thee
Help sure help[.] 20

Oh and if thou dost not call
Be but faithful that is all.
Go right on, and close behind thee
There shall follow still and find thee
Help sure help[.] 25

When the panic comes upon thee
When necessity seems on thee

214–15] Cp John 14:6. Houghton (1963) also compares John 10:14 and I Peter
2:25.
8–39] Inserted into this scene from a draft in the second book of MS1 by
1865. I have followed this procedure for two reasons: 1. The draft is preceded
by a version of lines 1–7 of this scene; 2. There is a gap in the text at this point
for a speech by Dipsychus.

Hope and choice have all forgone thee
Fate and force are closing o'er thee
And but one way stands before thee   30
     Call on us[.]

[S:]   This is what comes of drinking tea
         It doesn't matter much to me
         Only it's curious to see
         How beautifully this mild potion   35
         Facilitates the genial motion
         Of opening medicine and devotion[;]
         A thing one ought at church to take
         But that it [keeps] one *too* awake[.]

[D:] Not for thy service, thou imperious fiend   40
      Not to do thy work or the like of thine
      Not to please thee, O base and fallen Spirit
      But One Most High, Most True; whom without thee
      It seems I cannot.
                    O the misery
      That one must truck and practise with the World   45
      To gain the 'vantage ground to assail it from;
      To set upon the Giant one must first,
      O perfidy! have eat the Giant's bread.
      If I submit, it is but to gain time
      And arms and stature: 'tis but to lie safe   50
      Until the hour strike to arise and slay.
      'Tis the old story of the adder's brood
      Feeding and nestling till the fangs be grown.
      Were it not nobler done then to act fair
      To accept the service with the wages; do   55
      Frankly the devil's work for the devil's pay[?]
      O but another my allegiance holds
      Inalienably his. How much soe'er
      I might submit, it must be to rebel.
      Submit then sullenly, that's no dishonour.   60
      Yet I could deem it better too to starve
      And die untraitored. O who sent me, though?
      Some one, and to do something. O hard master

32–9] This speech is not attributed to either of the characters in the MS, but the metre and tone strongly suggest they belong to The Spirit.
63. O hard master] An echo of Milton's line 'For ever in my great Task-master's eye' (sonnet VII). There is another echo of Milton in the comparison with the blind Samson below (77–83). C. always associated Milton with the life of commitment, action and service; see the discussion of the contrast between Milton and Shakespeare, Introduction, pp. 9–10.

To do a treachery. But indeed 'tis done
I have already taken of the pay   65
And curst the payer; take I must, curse too.
Alas the little strength that I possess
Derives I think of him. So still it is,
The timid child that clung unto her skirts,
A boy, will slight his mother; and grown a man,   70
His father too. There's Scripture too for that[.]
Do we owe fathers nothing, mothers nought,
Is filial duty folly? Yet He says,
He that loves father, mother more than me –
Yea, and the man his parents shall desert   75
The ordinance says and cleave unto his wife[.]
O man behold thy wife, th'hard naked World;
Adam accept thy Eve. –
                        So still it is –
The tree exhausts the soil; creepers kill it;
Their insects them; the lever finds its fulcrum   80
On what it then o'erthrows; the homely spade
In Labour's hand unscrupulously seeks
Its first momentum on the very clod
Which next will be upturned. It seems a law.
And am not I, though I but ill recall   85
My happier days, a kidnapped child of heaven,
Whom these uncircumcised Philistines
Have by foul play shorn, blinded, maimed and kept
For what more glorious than to make then sport[?]
Wait then wait O my soul[,] grow grow ye locks,   90
Then perish they and if need is I too. –

S (aside):   A truly admirable proceeding!
              Could there be finer special pleading
              When scruples would be interceding[?]
              There's no occasion I should stay.   95

74] Matthew 10:37; cp 1.6.87 above.

75–6] Matthew 19:5; Mark 10:7–8; both citing Genesis 2:24.

77–8] The clearest expression of C.'s tendency to see marriage as the paradigmatic form of action in his poetry. It suggests parallels with Luke 16:9, 13 and Genesis 2:24.

86] An allusion to Wordsworth's 'Ode: Intimations of Immortality from Recollections of Early Childhood': 'Heaven lies about us in our infancy!/ Shades of the prison-house begin to close/ Upon the growing Boy[.]' (66–8).

87–91] The story of Samson, the Israelite hero who was captured, blinded and enslaved by the Philistines, and who gained his revenge by pulling the Philistines' temple down upon them, killing both them and himself, is told in Judges 16, and in Milton's poem *Samson Agonistes* (see note to 2.6.54–5 above).

He is working out, his own queer way,
The sum I set him, and this day,
Will bring it neither less nor bigger
Exact to my predestined figure.

SCENE 7

D: Twenty one past, twenty five coming on
One third of life departed, nothing done
Out of the Mammon of Unrighteousness
That we make friends, the Scripture is express.
Mephisto, come; we will agree   5
Content; you'll take a moiety.

S: A moiety, ye gods; he-he!

D: Three quarters then. One eye you close,
And lay your finger to your nose.
Seven eighths? nine tenths? O griping beast!   10
Leave me a decimal at least.

S: Oh one of ten! to infect the nine,
And make the devil a one be mine!
Oh one! to jib all day, God wot,
When all the rest would go full trot!   15
One very little one, eh? to doubt with,
Just to pause, think, and look about with?
In course! you counted on no less!
You thought it likely I'd say yes!

D: Be it then thus: since that it must, it seems.   20
Welcome, O world henceforth; and farewell dreams.
Yet know, Mephisto, know, nor you nor I
Can in this matter either sell or buy:
For the fee simple of this trifling lot

1–2] Another allusion to Milton's seventh sonnet: 'How soon hath Time the suttle thief of youth/ Stolne on his wing my three and twentith yeer!' (1–2) It is worth noticing that, although Dipsychus makes himself the same age as Milton was when he wrote his sonnet, C. was in his early to mid-thirties when he wrote *Dipsychus*.

3–4] Luke 16:9: 'And I say unto you, Make to yourselves friends of the mammon of unrighteousness; that, when ye fail, they may receive you into everlasting habitations.'

6. moiety] Half.

24. fee simple] A legal term meaning unconditional inheritance.

To you or me, trust me, pertaineth not.   25
I can but render what is of my will,
And behind it somewhat remaineth still.
Oh, your sole chance was in the childish mind
Whose darkness dreamed that vows like this could bind;
Thinking all lost, it made all lost, and brought,   30
In fact the ruin which had been but thought.
Thank heaven (or you!) that's past these many years,
And we have knowledge wiser than our fears.
So your poor bargain take, my man;
And make the best of it you can.   35

S: With reservations! – oh, how treasonable!
            When I had let you off so reasonable.
            However; I don't fear; be it so!
            Brutus is honourable, I know;
            So mindful of the dues of others   40
            So thoughtful for his poor dear brothers;
            So scrupulous, considerate, kind,
            He wouldn't leave the devil behind
            If he assured him he had claims
            For his good company to hell-flames.   45

            No matter, no matter; the bargain's made;
            And I, for my part, will not be afraid.
            Little Bo Peep, she lost her sheep
            And knew not where to find them.
            He he! With reservations, Christo!   50
            A child like you to cheat Mephisto!

            With reservations! oh ho ho!
            But Time, my friend, has yet to show
            Which of us two will closest fit
            The proverb of the Biter Bit. –   55
            Little Bo Peep, she lost her sheep –

D: Tell me thy name, now it is over.

S: Oh!
            Why Mephistopheles, you know –

39. Brutus is honourable] 'Brutus is an honourable man' – the refrain of Mark
Anthony's speech to the Romans after the assassination of Caesar; *Julius
Caesar* III.ii.
48–9] From the children's nursery rhyme; cp 2.3.186–90 above.
52–6] These lines might be an alternative to 46–51 above; the MS is unclear
at this point.
58–60] In the First Revision The Spirit is referred to as 'Mephisto' right up
until the end; Dipsychus uses the name 'Belial' for his tormentor at 1.3.24.

At least you've lately called me so;
Belial it was some days ago. 60
But take your pick; I've got a score –
Never a royal baby more.
For a brass plate upon a door
What think you of *Cosmocrator?*

D: Τοὺς κοσμοκράτορας τοῦ αἰῶνος τούτου 65
And that you are indeed, I do not doubt you.

S: Ephesians, ain't it? near the end
You dropt a word to spare your friend.
What follows too, in application
Would be absurd exaggeration. 70

D: The Power of this World! hateful unto God!

S: Cosmarchon's shorter, but sounds odd:
One wouldn't like, even if a true devil,
To be taken for a vulgar Jew devil.

D: Yet in all these things we, 'tis Scripture too, 75
Are more than conquerors – even over you.

S: Come come don't maunder any longer
Time tests the weaker and the stronger.
And we without procrastination
Must set you know to our vocation[.] 80
O goodness! Won't you find it pleasant
To own the positive and present
To see yourself like people round
And feel your feet upon the ground. –

Little Bo Peep, she lost her sheep[.] 85

Aside: In the Piazza di San Marco
O won't I try him after dark, oh

---

64. Cosmocrator] The power of this world.
65] Glossed by C. in the margin: Ephesians 6:12: 'For we wrestle not against flesh and blood, but against principalities, against powers, against *the rulers of the darkness of this world*, against spiritual wickedness in high places.' (Emphasis added.)
68] The missing words are τοῦ σκότου, i.e. 'darkness'.
75–6] From Romans 8:37: 'Nay, in all these things we are more than conquerors through him that loved us.'
77. maunder] Grumble.

O Jesus Christ! it will be funny
If I don't get my earnest money[.]

Exeunt ambo.

Epilogue

'I don't very well understand what it's all about,' said my uncle. 'I
won't say I didn't drop into a doze while the young man was
drivelling through his later soliloquies. But there was a great deal
that was unmeaning, vague, and involved; and what was most plain
was least decent and least moral.'   5

'Dear sir,' said I, 'Says the Proverb, Needs must when the devil
drives, and if the devil is to speak –'

'Well,' said my uncle, 'why should he? Nobody asked him. Not
that he didn't say much which if only it hadn't been for the way he
said it, and that it was he who said it, would have been sensible   10
enough.'

'But, sir,' said I, 'perhaps he wasn't a devil after all. That's the
beauty of the poem; nobody can say. You see, dear sir, the thing
which it is attempted to represent is the conflict between the tender Conscience and the World - now the over-tender conscience   15
will of course exaggerate the wickedness of the world, and the
Spirit in my poem may be merely the hypothesis or subjective
imagination, formed –'

'Oh for goodness' sake, my dear boy,' interrupted my uncle,
'don't go into the theory of it. If you're wrong in it, it makes bad   20
worse; if you're right, you may be a critic but you can't be a poet.
And then you know very well I don't understand all those new
words. But as for that, I quite agree that consciences are often
much too tender in your generation. Schoolboys' consciences too!
As my old friend the Canon says of the Westminster Students,   25

---

89. *earnest money]* A deposit; possibly also an allusion to Judas Iscariot's
thirty pieces of silver.
17-18. *hypothesis or subjective imagination]* Terms drawn from the latest critical jargon, designed to infuriate a partisan of common sense like the poet's
Uncle.

"They're all so pious" - It's all Arnold's doing. He spoilt the public schools.'

'My dear uncle,' said I, 'how can so venerable a sexagenarian
utter so juvenile a paradox? How often have I not heard you
lament the idleness and listlessness, the boorishness and vulgar   30
tyranny, the brutish manners alike and minds –'

'Ah' said my uncle, 'I may have fallen in occasionally with the
talk of the day; but at seventy one begins to see clearer into the
bottom of one's mind. In middle life one says so many things in
the way of business. – Not that I mean to say that the old schools   35
were perfect, any more than we old boys, that were there. But
whatever else they were or did, they certainly were in harmony
with the world – and they certainly did not disqualify the country's youth for after life and the country's service' –

'But my dear sir this bringing the schools of the country into   40
harmony with public opinion and feeling is exactly –'

'Don't interrupt me with public opinion, my dear nephew;
you'll quote me a leading article next. "Young men must be young
men" as the worthy head of your college said to me touching a case
of rustication. "My dear sir," answered I, "I only wish to heaven   45
they would be, but as for my own nephews, they seem to me a sort
of hobbadihoy cherub, too big to be innocent, and too simple for
anything else. – They're full of the notion of the world being so
wicked, and of their taking a higher line, as they call it. I only fear
they'll never take any at all." – What is the true purpose of educa-   50
tion? Simply to make plain to the young understanding the laws of
the life they will have to enter. – For example, that lying won't do,
thieving still less, that idleness will get punished, that if they are
cowards, the whole world will be against them; that if they will
have their own way, they must fight for it. – Etc. etc. As for the   55
conscience, Mamma I take it, such as mammas are nowadays at
any rate, has probably set that agoing fast enough already. What a
blessing to see her good little child come back a brave young devil-
may-care.'

'Exactly, my dear sir. As if at twelve or fourteen a roundabout   60
boy, with his three meals a day inside him, is likely to be over-
troubled with scruples.'

---

26. *Arnold]* Thomas Arnold, headmaster of Rugby and reformer of the
English public school system. His influence on C. has been extensively
chronicled; see esp. Woodward 1957: ch. 3, Veyriras 1964: ch. 3.
45. *rustication]* Temporary expulsion from the University.
47. *hobbadi-hoy]* Normally 'hobbledehoy'; an expression for an awkward
youth halfway between a boy and a man.

'Put him through a course of confirmation and sacraments
backed up with sermons and private admonitions, and what is
much the same as auricular confession, and really my dear nephew   65
I can't answer for it but he mayn't turn out as great a goose as you
– pardon me, *were* about the age of eighteen or nineteen.'

'But to have past *through* that, my dear sir! surely that can be no
harm.'

'I don't know. Your constitutions don't seem to recover it quite.   70
We did without these foolish measles, well enough, in my time.'

'Westminster had its Cowper, my dear sir; other schools theirs
also, mute and inglorious, but surely not few.'

'Ah, ah, the beginning of troubles. –'

'You see, my dear Sir you must not refer it to Arnold at all, at   75
all. Anything that Arnold did in this direction –'

'Why, my dear boy, how often have I not heard from you, how
he used to attack offences, not as offences, the right view, against
discipline, but as sin, heinous guilt, I don't know what beside.
Why didn't he flog them and hold his tongue? Flog them he did;   80
but why preach?'

'If he did err in this way, sir, which I hardly think, I ascribe it to
the spirit of the time. The real cause of the evil you complain of,
which to a certain extent I admit, was, I take it, the religious movement of the last century, beginning with Wesleyanism, and   85
culminating at last in Puseyism – This overexcitation of the religious sense, resulting in this irrational almost animal irritability of
conscience was in many ways as foreign to Arnold as it is proper to
. . .'

63–7. Put him through . . . eighteen or nineteen] The Uncle describes the kind of
regime characteristic of Arnold's Rugby; Arnold instituted something like the
Catholic practice of 'auricular confession' at the school, encouraging the boys
to confess their sins to him in private.

72. Cowper] The poet William Cowper (1731–1800), seen at the time (and
since) as a harbinger of the Romantic movement; his poem *Tirocinium; or, a
Review of Schools* (1784) criticises the English public school system in terms
which anticipate Dr Arnold's reforms at Rugby.

73. mute and inglorious] An allusion to Gray's *Elegy Written in a Country
Churchyard* (1751): 'Some mute inglorious Milton here may rest,/ Some
Cromwell guiltless of his country's blood' (59–60).

85. Wesleyanism] Methodism, the religious movement begun by John Wesley
in the eighteenth century.

86. Puseyism] See 1.7.147 and note. C. suggests that the century-long religious
movement encompassing these movements, with its 'animal irritability of conscience', has now ended.

'Well well my dear nephew if you like to make a theory of   90
it, pray write it out for yourself nicely in full: but your poor
old uncle does not like theories, and is moreover sadly sleepy
—'

'Good night, dear uncle, good night. Only let me say you
six more verses.'   95
        'Ah, whose are those? – ah – what? well . . .'
        'Good night, dear uncle, good night.'

93–4. *six more verses*] Possibly a reference to *Dipsychus Continued*, C.'s fragmentary 'sequel' to the poem.
96. *Good night, dear uncle, good night*] Cp *Hamlet* IV.v: 'Good night, ladies;
good night, sweet ladies, good night, good night.'

Shorter Poems

Text and MSS: Where available the version published during C.'s lifetime is followed. For posthumously published poems the latest available MS is preferred; exceptions to this procedure are explained in the Headnotes to individual poems. All MSS (unless otherwise stated) are in the Bodleian Library at Oxford. On the principles governing the choice of poems in this section, see Introduction, pp. 5–6.

Epi-Strauss-ium

1869. Two MSS: one in 1847 Notebook (MS1) entitled *Epi-Strauss-ion*, another on a loose sheet (MS2). MS2 is followed here. George Eliot's translation of David Friedrich Strauss's *Life of Jesus Critically Examined* was published in 1846. Strauss's book, one of the most important of the nineteenth century, was the first to apply the 'mythological' method of biblical criticism to the gospel narratives, and concluded that the records of the life of Jesus were almost entirely lacking in any genuine historical foundation. C.'s optimistic response to Strauss's work in this poem can be ascribed to the fact that, unlike most of his contemporaries, he was well aware of developments in German biblical criticism, and had long since ceased to base his faith on the historical evidence for Christianity. He was, however, also capable of seeing the loss of the gospel narratives in a bleaker light; cp *Easter Day* below, p. 256.

> Matthew and Mark and Luke and holy John
> Evanished all and gone!
> Yea, He that erst, his dusky Curtains quitting,

Title. Epi-Strauss-ium] 'A little poem about Strauss.'
3–10] The evangelists are compared to the stained-glass windows on the eastern side of the cathedral which intercept and diminish the clear white light of heaven.

Through Eastern pictured panes his level beams
    transmitting,
With gorgeous portraits blent,   5
On them his glories intercepted spent,
Southwestering now, through windows plainly glassed
On the inside face his radiance keen hath cast;
And in the lustre lost, invisible and gone,
Are, say you? Matthew, Mark, and Luke and holy John.   10
Lost, is it? lost, to be recovered never?
However,
The Place of Worship the meantime with light
Is, if less richly, more sincerely bright,
And in blue skies the Orb is manifest to sight.   15

The Song of Lamech

1862. Two almost identical MSS: 1849–50 (Lamech) Notebook (MS1) and
1852 (Smith) Notebook (MS2). MS1 is followed here; the copying in MS2 is
slipshod and the punctuation erratic. The poem is dated 'Liverpool February
1849' in both MSS. This and the following two poems draw on contemporary
historiographical techniques; see Introduction, pp. 6–7. The song of Lamech
occurs in Genesis 4:23–4: 'And Lamech said unto his wives, Adah and Zillah,
Hear my voice; ye wives of Lamech, hearken unto my speech: for I have slain
a man to my wounding, and a young man to my hurt./ If Cain shall be
avenged sevenfold, truly Lamech seventy and sevenfold.' Keble cites the
opinion of contemporary scholars that this brief song is 'the most ancient of
all songs that remain to us' (Keble 1912: i, 59). C.'s treatment of it suggests
that he sees it as the source of the myth of Cain and Abel.

Hearken to me, ye mothers of my tent;
Ye wives of Lamech, listen to my speech.
Adah, let Jabal hither lead his goats,
And Tubal-Cain, O Zillah, hush the forge;
Naamah her wheel shall ply beside, and thou,   5
My Jubal, touch, before I speak, the string.

3. *Jabal]* Son of Adah, 'the father of such as dwell in tents, and *of such as
have* cattle' (Genesis 4:20).
4. *Tubal-Cain]* Son of Zillah, 'an instructer of every artificer in brass and
iron' (Genesis 4:22). Byron uses the names Adah and Zillah for the wives of
Cain and Abel in his *Cain.*
5. *Naamah]* Sister of Tubal Cain.
6. *Jubal]* Brother of Jabal, 'the father of all such as handle the harp and
organ' (Genesis 4:21).

Yea, Jubal, touch before I speak, the string.
Hear ye my voice, beloved of my tent,
Dear ones of Lamech, hearken to my speech.

For Eve made answer, Cain my son, my own;   10
O first mysterious increase of my womb,
O if I cursed thee, O my child, I sinned;
And He that heard me, heard and said me nay;
My first, my only one, thou shalt not go.

And Adam answered also. Cain, my son,   15
He that is gone forgiveth; we forgive.
Rob not thy mother of two sons at once:
My child, abide with us, and comfort us.

Hear ye my voice, Adah and Zillah, hear;
Ye wives of Lamech, listen to my speech.   20

For Cain replied not, but an hour more sat,
Where the night through he sat, his knit brows seen,
Scarce seen, amidst the foldings of his limbs.
But when the Sun was bright upon the field,
To Adam still and Eve still waiting by,   25
And weeping, lift he up his voice and spake.

Cain said, The Sun is risen into the sky:
The day demands my going, and I go.
As you from Paradise, so I from you;
As you to exile, into exile I: 30
Into a barren and a naked earth
My Father and my Mother, I depart.

As betwixt you and Paradise of old,
So betwixt me, my Parents, now, and you
Cherubims I discern, and in their hand   35
A flaming sword that turneth every way,
To keep the way of my one tree of life,
The way, my spirit yearns to, of your love.

10 et seq.] The story of Cain and Abel immediately precedes the song of
Lamech in Genesis; see C.'s treatment of the story in *Adam and Eve* above,
pp. 49–72.
33–7] After expelling Adam and Eve from Paradise the Lord placed at the
east of it 'Cherubims, and a flaming sword which turned every way, to keep
the way of the tree of life' (Genesis 3:24).

Yet not, O Adam, and O Eve, fear not.
For He that asked me, Where is Abel? He   40
Who called me cursed from the Earth, and said,
A fugitive and vagabond thou art
He also said, when fear had struck my soul,
There shall not touch thee man nor beast; fear not.
Fear not, my father, nor, my mother, fear.   45
Lo I have spoke with God, and He hath said:
Fear not; and let me go as He hath said.
For also in the darkness of my mind
When the night's night of misery was most black,
A little star came twinkling up within,   50
And in myself I had a guide that led,
And in myself had knowledge of a soul:
Fear not, O Adam and O Eve. I go.

O Jubal touch, touch yet again the string.
Children of Lamech, listen to my speech.   55

For when the years were multiplied, and Cain
Eastward of Eden in this land of Nod
Had sons and sons of sons and sons of them,
Enoch and Irad and Mehujael
My father and my children's grandsire he,   60
It came to pass that Cain, who dwelt alone,
Met Adam at the nightfall in the field;
Who fell upon his neck, and wept and said,
My Son: hath God not spoken to thee, Cain?

And Cain replied, when weeping loosed his voice: 65
My dreams are double, O my father; good
And evil. Terror to my soul by night,
And agony by day, when Abel stands
A dead black shade and speaks not, neither looks:
Nor makes me any answer when I cry,   70

40] Genesis 4:9: 'And the LORD said unto Cain, Where *is* Abel thy brother?'
41–2] Genesis 4:11–12: 'And now *art* thou cursed from the earth . . . a fugitive and vagabond shalt thou be in the earth.'
44] Genesis 4:14–15.
50–2] C. sees sin as the origin of conscience and consciousness; cp *Adam and Eve* above and notes.
59. Mehujael] A slight error; Methusael is given as Lamech's father in Genesis 4:18.
66–7] A typically Cloughian double-mindedness.

Curse me, but let me know thou art alive.
But comfort also like a whisper comes
In visions of a deeper sleep, when he
Abel, as when we knew him yours and mine,
Comes with a sweet forgiveness in his face, 75
Seeming to speak, solicitous for words
And wearing ere he go the old first look
Of unsuspecting unforeboding love.
Three nights are gone, I saw him thus, my sire.

Dear ones of Lamech, listen to my speech. 80

For Adam said, Three nights ago to me
Came Abel in my sleep as thou hast said,
And spake and bade, Arise, my father, go
Where in the land of exile lives thy son:
Say to my brother, Abel bids thee come, 85
Abel would have thee; and lay thou thy hand
My father, on his head, that he may come.
Am I not weary, Father, for this hour?

Hear ye my voice, Adah and Zillah, hear:
Children of Lamech, listen to my speech; 90
And, son of Zillah, sound thy solemn string.

For Adam laid upon the head of Cain
His hand, and Cain bowed down, and slept and died:
And a deep sleep on Adam also fell,
And in his slumber's deepest he beheld 95
Standing before the gate of Paradise
With Abel hand in hand our father Cain.

Hear ye my voice, Adah and Zillah, hear;
Ye wives of Lamech, listen to my speech.
Though to his wounding did he slay a man, 100
Yea, and a young man to his hurt he slew,
Fear not, ye wives, nor sons of Lamech, fear;
If unto Cain was safety given and rest,
Shall Lamech surely and his people die?

100–4] Lamech construes the story of Cain and Abel as one of forgiveness and redemption, and deduces from it that he too will be forgiven for his crime.

Jacob's Wives

1869. One MS in 1849–50 (Lamech) Notebook. The MS is followed in pre-
ference to the printed version. The story of Rachel and Leah is told in Genesis
29 and 30. Jacob served Laban for seven years so that he could marry Rachel,
but at the end of this time was deceived into marrying Leah, her older sister.
C. sees this story as emblematic of the contrast between romantic expectation
and reality in marriage: 'Rachel we serve-for, long years, – that seem as a few
days only,/ E'en for the love we have to her, – and win her at last of Laban./
Is it not Rachel we take in our joy from the hand of her father?/ Is it not
Rachel we lead in the mystical veil from the altar?/ Rachel we dream-of at
night: in the morning, behold, it is Leah' (*The Bothie* ix.175–9).

These are the words of Jacob's wives; the words
Which Leah spake and Rachel to his ears,
When in the shade at eventide he sat
By the tent-door, a palm tree overhead,
A spring beside him, and the sheep around.   5

And Rachel spake and said, The nightfall comes;
Night which all day I wait for, and for thee.

And Leah also spake, The day is done;
My lord with toil is weary, and would rest.

And Rachel said, Come, O my Jacob, come.   10
And we will think we sit beside the well
As in that day the long long years agone
When first I met thee with my father's flock.

And Leah said, Come, Israel, unto me:
And thou shalt reap an harvest of fair sons,   15
E'en as before I bare thee goodly babes;
For when was Leah fruitless to my lord?

And Rachel said, Ah come, as then thou cam'st;
Come once again to set thy seal of love,
As then down bending when the sheep had drunk   20
Thou settedst it, my shepherd, O sweet seal,
Upon the unwitting half-foretasting lips
Which shy and trembling thirsted yet for thine
As cattle thirsted never for the spring.

And Leah answered, Are not these their names   25
As Reuben, Simeon, Levi, Judah, four?
Like four young saplings by the water's brim

14–17] Genesis 29:31: 'And when the LORD saw that Leah *was* hated, he
opened her womb: but Rachel *was* barren.'

Where straining rivers through the great plain wind,
Four saplings soon to rise to goodly trees,
Four trees whose growth shall cast an huger shade 30
Than ever yet on river side was seen.

And Rachel said, And shall it be again
As when dissevered far, unheard, alone,
Consumed in bitter anger all night long,
I moaned and wept, while silent and discreet 35
One reaped the fruit of love that Rachel's was
Upon the breast of him that knew her not[?]

And Leah said, And was it then a wrong,
That in submission to a father's word
Trembling yet hopeful to that bond I crept, 40
Which God hath greatly prospered, and my lord
Content in after-wisdom not disowned,
Joyful in after-thankfulness approved?

And Rachel said, But we will not complain,
Though all life long an alien unsought third 45
She trouble our companionship of love.

And Leah answered, No; complain we not,
Though year on year she loiter in the tent
A fretful vain unprofitable wife.

And Rachel answered, Ah she little knows 50
What in old days to Jacob Rachel was.

And Leah said, And wilt thou dare to say
Because my lord was gracious to thee then
No deeper thought his riper cares hath claimed
No stronger purpose passed into his life: 55
That, youth and maid once fondly softly touched
Time's years must still the casual dream repeat,
And all the river far from source to sea
One flitting moment's chance reflexion bear?

Also she added, who is she to judge 60
Of thoughts maternal and a father's heart?

And Rachel said, But what to supersede
The rights which choice bestowed hath Leah done[?]
What which my handmaid or which hers hath not?

64–7] Billah [Bilhah], Rachel's handmaid, was given to Jacob 'to wife' by
Rachel in order to bear children for her; her sons were called Dan and
Naphtali (Genesis 30:3–8). Zilpah was Leah's handmaid, and performed a
similar service.

Is Simeon more than Naphthali, is Dan   65
Less than his brother Levi in the house?
That part that Billah and that Zilpah have
That and no more, hath Leah in her lord,
And let her with the same be satisfied.

Leah asked then, And shall these things compare   70
(Fond wishes, and the pastime and the play)
With serious aims and forward-working hopes
Aims as far reaching as to Earth's last age
And hopes far-travelling as from East to West[?]

Rachel replied – That love which in his youth   75
Through trial proved consoles his perfect age
Shall this with project and with plan compare?
Or is forever shorter than all time,
And love more straitened than from East to West[?]

Leah spake further, Hath my lord not told   80
How in the visions of the night his God
The God of Abraham and of Isaac spake
And said, Increase and multiply and fill
With sons to serve me this thy land and mine,
And I will surely do thee good, and make   85
Thy seed as is the sand beside the sea,
Which is not numbered for its multitude[?]
Shall [Rachel] bear this progeny to God?

But Rachel wept and answered, And if God
Hath closed the womb of Rachel until now,   90
Shall he not at his pleasure open it?
Hath Leah read the counsels of the Lord?
Was it not told to her in the ancient days
How Sarah, mother of great Israel's sire
Lived to long years insulted of her slave   95
Or e'er to light the Child of Promise came,
Whom Rachel too to Jacob yet may bear[?]

Moreover Rachel said, Shall Leah mock?
Who stole the prime embraces of my love,
My first long-destined, long-withheld caress.   100

But not, she said, methought, but not for this

80–8] Genesis 28:13–14: 'And, behold, the LORD stood above it, and said, I
am the LORD God of Abraham thy father, and the God of Isaac: the land
whereon thou liest, to thee will I give it, and to thy seed;/ And thy seed shall
be as the dust of the earth, and thou shalt spread abroad to the west, and to
the east, and to the north, and to the south[.]'
94–6] Sarah, Abraham's wife, was promised by the Lord that she would give
birth to a child despite being 'well stricken in age' (Genesis 18:11).

In the old days did Jacob seek his bride;
Where art thou now, O thou that sought'st me then[?]
Where is thy loving tenderness of old[?]
And where that fervency of faith to which   105
Seven weary years were even as a few days?
And Rachel wept and ended, Ah, my life!
Though Leah bear thee sons on sons, methought
The Child of love, late-born, were worth them all.

And Leah groaned and answered, It is well: 110
She that hath kept me from my husband's heart
Will set their father's soul against my sons.

Yet, also, not, she said, I thought, for this
Not for the feverish nor the doting love
Doth Israel, father of a Nation, seek;   115
Nor to light dalliance as of boy and girl
Incline the thoughts of matron and of man,
Or lapse the wisdoms of maturer mind.

And Leah ended, Father of my sons,
Come, thou shalt dream of Rachel if thou wilt,   120
So Leah fold thee in a wife's embrace.

These are the words of Jacob's wives, who sat
In the tent door, and listened to their speech
The spring beside him, and above the palm
While all the sheep were gathered for the night.   125

Jacob

1862. Two MSS: a draft consisting of five loose sheets (MS1) and a fair copy
(MS2) in the 1852 (Smith) Notebook. MS2 is followed. The poem is dated
'London 1851' in MS2. Based on Jacob's valedictory speech to his sons in
Genesis 49, C.'s sister suggested that the poem might have been written 'as a
sort of remembrance of [their] Father – & the struggles and trials of mercantile life – the hard battle that a real gentleman and a Christian man with an
affectionate honourable too yielding character had had with his life' (unpublished MS life of C.; cited in Houghton 1963: 77).

My sons, and ye the children of my sons,
Jacob your father goes upon his way,
His pilgrimage is being accomplished.
Come near, and hear him ere his words are o'er.

105–6] Genesis 29:20: 'And Jacob served seven years for Rachel; and they
seemed unto him *but* a few days, for the love he had to her.'

Not as my father's or his father's days   5
As Isaac's days or Abraham's have been mine,
Not as the days of those that in the field
Walked at the eventide to meditate
And haply to the tent returning found
Angels at nightfall waiting at their door.   10
They communed, Israel wrestled with the Lord.
No not as Abraham's or as Isaac's days,
My sons, have been Jacob your father's days,
Evil and few, attaining not to theirs
In number, and in worth inferior much.   15
As a man with his friend, walked they with God,
In his abiding presence they abode,
And all their acts were open to his face.
But I have had to force mine eyes away,
To lose, almost to shun the thoughts I loved   20
To bend down to the work, to bare the breast
And struggle feet and hands with enemies,
To buffet and to battle with hard men,
With men of selfishness and violence
To watch by day and calculate by night   25
To plot and think of plots, and through a land
Ambushed with guile and with strong foes beset
To win with art safe Wisdom's peaceful way.
Alas, I know and from the outset knew,
The first-born faith, the singleness of soul   30
The antique pure simplicity with which
God and good angels communed undispleased
Is not: – it shall not any more be said
That of a blameless and a holy kind
The chosen race, the seed of promise comes.   35
The royal high prerogatives, the dower
Of innocence and perfectness of life
Pass not unto my children from their sire
As unto me they came of mine; they fit
Neither to Jacob nor to Jacob's race.   40

13–15] Possibly a reminiscence of Milton's lines from *Paradise Lost* 7.26–7:
'On evil days though fallen, and evil tongues;/ In darkness, and with dangers
compassed round.' These lines are cited in C's 'Lecture on the Development
of English Literature' (*PR* 340).

Think ye, my sons, in this extreme old age
And in this failing breath that I forget
How on the day when from my father's door
In bitterness and ruefulness of heart
I from my parents set my face and felt   45
I never more again should look on theirs, –
How on that day I seemed unto myself
Another Adam from his home cast out
And driven abroad into a barren land
Cursed for his sake and mocking still with thorns   50
And briars that labour and that sweat of brow
He still must spend to live. Sick of my days
I wished not life but cried out, let me die;
But at Luz God came to me; in my heart
He put a better mind, and showed me how   55
While we discern it not and least believe
On stairs invisible betwixt his heaven
And our unholy sinful toilsome earth
Celestial messengers of loftiest good
Upward and downward pass continually.   60
Many, since Jacob on the field of Luz
Set up the stone he slept on, unto God,
Many have been the troubles of my life;
Sins in the field and sorrows in the tent,
In mine own household anguish and despair,   65
And gall and wormwood mingled with my love.
The time would fail me, should I seek to tell
Of a child wronged and cruelly revenged
(Accursed was that anger, it was fierce,
That wrath, for it was cruel), or of strife   70
And jealousy and cowardice with lies
Mocking a father's misery: deeds of blood
Pollutions, sicknesses, and sudden deaths,

41–6] Jacob was sent away from his home after having usurped his brother
Esau's birthright; see Genesis 27.
47–52] Another instance of the motif of the Fall (cp *The Song of Lamech*).
54–60] Jacob dreamed he saw 'a ladder set up on the earth, and the top of it
reached to heaven: and behold the angels of God ascending and descending
on it' (Genesis 28:12).
68–70] Jacob's daughter Dinah was 'defiled' by Shechem; two of Jacob's
sons, Simeon and Levi, exacted revenge by killing Shechem and all his kins-
men (Genesis 34).
70–3] A reference to the story of Joseph and his brothers (Genesis 37)
amongst others.

These many things against me many times.
The ploughers have ploughed deep upon my back,   75
And made deep furrows; blessed be his name
Who hath delivered Jacob out of all;
And left within his spirit hope of good.
Come near to me, my sons; your father goes,
The hour of his departure draweth nigh.   80
Ah me, this eager rivalry of life,
This cruel conflict for pre-eminence,
This keen supplanting of the dearest kin,
Quick seizure and fast unrelaxing hold
Of vantage-place; the stony-hard resolve,   85
The chase, the competition and the craft,
Which seems to be the poison of our life
And yet is the condition of our life.
To have done things on which the eye with shame
Looks back, the closed hand clutching still the prize   90
Alas, what of all these things shall I say[?]
Take me away unto thy sleep, O God.
I thank thee it is over, yet I think
It was a work appointed me of thee.
How is it? I have striven all my days   95
To do my duty to my house and hearth
And to the purpose of my father's race.
Yet is my heart therewith not satisfied.

MS1 continues:

Take me away unto thy rest, my God.
There Abraham and Isaac evermore   100
Under celestial palms are set in peace
And with Rebekah and with Sarah there
My Rachel and my Leah shall I see.

But falter not, my children, falter not
Quit not the appointed path, let none step in;   105
The promise is secure and shall not fail
The land and all the fat of it is ours
You or your children shall inherit it
A land of pleasant places, flowing full
With milk and honey, rich with grapes and figs: 110

99–119] C.'s omission of the concluding lines from MS1 would seem to indicate a loss of confidence in the possibility of ever reaching the Promised Land.

A land of springs of water and of hills
Whence you may dig the iron and the brass
Into it bear your father's bones before:
Lay me within the field I purchased there
(There laid I Rachel): in the field I bought   115
And with my money paid for it, lay me.
The land is yours and all the good of it
Falter not sons of Jacob falter not
I go before and you must follow me.

Bethesda: A Sequel

1862. Three MSS: 1. 1849 (Roma) Notebook (ll. 1–21 only) in Balliol College
Oxford; 2. British Museum; 3. Harvard bMS 1036(2). MS3 is followed.
Companion poem to 'The human spirits saw I on a day' (see above, p. 32).
The biblical text upon which both this and the earlier poem are based is John
5:2–4: 'Now there is at Jerusalem by the sheep *market* a pool, which is called
in the Hebrew tongue Bethesda, having five porches./ In these lay a great
multitude of impotent folk, of blind, halt, withered, waiting for the moving of
the water./ For an angel went down at a certain season into the pool, and
troubled the water: whosoever then first after the troubling of the water
stepped in was made whole of whatsoever disease he had.'

I saw again the spirits on a day,
Where on the earth in mournful case they lay;
Five porches were there, and a pool, and round,
Huddling in blankets, strewn upon the ground,
Tied-up and bandaged, weary, sore and spent,   5
The maimed and halt, diseased and impotent.

For a great angel came, 'twas said, and stirred
The pool at certain seasons, and the word
Was, with this people of the sick, that they
Who in the waters here their limbs should lay   10
Before the motion on the surface ceased
Should of their torment straightway be released.

So with shrunk bodies and with heads down-dropt,
Stretched on the steps and at the pillars propt,
Watching by day and listening through the night,   15
They filled the place, a miserable sight.

And I beheld that on the stony floor

He too, that spoke of duty once before,
No otherwise than others here to-day
Fordone and sick and sadly muttering lay.   20
'I know not, I will do, – what is it I would say?
What was that word which once sufficed alone for all,
Which now I seek in vain and never can recall?'

'I know not I will do the work the world requires
Asking no reason why, but serving its desires;   25
Will do for daily bread, for wealth, respect, good name,
The business of the day – alas, is that the same[?]'
And then as weary of in vain renewing
His question, thus his mournful thought pursuing,
'I know not, I must do as other men are doing.'   30

But what the waters of that pool might be,
Of Lethe were they, or Philosophy;
And whether he long waiting did attain
Deliverance from the burden of his pain
Here with the rest; or whether, yet before,   35
Some more diviner stranger passed the door
With his small company into that sad place,
And breathing hope into the sick man's face
Bade him take up his bed and rise and go,
What the end were, and whether it were so,   40
Further than this I saw not neither know. –

Resignation – to Faustus

1869: Title 'At Rome'. Two MSS, the first of which contains an expanded version of lines 1–34 only; MS2 is followed here. The title alludes to Matthew Arnold's *Resignation - to Fausta* which was published in February 1849. The poem dates from C.'s visit to Rome in the same year.

O Land of Empire, art and love!
        What is it that you show me?
A sky for Gods to tread above,
        A soil for pigs below me!

18] See 'The Human Spirits', p. 33; l. 25 et seq.: 'I know not, I will do my duty . . .'
32. Lethe] The river of forgetfulness across which the dead were ferried in Greek mythology.
36–9] A reference to John 5:5–9, in which Jesus cures one of the sick people sitting around the pool with the words 'Rise, take up thy bed, and walk'.

O in all place and shape and kind 5
    Beyond all thought and thinking,
The graceful with the gross combined,
    The stately with the stinking!
Whilst words of mighty love to trace,
    Which thy great walls I see on, 10
Thy porch I pace or take my place
    Within thee, great Pantheon,
What sights untold of contrast bold
    My ranging eyes must be on!
What though uprolled by young and old 15
    In slumbrous convolution
Neath pillared shade must lie displayed
    Bare limbs that scorn ablution
Should husks that swine would never pick
    Bestrew that patterned paving, 20
And sores to make a surgeon sick
    For charity come craving?
Though oft the meditative cur
    Account it small intrusion
Through that great gate to quit the stir 25
    Of market-place confusion,
True brother of the bipeds there,
    If Nature's need requireth,
Lifts up his leg with tranquil air
    And tranquilly retireth: 30
Though priest think fit to stop and spit
    Beside the altar solemn,
Yet, boy, that nuisance why commit
    On this Corinthian column? –

O richly soiled and richly sunned, 35
Exuberant, fervid, and fecund!
    Are these the fixed condition
On which may Northern pilgrim come

After 8] MS1 has: 'Was ever seen in tie so close/ With beauty dirt in union?/ Did ever glorious things and gross/ Hold such serene communion?/ For though for open bridge and street/ I will not feel compunction,/ Is palace proud a place allowed/ For bestial-filthy function?/ Must vile expectorations greet/ Angelic limbs with unction,/ And marble flags attest the feat/ Of digital emunction?' ('Emunction' means nose-blowing).

33–4] MS1: 'Must therefore boys turn up to —/ By this Corinthian column?'

35] Note the pun on 'soiled'.

To imbibe thine ether-air, and sum
    Thy store of old tradition?   40
Must we be chill, if clean, and stand
Foot-deep in dirt in classic land?

So is it: in all ages so,
And in all places man can know,
From homely roots unseen below   45
In forest-shade in woodland bower
The stem that bears the ethereal flower
Derives that emanative power;
From mixtures fetid foul and sour
Draws juices that those petals fill.   50

Ah Nature, if indeed thy will
Thou own'st it, it shall not be ill!
And truly here, in this quick clime
Where, scarcely bound by space or time,
The elements in half a day   55
Toss off with exquisitest play
What our cold seasons toil and grieve,
And never quite at last achieve;
Where processes, with pain and fear
Disgust and horror wrought, appear   60
The quick mutations of a dance,
Wherein retiring but to advance,
Life, in brief interpause of death,
One moment sitting, taking breath,
Forth comes again as glad as e'er   65
In some new figure full as fair,
Where what has scarcely ceased to be,
Instinct with newer birth we see -
What dies already, look you, lives;
In such a clime, who thinks, forgives;   70
Who sees, will understand; who knows,
In calm of knowledge find repose,
And thoughtful as of glory gone,
So too of more to come anon,
Of permanent existence sure,   75
Brief intermediate breaks endure.
    O Nature, if indeed thy will,

---

39. *ether-air*] Nineteenth-century physicists assumed that there was a substance called ether which occupied all space and facilitated the transmission
of electric and magnetic waves.
43–50] C. argues that the dirt and filth of Italy are the soil out of which the
works of art which they appear to deface grow.

Thou ownest it, it is not ill!
And e'en as oft on heathy hill,
On moorland black, and ferny fells,   80
Beside thy brooks and in thy dells,
Was welcomed erst the kindly stain
Of thy true earth, e'en so again
With resignation fair and meet
The dirt and refuse of the street   85
My philosophic foot shall greet,
So leave but perfect to my eye
Thy columns set against the sky!

Uranus

1869. MS in 1849 (Roma) Notebook (Balliol). The MS is followed. 'This thought is taken from a passage on astronomy in Plato's *Republic*, in which the following sentence occurs, vii.529, D: "We must use the fretwork of the sky as patterns, with a view to the study which aims at these higher realities, just as if we chanced to meet with diagrams cunningly drawn and devised by Dedalus or some other craftsman or painter" ' (footnote first included in 1869). Uranus was the personification of heaven, first ruler of the universe, in Greek mythology. The planet Uranus was discovered in 1781 by William Herschel; it was the first planet to be discovered in modern times with the aid of a telescope. The word therefore encapsulates two wholly opposed ways of understanding the universe, and C. uses it as the starting point for a meditation on the pretensions of modern science.

When on the primal peaceful blank profound
Which in its still unknowing silence holds
All knowledge, ever by withholding holds
When on that void – (like footfalls in far rooms),
In faint pulsations from the whitening East   5
Articulate voices first were felt to stir
And the great child in dreaming grown to man
Losing his dream to piece it up began
Then Plato in me said –
'Tis but the figured ceiling overhead   10
With cunning diagrams bestarred that shine
In all the three dimensions, are endowed
With motion too by skill mechanical
That thou in height and depth and breadth and power
Schooled unto pure Mathesis [,in thyself behold   15

15. Mathesis] Mental discipline, especially of a mathematical kind.

The things of space, so disciplined] might proceed
To higher entities whereof in us.
Copies are seen existent they themselves
In the sole Kingdom of the Mind and God
Mind not the stars, mind thou thy Mind and God.   20
By that supremer Word
O'ermastered, deafly heard
Were hauntings dim of old astrologies
Chaldean mumblings vast, with gossip light
From modern ologistic fancyings mixed   25
Of suns and stars by hypothetic men
Of other frame than ours inhabited
Of lunar seas and lunar craters huge
And was there atmosphere or was there not
And without oxygen could life subsist[?]   30
And was the world originally mist. –
Talk they as talk they list
I in that ampler voice
Unheeding did rejoice.

Sa Majesté Très Chrétienne

1951. Two MSS: 1. A version entitled 'L. XV' in 1849 (Roma) Notebook
(Balliol) containing mostly alternative material, including fifty lines before
line 1 (published in Mulhauser 1974: 670–1 and in McCue 1991: 80–1); 2.
1849-50 (Lamech) Notebook. MS2 is followed here. 'His most Christian
majesty' was the title traditionally bestowed on Kings of France. The MS1
title 'L. XV' suggests that C. was thinking of Louis XV. This king features in
the opening chapters of Carlyle's *French Revolution* where he is referred to as
'the Most Christian King' on a number of occasions, and the title cancelled in
MS2, '*Le Plus Chrétien Roi*', may be a direct translation from Carlyle.

'Tis true, Monseigneur, I am much to blame;
But we must all forgive; especially
Subjects their King; would I were one to do so
What could I do? and how was I to help it[?]

17–19] An allusion to the Platonic argument that existing things are imperfect copies of transcendent perfect realities.
24. Chaldean mumblings] Babylonia, also known as Chaldea during the New
Empire (625–538 BC), was the ancient centre of astronomical learning.
25. ologistic] Scientific.
26–31] There was a good deal of speculation on the origins of the universe
and the possibility of life on other planets in the early nineteenth century.

'Tis true it should not be so; true indeed,   5
I know I am not what I would I were.
I would I were, as God intended me,
A little quiet harmless acolyte
Clothed in long serge and linen shoulder-piece
Day after day   10
To pace serenely through the sacred fane,
Bearing the sacred things before the priest,
Curtsey before that altar as we pass,
And place our burden reverently on this.
There – by his side to stand and minister,   15
To swing the censer and to sound the bell,
Uphold the book, the patin change and cup –
Ah me –
And why does childhood ever change to man[?]
Oh underneath the black and sacred serge   20
Would yet uneasy uncontented blood
Swell to revolt; beneath the tippet's white
Would harassed nerves by sacred music soothed,
By solemn sights and peaceful tasks composed,
Demand more potent medicine than these   25
Or ask from pleasure more than duty gives?

————

Ah, holy father, yes.
Without the appointed
Without the sweet confessional relief,
Without the welcome all-absolving words,   30
The mystic rite, the solemn soothing forms
Our human life were miserable indeed.
And yet methinks our holy Mother Church
Deals hardly, very, with her eldest born
Her chosen, sacred, and most Christian Kings.   35
To younger pets the blind, the halt, the sick

8. *acolyte]* Somebody in minor orders, below the rank of Subdeacon.
11. *fane]* Temple.
16–17] References to Catholic ritual: the censer is the pan in which incense is burned, and the patin is the communion-plate.
22] The tippet is a white scarf worn by clerics.
27 *et seq.]* The value of auricular confession, as practised by Roman Catholics, was a subject of fierce debate in the Church of England after its partial reintroduction by E.B. Pusey in the 1840s; C., here and elsewhere, sees it as a device which impedes the moral development of the individual.
34. *her eldest born]* France is known as the eldest daughter of the Roman Catholic Church.

The outcast child, the sinners of the street,
Her doors are open and her precinct free:
The beggar finds a nest, the slave a home
Even thy altars, O my Mother Church   40
O templa quam delicta. We the while,
Poor Kings, must forth to action, as you say;
Action, that slaves us, – drives us, fretted, worn,
To pleasure which anon enslaves us too;
Action, and what is Action, O my God?   45
Alas, and can it be
In this perplexing labyrinth I see,
This waste and wild infinity of ways
Where all are like, and each each other meets,
Quits, meets, and quits a many hundred times,   50
That this path more than that conducts to Thee?
Alas, and is it true
Ought I can purpose, say, or will, or do,
My fancy choose, my changeful silly heart
Resolve, my puny petty hand enact   55
To that great glory can in ought conduce
Which from the old eternities is Thine –
Ah never, no!
If ought there be for sinful souls below
To do, 'tis rather to forbear to do;   60
If ought there be of action that contains
The sense of sweet identity with God
It is, methinks, it is inaction only.
To walk with God I know not; let me kneel.
Ah yes, the livelong day.   65
To watch before the altar where they pray:
To muse and wait,
On sacred stones lie down and meditate.
No, through the long and dark and dismal night
We will not turn and seek the city streets,   70
We will not stir, we should but lose our way,

---

41. O templa quam delicta] An adaptation of the Vulgate text of Psalm
84:1 (Psalm 83 in the Vulgate): 'Quam delicta tabernacula tua Domine
exercituum' – 'O how amiable are thy dwellings: thou Lord of hosts!'
46–51] Cp C.'s description of 'the garden of the infinite choices' cited in
Introduction, p. 9.
59–63] Carlyle also stresses Louis's inability to act, calling him '*Roi
Fainéant*, King Donothing': 'He may say ... What have I done to be so
hated? Thou hast done nothing, poor Louis! Thy fault is properly even this,
that thou didst *nothing*' (*French Revolution*, Part 1, Bk i, ch. iv).

But faithful stay
And watch the tomb where He, our Saviour, lies
Till his great day of Resurrection rise.

Yes, the commandments you remind me, yes,   75
The Sacred Word has pointed out the way,
The Priest is here for our unfailing guide,
Do this, not that, to right hand and to left,
A voice is with us ever at our ear.
Yes, holy Father, I am thankful for it.   80
Most thankful I am not, as other men
A lonely Lutheran English Heretic.
If I had so by God's despite been born,
Alas, methinks I had but passed my life
In sitting motionless beside the fire   85
Not daring to remove the once-placed chair,
Nor stir my foot for fear it should be sin.
Thank God indeed
Thank God for his infallible certain creed.
Yes, the commandments, precepts of good life,   90
And counsels of perfection, and the like,
'Thou knowest the commandments'. Yes indeed,
Yes, I suppose. But it is weary work,
For Kings I think they are not plain to read,
Ministers somehow have small faith in them.   95
Ah, holy father, would I were as you.
But you, no less, have trials as you say,
Inaction vexes you, and action tempts,
And the bad prickings of the animal heats,
As in the palace, to the cell will come.   100
Ah, well a day,
Would I were out in quiet Paraguay
Mending the Jesuits' shoes! –

———

You drive us into action as our duty.
Then action persecutes and tortures us,   105
To pleasures and to loving soft delights
We fly for solace and for peace; and gain
Vexation, Persecution also here.

82] A hyperbolical description of English Protestantism.
100. the cell] i.e. the monk's cell.
102–3] The Jesuits were famous for their missionary and educational work
in Paraguay during the eighteenth century.

We hurry from the tyranny of man
Into the tyranny yet worse of woman.   110
No satisfaction find I any more
In the old pleasant evil ways; but less,
Less, I believe of those uneasy stirs
Of discontented and rebellious will
That once with self contempt tormented me.   115
Depraved, that is, degraded am I – Sins,
Which yet I see not how I should have shunned,
Have in despite of all the means of grace
Submission perfect to the appointed creed
And absolution-plenary and prayers   120
Possessed me held, and changed – Yet after all
Somehow I think my heart within is pure.

Easter Day. Naples, 1849

1865. Three MSS: MS2 is headed 'Naples, 1849', while MS3 is in Mrs. C.'s
handwriting and bears the current title. MS2 is followed here. The title
should not be understood as implying that the poem was written in Naples on
Easter Day 1849; C. was in Naples in 1849, but not until July. The poem
draws out the consequences of some remarks in Paul's first letter to the
Corinthians: 'Now if Christ be preached that he rose from the dead, how say
some among you that there is no resurrection of the dead?/ But if there be no
resurrection of the dead, then is Christ not risen:/ And if Christ be not risen,
then *is* our preaching vain, and your faith *is* also vain. . . . If in this life only
we have hope in Christ, we are of all men most miserable' (I Corinthians
15:12–19). It represents an altogether bleaker response to the findings of the
Higher Criticism than *Epi-Strauss-ium* (see above, pp. 235–6 and notes). C.
reflects further on the implications of the thesis advanced in the poem in the
sequel, 'So while the blear-eyed pimp beside me walked' (see below), and in
Dipsychus (see above, pp. 159–62 and pp. 199–202).

Through the great sinful streets of Naples as I past,
With fiercer heat than flamed above my head
My heart was hot within me; till at last
My brain was lightened, when my tongue had said

120. absolution-plenary] Plenary absolution is the full and complete remis-
sion of sins granted by the priest after confession.
3–4] Psalm 39:3: 'My heart was hot within me, while I was musing the fire
burned: *then* spake I with my tongue.' This Psalm is cited by Keble in support of his theory of poetry as relief for the overburdened mind in his
Lectures on Poetry; see Keble 1912: i, lecture 4.

Christis not risen!   5

Christ is not risen, no,
He lies and moulders low;
   Christ is not risen.

What though the stone were rolled away, and though
   The grave found empty there! –   10
   If not there, then elsewhere;
If not where Joseph laid Him first, why then
   Where other men
Translaid Him after; in some humbler clay
   Long ere to-day   15
Corruption that sad perfect work hath done,
Which here she scarcely, lightly had begun.
   The foul engendered worm
Feeds on the flesh of the life-giving form
Of our most Holy and Anointed One.   20

   He is not risen, no,
   He lies and moulders low;
      Christ is not risen.

   Ashes to ashes, dust to dust;
As of the unjust, also of the just –   25
      Christ is not risen.

What if the women, ere the dawn was grey,
Saw one or more great angels, as they say,
Angels, or Him himself? Yet neither there, nor then,
Nor afterward, nor elsewhere, nor at all,   30
Hath He appeared to Peter or the Ten,
Nor, save in thunderous terror, to blind Saul;

5] Cp the Easter day chorus from Goethe's *Faust I* (I.i.384–8) beginning
'Christ ist erstanden!' (Christ is risen!)

12. Joseph] Joseph of Arimathea, who laid out the body of Jesus (Matthew
27:57–9).

24] From the Prayer Book Order for the Burial of the Dead: '[We] therefore
commit *his* body to the ground; earth to earth, ashes to ashes, dust to dust; in
sure and certain hope of the Resurrection to eternal life.' Psalm 39, alluded
to in the opening lines, also features in this service.

27–9] Matthew 28:1–8.

31. Peter or the Ten] The Disciples after the departure of Judas Iscariot.

32. blind Saul] Saul (St Paul) was blind for three days after his vision of the
Lord; Acts 9:9.

Save in an after–Gospel and late Creed
    He is not risen indeed,
        Christ is not risen.   35

Or what if e'en, as runs the tale, the Ten
Saw, heard, and touched, again and yet again?
What if at Emmaus' inn and by Capernaum's lake
    Came One the bread that brake,
Came One that spake as never mortal spake,   40
And with them ate and drank and stood and walked about?
    Ah! 'some' did well to 'doubt'!
Ah! the true Christ, while these things came to pass,
Nor heard, nor spake, nor walked, nor dreamt, alas!
    He was not risen, no,   45
    He lay and mouldered low,
        Christ was not risen.

As circulates in some great city crowd
A rumour changeful, vague, importunate, and loud,
From no determined centre, or of fact,   50
      Or authorship exact,
      Which no man can deny
      Nor verify;
      So spread the wondrous fame;
        He all the same   55
      Lay senseless, mouldering, low.
    He was not risen, no,
        Christ was not risen!

Ashes to ashes, dust to dust;
As of the unjust, also of the just –   60
      Yea, of that Just One too.

---

33. after–Gospel and late Creed] A reference to the late dating given to the Christian gospels and doctrinal formulae by the German Higher Critics. The phrase 'after–Gospel' prefigures Matthew Arnold's use of the term *Aberglaube* (After-belief) in his 1873 *Literature and Dogma*.

38. Emmaus] Jesus appeared to two of the disciples at Emmaus; Luke 24:13.

38. Capernaum] One of the places visited by Jesus: see Matthew 17:24; Mark 9:33.

42] Thomas Didymus ('twin') refused to believe in Jesus's resurrection until he saw the marks of the nails on his hands and feet, thus earning for himself the title of 'Doubting Thomas'; John 20:24–9. Doubting Thomas was the favourite disciple of Thomas Arnold.

48–53] Cp the account of the generation of historical fact from rumour in *Amours* II.vii.

This is the one sad Gospel that is true,
    Christis is not risen.

———————

Is He not risen, and shall we not rise?
    Oh, we unwise!   65
What did we dream, what wake we to discover?
Ye hills, fall on us, and ye mountains, cover!
    In darkness and great gloom
Come ere we thought it is our day of doom,
From the cursed world which is one tomb,   70
    Christ is not risen!

Eat, drink, and die, for we are men deceived,
Of all the creatures under heaven's wide cope
We are most hopeless who had once most hope,
We are most wretched that had most believed.   75
    Christ is not risen.

Eat, drink, and play, and think that this is bliss!
    There is no Heaven but this!
    There is no Hell; –
Save Earth, which serves the purpose doubly well,   80
    Seeing it visits still
With equallest apportionments of ill
Both good and bad alike, and brings to one same dust
    The unjust and the just
    With Christ, who is not risen.   85

Eat, drink, and die, for we are souls bereaved,
Of all the creatures under this broad sky
We are most hopeless, that had hoped most high,
And most beliefless, that had most believed.
    Ashes to ashes, dust to dust;   90
    As of the unjust, also of the just –
    Yea, of that Just One too.

67] Luke 23:28–30: 'But Jesus turning unto them said, Daughters of Jerusalem, weep not for me, but weep for yourselves, and for your children./ For, behold, the days are coming, in the which they shall say, Blessed *are* the barren, and the wombs that never bare, and the paps which never gave suck./ Then shall they begin to say to the mountains, Fall on us; and to the hills, Cover us.'
72] I Corinthians 15:32: 'If after the manner of men I have fought with beasts at Ephesus, what advantageth it me, if the dead rise not? let us eat and drink; for to morrow we die.'

It is the one sad Gospel that is true,
Christ is not risen.

Weep not beside the Tomb,   95
  Ye women, unto whom
He was great solace while ye tended Him;
  Ye who with napkin o'er His head
And folds of linen round each wounded limb
      Laid out the Sacred Dead;   100
And thou that bar'st Him in thy Wondering Womb.
Yea, Daughters of Jerusalem, depart,
Bind up as best ye may your own sad bleeding heart;
Go to your homes, your living children tend,
      Your earthly spouses love;   105
  Set your affections not on things above,
Which moth and rust corrupt, which quickliest come to
      end:
Or pray, if pray ye must, and pray, if pray ye can,
For death; since dead is He whom ye loved more than
      man,
      Who is not risen, no,   110
      But lies and moulders low,
        Who is not risen.

      Ye men of Galilee!
Why stand ye looking up to heaven, where Him ye
      ne'er may see,
Neither ascending hence, nor hither returning again?   115

98–100] John 20:7.
106–7] Matthew 6:19–20: 'Lay not up for yourselves treasures upon earth,
where moth and rust doth corrupt, and where thieves break through and
steal:/ But lay up for yourselves treasures in heaven, where neither moth nor
rust doth corrupt, and where thieves do not break through nor steal[.]'
113–15] A reference to the Ascension of Christ: 'And while they looked
stedfastly toward heaven as he went up, behold, two men stood by them in
white apparel;/ Which also said, Ye men of Galilee, why stand ye gazing up
into heaven? this same Jesus, which is taken up from you into heaven, shall
so come in like manner as ye have seen him go into heaven' (Acts 1:10–11).

Ye ignorant and idle fishermen!
Hence to your huts and boats and inland native shore,
    And catch not men, but fish;
    Whate'er things ye might wish,
Him neither here nor there ye e'er shall meet with more.   120
    Ye poor deluded youths, go home,
    Mend the old nets ye left to roam,
    Tie the split oar, patch the torn sail;
    It was indeed 'an idle tale',
    He was not risen.   125

And oh, good men of ages yet to be,
Who shall believe because ye did not see,
    Oh, be ye warned! be wise!
    No more with pleading eyes,
    And sobs of strong desire,   130
    Unto the empty vacant void aspire,
Seeking another and impossible birth
That is not of your own and only Mother Earth.
But if there is no other life for you,
Sit down and be content, since this must even do: 135
    He is not risen.

    One look, and then depart,
    Ye humble and ye holy men of heart!
And ye! ye ministers and stewards of a word
Which ye would preach, because another heard, –   140
    Ye worshippers of that ye do not know,
    Take these things hence and go;
    He is not risen.

116–23] Matthew 4:18–22: 'And Jesus, walking by the sea of Galilee, saw two brethren . . . casting a net into the sea: for they were fishers./ And he saith unto them, Follow me, and I will make you fishers of men./ And they straightway left *their* nets, and followed him./ And going on from thence, he saw other two brethren . . . mending their nets; and he called them./ And they immediately left the ship and their father, and followed him.'

124] The words of Mary Magdalene and the other women who discovered the empty tomb at first seemed 'as idle tales' to the Disciples, 'and they believed them not' (Luke 24:11).

127] Jesus's words to Doubting Thomas: 'Thomas, because thou hast seen me, thou hast believed: blessed *are* they that have not seen, and *yet* have believed' (John 20:29). See also 'Blessed are those that have not seen', below, p. 271.

142. Take these things hence] Jesus's words to the money-changers in the Temple; John 2:16.

Here on our Easter Day
We rise, we come, and lo! we find Him not;   145
      Gardener nor other on the sacred spot,
Where they have laid Him is there none to say!
No sound, nor in, nor out; no word
Of where to seek the dead or meet the living Lord;
There is no glistering of an angel's wings,   150
There is no voice of heavenly clear behest:
Let us go hence, and think upon these things
In silence, which is best.
      Is He not risen? No –
      But lies and moulders low –   155
            Christ is not risen.

Easter Day II

1865. One MS, untitled; the title, given by Mrs C., has been retained to emphasise the poem's connection with *Easter Day*. This poem illustrates C.'s tendency to update or revise conclusions expressed in earlier work (see Introduction, p. 2). C. suggests that the resurrection might still be true in some sense even if the physical return from the dead is not.

So while the blear-eyed pimp beside me walked,
And talked,
For instance, of the beautiful danseuse,
And 'Eccellenza sure must see, if he would choose'
Or of the lady in the green silk there,   5
Who passes by and bows with minx's air,
Or of the little thing not quite fifteen,
Sicilian-born who surely should be seen.
So while the blear-eyed pimp beside me walked
And talked, and I too with fit answer talked,   10
So in the sinful streets, abstracted and alone,
I with my secret self held communing of mine own.

So in the southern city spake the tongue
      Of one that somewhat overwildly sung
      But in a later hour I sat and heard   15

152. Let us go hence] John 14:31.
4. Eccellenza] His Excellency – an attempt at flattery.
13. the southern city] Naples.

Another voice that spake, another graver word.
Weep not, it bade, whatever hath been said,
Though He be dead, He is not dead.
    In the true Creed
    He is yet risen indeed,   20
        Christ is yet risen.

    Weep not beside His tomb,
    Ye women unto whom
He was great comfort and yet greater grief;
Nor ye faithful few that wont with Him to roam,   25
Seek sadly what for Him ye left, go hopeless to your home;
Nor ye despair, ye sharers yet to be of their belief;
    Though He be dead, He is not dead,
        Nor gone, though fled,
        Not lost, though vanished;   30
    Though He return not, though
    He lies and moulders low;
        In the true Creed
    He is yet risen indeed,
        Christ is yet risen.   35

Sit if ye will, sit down upon the ground,
Yet not to weep and wail, but calmly look around.
        Whate'er befell
        Earth is not hell;
Now, too, as when it first began,   40
Life yet is Life and Man is Man.
For all that breathe beneath the heaven's high cope,
    Joy with grief mixes, with despondence hope.
    Hope conquers cowardice, joy grief:
    Or at the least, faith unbelief.   45
        Though dead, not dead;
        Not gone, though fled;
        Not lost, not vanished.
    In the great Gospel and true Creed,
    He is yet risen indeed;   50
        Christ is yet risen.

36–7] Cp Psalm 137:1: 'By the rivers of Babylon, there we sat down, yea, we wept, when we remembered Zion.'
44–5] C. finds a minimum of faith to rest on; cp the *Seven Sonnets* below, pp. 268–7 and notes.

The Latest Decalogue

1.*1862*. 2.*1974*. MS1. British Museum; MS2. Norton bMS. 1. has been followed universally hitherto, but 2. is certainly later; I have, therefore decided to print the two texts in parallel with one another. The poem refers to the Ten Commandments (Exodus 20:2–17); Walter Houghton notes that C. had pointed out the modern age's self-serving gloss on the Commandments in a letter to *The Balance* of February 1846: 'The very Decalogue itself – the definitive "Thou shalt not do murder," and "Thou shalt not steal," may pass into a very dubious "Thou shalt not do murder, *without great provocation*," and "Thou shalt not steal, *except now and then*" ' (Houghton 1963: 72n).

1. Thou shalt have one God only; who
    Would be at the expense of two?
    No graven images may be
    Worshipped, except the currency:
    Swear not at all; for for thy curse   5
    Thine enemy is none the worse:
    At Church on Sunday to attend
    Will serve to keep the world thy friend:
    Honour thy parents; that is, all
    From whom advancement may befall: 10
    Thou shalt not kill; but needst not strive
    Officiously to keep alive:
    Do not adultery commit;
    Advantage rarely comes of it:
    Thou shalt not steal; an empty feat,   15
    When it's so lucrative to cheat:
    Bear not false witness; let the lie
    Have time on its own wings to fly:
    Thou shalt not covet; but tradition
    Approves all forms of competition.   20

    The sum of all is, thou shalt love,
    If any body, God above:
    At any rate shall never labour
    More than thyself to love thy neighbour.

2. Thou shalt have one God only; who
    Would tax himself to worship two?
    God's image nowhere shalt thou see,
    Save haply in the currency.

1. 21–4] Cp Jesus's answer to the question 'which *is* the greatest commandment in the law?': 'Thou shalt love the Lord thy God with all thy heart, and with all thy soul, and with all thy mind./ This is the first and great commandment./ And the second *is* like unto it, Thou shalt love thy neighbour as thyself.'

Swear not at all: since for thy curse   5
Thine enemy is not the worse.
At Church on Sunday to attend
Will help to keep the world thy friend.
Honour thy parents: that is, all
From whom promotion may befall.   10
Thou shalt not kill: but needst not strive
Officiously to keep alive.
Adultery it is not fit,
Or safe, for women, to commit.
Thou shalt not steal: an empty feat,   15
When it's so lucrative to cheat.
False witness not to bear be strict;
And cautious, ere you contradict.
Thou shalt not covet; but tradition
Sanctions the keenest competition.   20

The Struggle

The Crayon, Vol. 2, No. 5 (August 1855). Alt. MS titles 'In profundis' ('in the depths') and 'Dum Spiro' ('While I breathe') – the latter from *Dum spiro, spero* (While I breathe, I hope). The published text is followed. This poem was begun during the siege of Rome; cp the reflections on the value of struggle and sacrifice in *Amours* II.vi and V.vi, and the following three poems.

Say not the struggle naught availeth,
    The labour and the wounds are vain,
The enemy faints not nor faileth,
    And as things have been, things remain.

If hopes were dupes, fears may be liars;   5
    It may be, in yon smoke concealed,
Your comrades chase e'en now the fliers –
    And, but for you, possess the field.

For while the tired waves vainly breaking
    Seem here no painful inch to gain,   10

2. *13–14*] Opposite these lines C. has written 'nb observe the commas'.
5–8] Cp the image of the night-battle from the end of *The Bothie*: 'If there is battle, 'tis battle by night: I stand in the darkness,/ Here in the melee of men, Ionian and Dorian on both sides,/ Signal and password known; which is friend and which is foeman?' (IX.51–3). The source of this figure is the battle of Epipolae in Thucydides, *The Peloponnesian War*, Bk VII, ch. iv; cp Matthew Arnold's *Dover Beach* 35–7.

Far back through creeks and inlets making,
        Comes silent, flooding-in, the main.

And not by eastern windows only,
        When daylight comes, comes in the light,
In front the sun climbs slow, how slowly,   15
        But westward, look! the land is bright.

1869: *Title* Noli Aemulari ('Do not strive'). One MS. I have followed the MS
but incorporated conjectural readings from *1869* at ll. 10 and 14. The poem is
a response to *The Struggle*; cp Matthew Arnold's letter to Clough of 6
September 1853: 'As to conformity I only recommend it in so far as it frees us
from the unnatural and unhealthy attitude of contradiction and opposition –
the *Qual der Negation* as Goethe calls it. Only positive convictions and feelings are worth anything' (Lowry 1932: 142).

In controversial foul impureness
        The peace that is thy light to thee
Quench not: in faith and inner sureness
        Possess thy soul and let it be.

No violence – perverse, persistent –   5
        What cannot be can bring to be,
No zeal what is make more existent,
        And strife but blinds the eyes that see.

What though in blood their souls embruing,
        The [great,] the good, and wise they curse,   10
Still sinning, what they know not doing;
        Stand still, forbear, nor make it worse.

By cursing, by denunciation,
        [The coming fate] they cannot stay;
Nor thou, by fiery indignation,   15
        Though just, accelerate the day.

While circling, chasing, unescaping,
        The waters here these eddies tease,
Unconscious, far its free course shaping,
        The great stream silent seeks the seas.   20

While here, to nooks and shallows drifted,
        Leaf, stick, and foam dispute the shore,

9. embruing] soaking or drenching.
10. great] Supplied by *1869* to fill a gap in the MS.
11. what they know not doing] Cp Jesus's words on the cross: 'Father, forgive
them; for they know not what they do' (Luke 23:34).
14. The coming fate] Supplied in place of 'By [   ]' by *1869*.

The boatman there his sail has lifted
Or plies his unimpeded oar.

Peschiera

Putnam's Magazine, Vol. 3 (May 1854). Peschiera was part of the 'quadri-
lateral' of fortified towns to which the Austrians retreated after having been
driven out of Milan and Venice by popular uprisings in March 1848. It was
captured by the Piedmontese army in the ensuing war, but lost again soon
afterwards. C.'s poem, a characteristic meditation on the value of heroic self-
sacrifice, also refers to the 'ten days of Brescia' in *1849* (see notes to ll. 13–16
below).

What voice did on my spirit fall,
Peschiera, when thy bridge I crost?
' 'Tis better to have fought and lost
Than never to have fought at all.'

The Tricolor a trampled rag,   5
Lies, dirt and dust; the lines I track,
By sentry-boxes yellow-black,
Lead up to no Italian flag.

I see the Croat soldier stand
Upon the grass of your redoubts;   10
The Eagle with his black wing flouts
The breadth and beauty of your land.

Yet not in vain, although in vain
O! men of Brescia, on the day

3–4] Cp 1850, *In Memoriam* XXVII.15–16: ' 'Tis better to have loved and
lost/ Than never to have loved at all.' The poem also makes use of *In
Memoriam*'s stanza form.
5. Tricolor] The Italian flag of red, white and green.
7. yellow-black] The colours of the Austrian Empire.
9. Croat] Croatia was at this time under Austrian control, and furnished the
Empire with a large number of its soldiers; the term 'Croat' was virtually
synonymous with 'mercenary' in the nineteenth century (see *Dipsychus*
1.6.20 and note).
11. The Eagle] The symbol of the Hapsburg Emperors.
13–16] The success of the Austrians in recapturing Tuscany, Modena and
Parma, and the impending defeat of Sicily by the Neapolitans, prompted a
brave but doomed uprising in March 1849. A small number of men from the
surrounding mountains encircled the garrison town of Brescia, near
Peschiera, and roused its inhabitants to revolt. The populace held out for ten
days, from 23 March until 2 April 1849, before finally capitulating.

Of loss past hope, I heard you say   15
Your welcome to the noble pain.

You said, 'Since so it is, good-bye
Sweet life, high hope; but whatsoe'er
May be or must, no tongue shall dare
To tell, "The Lombard feared to die".'   20

You said, (there shall be answer fit,)
'And if our children must obey
They must, but thinking on this day
'Twill less debase them to submit.'

You said (O! not in vain you said,)   25
'Haste, brothers, haste while yet we may;
The hours ebb fast of this one day
When blood may yet be nobly shed.'

Ah! not for idle hatred, not
For honour, fame, nor self-applause,   30
But for the glory of your cause,
You did what will not be forgot.

And though the stranger stand, 'tis true
By force and fortune's right he stands;
By fortune which is in God's hands,   35
And strength which yet shall spring in you.

This voice did on my spirit fall,
Peschiera, when thy bridge I crost,
' 'Tis better to have fought and lost
Than never to have fought at all.'   40

Alteram Partem

1862. Three MSS: 1. 1850 (Venice) Notebook; 2. 1849–50 (Lamech)
Notebook; 3. 1852 (Smith) Notebook. MS3 is followed here. The title means
'The other side [of the question]'.

Or shall I say, Vain word, false thought
Since Prudence hath her martyrs too

20. The Lombard] Brescia is part of the region of Lombardia.
21–4] The 'ten days of Brescia' became part of the mythology of the Italian
war of liberation.
33. stranger] Emended from the misprint 'strangers' in Putnam's.
33–4] At the time of the poem's publication the Austrians were still in control of their territories in northern Italy.
1–8] With the argument of ll. 1–8, cp *Amours* II.ii.

And Wisdom dictates not to do
Till doing shall be not for naught[?]

[Ah blood is blood and life is life:]   5
Will Nature then when brave ones fall
Remake her work, or songs recall
Death's victim slain in useless strife?

– That rivers flow into the sea
Is loss and waste the foolish say,   10
Nor know that back they find their way
Unseen to where they wont to be

Showers fall upon the hills, springs flow,
The river runneth still at hand,
Brave men are born into the land   15
And whence the foolish do not know.

No! no vain voice did on me fall
Peschiera! when thy bridge I crost
'*Tis* better to have fought and lost
Than never to have fought at all[.]   20

1862. Two MSS: 1. 1850 (Venice) Notebook; 2. Harvard bMS Eng. 1036 (2).
MS2 is followed.

It fortifies my soul to know
That though I perish, Truth is so:
That howsoe'er I stray and range,
Whate'er I do, Thou dost not change:
I steadier step, when I recall   5
That if I slip, Thou dost not fall.

In Stratis Viarum

Adapted from Virgil, *Aeneid* I.421–2: 'miratur molem Aeneas, magalia quon-
dam,/ miratur portas strepitumque et *strata viarum*' – 'Aeneas was amazed by
the size of [Rome] where recently there had been nothing but shepherds'
huts, amazed too by the gates, *the paved streets* and all the stir.' This title,
grouping together four poems written at different times, was suggested by C.
in a letter of April 1859 to C.E. Norton (Harvard bMS Eng 1036 (2)).

5. [Ah blood is blood and life is life:]] This line is taken from MS2; MS3 has
a gap. *1862* has 'Not ours to give or lose is life', which is not in any of the
extant MSS; Mulhauser (1974) adopts it on the grounds that it might be
based on a lost MS.

I

1863. Three MSS: 1. 1852 (Smith) Notebook entitled 'In the Great Metropolis'; 2 and 3 undated. MS1 is followed. With the poem's refrain cp C.'s remarks in a letter to Burbidge of June 1844: 'I do believe . . . that capital tyrannises over labour . . . [and that in] some way or other the problem now solved by universal competition or the devil take the hindmost may receive a more satisfactory solution' (*Corr.* i, 126–7).

Each for himself is still the rule,
We learn it when we go to school,
 The devil take the hindmost, O.

And when the schoolboys grow to men
In life they learn it o'er again   5
 The devil take the hindmost, O.

For in the church, and at the bar,
On change, at court, where'er they are,
 The devil takes the hindmost, O.

Husband for husband wife for wife   10
Are careful that in married life
 The devil take the hindmost, O.

From youth to age whate'er the game
The unvarying practice is the same,
 The devil take the hindmost, O.   15

And after death, we do not know
But scarce can doubt where'er we go
 The devil takes the hindmost, O.

Tol rol di rol, tol rol di ro,
The devil take the hindmost O!   20

II

1865 (as part of *Dipsychus and The Spirit*). Three MSS: 1. *Dipsychus* MS1 (canc.); 2. 1852 (Smith) Notebook; 3. *Dipsychus* MS2. MS3 is followed. The poem is dated '1851' in MS2.

Our gaieties, our luxuries
 Our pleasures and our glee

8. change] The Stock Exchange.

Mere insolence and wantonries
    Alas, they feel to me.

How shall I laugh and sing and dance[?]   5
    My very heart recoils
While here to give my mirth a chance
    A hungry brother toils.

The joy that does not spring from joy
    Which I in others see   10
How can I venture to employ
    Or find it joy for me?

III

Boston *1862*. One MS: Harvard bMS Eng 1036 (2). This poem was described by C. in a letter to Norton as 'in Heyne's manner'. The German poet Heinrich Heine was in vogue in England in the 1850s; his poetry is often sardonic and anti-religious in tone. The poem draws on the words of Jesus to Doubting Thomas in John 20:29; see above, *Easter Day* 127 and note.

Blessed are those, who have not seen,
    And who have yet believed,
The witness, here that has not been,
    From heaven they have received.

Blessed are those who have not known   5
    The things that stand before them,
And for a vision of their own
    Can piously ignore them.

So let me think, whate'er befall,
    That in the city duly   10
Some men there are who love at all,
    Some women who love truly;

And that upon two million odd
    Transgressors in sad plenty
Mercy will of a gracious God   15
    Be shown – because of twenty.

15–16] A reference to God's promise to Abraham that he would not destroy Sodom if twenty or even ten righteous people could be found there; see Genesis 18:31–2.

IV

1862: Title 'In a London Square'. One MS; Harvard bMS Eng 1036 (2).

Put forth thy leaf, thou lofty plane,
    East wind and frost are safely gone,
With zephyrs mild and balmy rain
    The summer comes serenely on,
Earth, air, and sun and skies combine   5
    To promise all that's kind and fair. –
But thou, O human heart of mine,
    Be still, contain thyself and bear.

December days were brief and chill,
    The winds of March were wild and drear,   10
And nearing, and receding still
    Spring never would, we thought, be here;
The leaves that burst, the suns that shine
    Had, not the less, their certain date –
But thou, O human heart of mine,   15
    Be still, refrain thyself and wait.

ὕμνος ἄϋμνος

1862. Two MSS: 1. 1851 (C) Notebook; 2. 1852 (Smith) Notebook. MS2 is
followed. The poem is dated 'London 1851'. The importance of this poem to
C. seems to have varied; in a letter to Blanche of May 1853 from the United
States he wrote 'I was just looking into a book which I brought with me at
what is called there *ὕμνος ἄϋμνος* – have you got it in yours – it wants a good
deal of mending as it stands chez moi, but it is on the whole in sense very satisfactory to me still' (*Corr.* ii, 427). By March 1859, however, he appears to
have forgotten it; see letter to C.E. Norton in *Corr.* ii, 565. It has attracted a
good deal of critical comment as the most striking example of C.'s habitual
mistrust of the human image-making faculty; see, e.g., Thorpe 1972: 147,
165; Kenny 1988: 66–8. Cp C.'s observation in his 'Review of Mr. Newman's
"The Soul" ': '[Is] it safe to ascribe an objective actual character to any picture of our imagination even in highest moments of beatitude?' (Trawick
1964: 282).

    O thou whose image in the shrine
    Of human spirits dwells divine
    Which from that precinct once conveyed
    To be to outer day displayed

3. zephyrs] West winds.
Title. ὕμνος ἄϋμνος] 'Hymnos ahymnos' ['A hymn, yet not a hymn'].

Doth vanish, part, and leave behind   5
Mere blank and void of empty mind
Which wilful fancy seeks in vain
With casual shapes to fill again –

O thou that in our bosoms' shrine
Dost dwell because unknown divine   10
I thought to speak, I thought to say
'The light is here,' 'behold the way'
'The voice was thus' and 'thus the word,[']
And 'thus I saw' and 'that I heard,'
But from the lips but half essayed   15
The imperfect utterance fell unmade.

O thou in that mysterious shrine
Enthroned, as we must say, divine.
I will not frame one thought of what
Thou mayest either be or not.   20
I will not prate of 'thus' and 'so'
And be profane with 'yes' and 'no,'
Enough that in our soul and heart
Thou whatsoe'er thou may'st be art.

Unseen, secure in that high shrine   25
Acknowledged present and divine
I will not ask some upper air,
Some future day, to place thee there.
Nor say nor yet deny, Such men
Or women saw thee thus and then;   30
Thy name was such, and there or here
To him or her thou didst appear.

Do only thou in that dim shrine
Unknown or known remain divine.
There or if not, at least in eyes   35
That scan the fact that round them lies.
– The hand to sway, the judgment guide
In sight and sense thyself divide
Be thou but there; in soul and heart,
I will not ask to feel thou art[.]   40

12–14] Cp Luke 17:20–1: 'The kingdom of God cometh not with observation:/ Neither shall they say, Lo here! or, lo there! for, behold, the kingdom
of God is within you.' Cp also *In Memoriam* VI, in which the poet describes
his anticipated response to Hallam's return: 'And ever met him on the way/
With wishes, thinking "here to-day,"/ Or "here to-morrow will he come".'

Putnam's Magazine, Vol. 2 (July 1853) (as part of the first *Letter of Parepidemus*). Reprinted as a separate poem with the title 'Perche Pensa? Pensando s'invecchia' in *1869.* The title means 'Why are you thinking? Thinking makes you old', and is taken from an anecdote in Goethe's *Italian Journey* (Goethe 1987: 118). The poem's sentiment is characteristically Cloughian; cp *Dipsychus and The Spirit* 4.31–4 and C.'s 'Notes on the Religious Tradition': 'I would scarcely have any man dare to say that he has found [the religious tradition], till that moment when death removes his power of telling it' (*PR* 418). The MS of the poem has two more stanzas which were not published – see Mulhauser 1974: 731.

> To spend uncounted years of pain
> Again, again, and yet again,
> In working out in heart and brain
>   The problem of our being here;
> To gather facts from far and near;   5
> Upon the mind to hold them clear,
> And, knowing more may yet appear,
> Unto one's latest breath to fear
> The premature result to draw, –
> Is this the object, end, and law   10
> And purpose of our being here?

Seven Sonnets

1869: Title 'Seven Sonnets on the Thought of Death'. One MS in 1851 (B) Notebook. A number of conjectural readings have been adopted due to the numerous alterations and omissions in the MS.

I

> That children in their loveliness should die
> Before the dawning beauty, which we know
> Cannot remain, has yet begun to go;
> That when a certain period has passed by
> People of genius and of faculty   5
> Leaving behind them some result to show
> Having performed some function should forgo
> A task which younger hands can better ply
> Appears entirely natural. But that one
> Whose perfectness did not at all consist   10

In things towards [framing] which time could have done
Anything – whose sole office was to exist,
Should suddenly dissolve and cease to be
Calls up the hardest questions.

II

That there are better things within the womb
Of Nature than to our unworthy view
She grants for a possession may be true
The cycle of the birthplace and the tomb
Fulfils at least the order and the doom   5
Of her that has not ordinance to do
More than to withdraw and to renew
To show one moment and the next resume.
The law that we return from whence we came
May for the flowers, beasts, and most men remain   10
If for ourselves we [question] not nor complain.
But for a being that demands the name
We highest deem, a Person and a Soul,
It troubles us if this should be the whole[.]

III

To see the rich autumnal tints depart
And view the fading of the roseate glow
That veils some Alpine altitude of snow
To hear some mighty masterpiece of art
Lost or destroyed, may to the adult heart   5
Impatient of the transitory show
Of lovelinesses that but come and go
A positive strange eager thankfulness impart.
When human pure perfections disappear
Not at the first but at some later day   10
The buoyancy of such reaction may
With strong assurance conquer blank dismay.

I. 11. framing] possibly 'forming'.
I. 14] Clearly 'perplexity' is needed for the rhyme, but C. did not find a way
of incorporating it into the line.
II. 3. grants for a possession] alt. 'condescends to publish'.
III. 12] The last two lines of the sonnet are indecipherable due to numerous
cancellations and revisions; McCue (1991) suggests 'Make Hope triumphant
over Doubt and fear/ To prove that spiritual victory clear'.

IV

If it is thou whose casual hand withdraws
What it at first as casually did make
Say what amount of ages it will take
With tardy rare concurrences of laws,
And subtle multiplicities of cause   5
The thing they once had made us to remake[?]
May hopes dead–slumbering dare to reawake
E'en after utmost interval of pause[?]
What revolutions must have passed, before
The great celestial cycles shall restore   10
The starry [sign] whose present hour is gone;
What worse than dubious chances interpose,
With cloud and sunny gleam to recompose
The skiey picture we had gazed upon?

V

But if as (not by what the soul desired
Swayed in the judgment) wisest men have thought
And furnishing the evidence it sought
Man's heart hath ever fervently required,
And story, for that reason deemed inspired   5
To every clime in every age hath taught
If in this human complex there be aught
Not lost in death as not in birth acquired
O then though cold the lips that did convey
Rich freights of meaning, dead each living sphere   10
Where thought abode and fancy loved to play
Thou, yet we think, somewhere somehow still art
And satisfied with that the patient heart
The where and how doth not desire to hear.

IV. 11. sign] conj.
V. 5–6] A reference to religious traditions concerning the immortality of the
soul.

VI

But whether in the uncoloured light of truth
This inward strong assurance be indeed
More than the self willed arbitrary creed
Manhood's inheritor to the dream of youth
Whether to shut out fact because forsooth 5
To live were insupportable, unfreed,
[   ]
Be not or be the service of untruth:
Whether this vital confidence be more
Than his, who upon death's immediate brink 10
Knowing, perforce determines to ignore
Or than the bird's, that with the hunter near
Burying her eyesight can forget her fear
Who about this shall tell us what to think?

VII

Shall I decide it by a random shot[?]
Our happy hopes, so happy and so good
Are not mere idle motions of the blood
And when they seem most baseless, most are not.
A seed there must have been [up]on the spot 5
Where the flowers grow[,] without it ne'er they could[.]
The confidence of growth least understood
Of some deep intuition was begot.
What if despair and hope alike be true[?]
The heart, 'tis manifest, is free to do 10
Whichever Nature and itself suggest;
And always 'tis a fact that we are here;
And with being here, doth palsy-giving fear
Whoe'er can ask or hope accord the best?

VI. 1–3] Cp *Epi-Strauss-ium*. The question of whether or not human religious beliefs are more than a 'self-willed arbitrary creed' is central to C.'s thought.
VI. 7] This line is missing in the MS.
VII. 5–8] A crucial use of the trope of growth; see Introduction, p. 16.

Last Words. Napoleon and Wellington

Fraser's Magazine, Vol. 47, No. 278 (February 1853). The poem is signed τηλόθεν ('from afar') – C. was in the United States at the time. C. wrote to Blanche Smith in February 1853: 'Look in the "Fraser" of this month for some verses about Napoleon and the Duke of Wellington; Napoleon's dying words "Tête d'Armée" [Head of the Army]. The Duke didn't say anything, did he? I went on that supposition' (*PR* 202). The following month he added: 'I don't know whether to like my verses in Fraser or to think them bad. I see that they are too hastily composed. At least the first piece, but I thought if they went at all, they must go at once' – Corr. ii, 382.

NAPOLEON

Is it this, then, O world-warrior,
    That, exulting, through the folds
Of the dark and cloudy barrier
    Thine enfranchised eye beholds?
Is, when blessed hands relieve thee   5
    From the gross and mortal clay,
This the heaven that should receive thee?
        [']Tête d'armée.'

Now the final link is breaking,
    Of the fierce, corroding chain,   10
And the ships, their watch forsaking,
    Bid the seas no more detain.
Whither is it, freed and risen,
    The pure spirit seeks away,
Quits for what the weary prison?   15
        'Tête d'armée.'

Doubtless – angels, hovering o'er thee
    In thine exile's sad abode,
Marshalled even now before thee,
    Move upon that chosen road!   20
Thither they, ere friends have laid thee
    Where sad willows o'er thee play,
Shall already have conveyed thee!
        'Tête d'armée.'

Shall great captains, foiled and broken,   25
    Hear from thee on each great day,
At the crisis, a word spoken –

Word that battles still obey –
'Cuirassiers here, here those cannon;
  Quick, those squadrons, up – away!   30
To the charge, on – as one man, on!'
    'Tête d'armée.'

(Yes, too true, alas! while, stated
  Of the wars so slow to cease,
Nations, once that scorned and hated,   35
  Would to Wisdom turn, and Peace;
Thy dire impulse still obeying,
  Fevered youths, as in the old day,
In their hearts still find thee saying,
    'Tête d'armée.')   40

Oh, poor soul! – Or do I view thee,
  From earth's battle-fields withheld,
In a dream, assembling to thee
  Troops that quell not, nor are quelled,
Breaking airy lines, defeating   45
  Limbo-kings, and, as to-day,
Idly to all time repeating
    'Tête d'armée'?

WELLINGTON

And what the words, that with his failing breath
  Did England hear her aged soldier say? 50
I know not. Yielding tranquilly to death,
  With no proud speech, no boast, he passed away.

Not stirring words, nor gallant deeds alone,
  Plain patient work fulfilled that length of life;
Duty, not glory – Service, not a throne,   55
  Inspired his effort, set for him the strife.

Therefore just Fortune, with one hasty blow,
  Spurning her minion, Glory's, Victory's lord,

29. Cuirassiers] Cavalrymen; *Fraser's* originally printed 'cuirassier' by mistake, as C. noted in his letter to Blanche.
33–40] Perhaps a reference to the revival of French militarism under Napoleon III; there was a baseless invasion scare in England in the early 1850s. The edition of *Fraser's* in which the poem appears includes an article on this very subject.

Gave all to him that was content to know
    In service done its own supreme reward.   60

The words he said, if haply words there were,
    When full of years and works he passed away,
Most naturally might, methinks, refer
    To some poor humble business of to-day.

'That humble simple duty of the day   65
    Perform,' he bids; 'ask not if small or great:
Serve in thy post; be faithful, and obey;
    Who serves her truly, sometimes saves the State.'

68] Cp Milton's Sonnet XX on his blindness: 'They also serve who only stand and waite.'

Works Cited in the Text

Arnold 1842: Thomas Arnold, D.D., *Introductory Lectures on Modern History*, Oxford: John Henry Parker, 1842.

Bagehot 1895: Walter Bagehot, *Literary Studies* (ed. R.H. Hutton), 3 vols, Longman, Green & Co., 1895.

Ball 1976: Patricia Ball, *The Heart's Events: The Victorian Poetry of Relationships*, Athlone Press, 1976.

Bertram 1966: James Bertram (ed.), *New Zealand Letters of Thomas Arnold the Younger, 1847–51*, OUP, 1966.

Blake 1978: Robert Blake, *Disraeli*, Methuen, 1966; rpt 1978.

Carlyle 1899: *The Centenary Edition of the Works of Thomas Carlyle*, 30 vols, Chapman & Hall, 1899.

Chorley 1962: Katharine Chorley, *Arthur Hugh Clough: The Uncommitted Mind*, OUP, 1962.

Clegg 1981: Jeanne Clegg, *Ruskin and Venice*, Junction Books, 1981.

Clough 1925: A.H. Clough, *Plutarch's Lives*, 3 vols, Dent, 1925.

Coleridge 1835: S.T. Coleridge, *Table Talk*, 2 vols, John Murray, 1835.

Coleridge 1949: S.T. Coleridge, *Philosophical Lectures* (ed. K. Coburn), Routledge & Kegan Paul, 1949.

Coleridge 1969: S.T. Coleridge and Robert Southey, *Omniana; or Horae Otiosiores* (ed. Robert Gittings), Fontwell, Sussex: Centaur Press, 1969.

De Wette 1843: F.L. De Wette, *A Critical Introduction to the Canonical Scriptures of the Old Testament* (trans. Theodore Parker), Boston: Little & Brown, 1843.

Emerson 1984: *Essays* (ed. Sherman Paul), Dent: Dutton, 1906; rpt 1984.

Farini 1854: Luigi Carlo Farini, *The Roman State from 1815 to 1850* (trans. W.E. Gladstone), 4 vols, London: John Murray, 1851–4.

Frei 1974: Hans W. Frei, *The Eclipse of Biblical Narrative*, New Haven and London: Yale UP, 1974.

Froude 1838: *Remains of the Late Revd. Richard Hurrell Froude*, 2 vols, J.G. & F. Rivington, 1838.

Froude 1849: J.A. Froude, *The Nemesis of Faith*, John Chapman, 1849.

Froude 1899: J.A. Froude, *Short Studies on Great Subjects*, 4 vols, Longman, Green & Co, 1899.

Goethe 1987: J.W. von Goethe, *Italian Journey* (trans. Auden and Mayer), Harmondsworth, Middx: Penguin, 1987.

Greenberger 1970: E.B. Greenberger, *Arthur Hugh Clough: The Growth of a Poet's Mind*, Cambridge, Mass.: Harvard UP, 1970.

Harris 1970: Wendell V. Harris, *Arthur Hugh Clough*, New York: Twayne Publishers Inc., 1970.

Houghton 1963: Walter Houghton, *The Poetry of Clough*, Cambridge, Mass. and London: Harvard UP, 1963.

Keble 1912: John Keble, *Lectures on Poetry* (trans. (from Latin) by E.K. Francis), 2 vols, OUP, 1912.

Kenny 1988: Anthony Kenny, *God and Two Poets*, Sidgwick & Jackson, 1988.

Kenny 1990: Anthony Kenny, *The Oxford Diaries of Arthur Hugh Clough*, OUP, 1990.

Kierkegaard 1964: *The Concept of Dread* (trans. W. Lowrie), Princeton NJ: Princeton UP, 1964.

Lowry 1932: H.F. Lowry (ed.), *The Letters of Matthew Arnold to Arthur Hugh Clough*, OUP, 1932.

Mazzini n.d.: *Scritti di Giuseppe Mazzini*, Bologna: Nicola Zanichelli, undated.

McCue 1991: Jim McCue (ed.), *Clough: Selected Poems*, Harmondsworth, Middx: Penguin, 1991.

Milnes 1927: R.M. Milnes (ed.), *The Life and Letters of John Keats*, Dent: Dutton, 1927.

Mulhauser 1974: Frederick Mulhauser (ed.), *The Poems of Arthur Hugh Clough*, 2nd edn, OUP, 1974. (Unless otherwise stated, all quotations from poems by Clough not included in the present volume are taken from this edition.)

Murray 1843: *Handbook for Travellers in Central Italy, including the Papal States, Rome, and the Cities of Etruria*, John Murray, 1843.

Murray 1846: *A Handbook for Travellers in Switzerland, and the Alps of Savoy and Piedmont*, 3rd edn, John Murray, 1846.

Murray 1847: *Handbook for Travellers in Northern Italy*, 3rd edn, John Murray, 1847.

Newman 1868: J.H. Newman, *Parochial and Plain Sermons*, Rivingtons, 1868.

Newman 1986: J.H. Newman, *Loss and Gain* (ed. Alan G. Hill), OUP, 1986.

Partington 1962: J.R. Partington, *A History of Chemistry*, 4 vols, Macmillan, 1964.

Pattison 1885: Mark Pattison, *Memoirs*, 1885; rpt (as *Memoirs of an Oxford Don*) Cassell, 1988.

Poirier 1990: Richard Poirier (ed.), *The Oxford Authors: Ralph Waldo Emerson*, OUP, 1990.

Pugin 1841: A.W.N. Pugin, *Contrasts: or, a Parallel between the Noble Edifices of the Middle Ages, and Corresponding Buildings of the Present Day; Shewing the Present Decay of Taste*, 2nd edn, Charles Dolman, 1841.

Rogerson 1984: John Rogerson, *Old Testament Criticism in the Nineteenth Century*, SPCK, 1984.

Ruskin 1899: John Ruskin, *Praeterita*, 3 vols, George Allen, 1899.

Ruskin 1903: *The Works of John Ruskin* (eds E.T. Cook and Alexander Wedderburn), George Allen, 1903.

Ruskin 1975: John Ruskin, *The Nature of Gothic*, Portland Oregon: Charles Lehman, 1975.

Schopenhauer 1986: Arthur Schopenhauer, *Essays and Aphorisms* (trans. R.J. Hollingdale), Harmondsworth, Middx: Penguin, 1986.

Scott 1974: Patrick Scott (ed.), *Amours de Voyage*, St Lucia: Univ. of Queensland Press, 1974.

Scott 1981: Patrick Scott, *The Editorial Problem in Clough's* Adam and Eve; Browning Institute Studies 9 (1981), 79–103.

Shaw 1987: W. David Shaw, *The Lucid Veil: Poetic Truth in the Victorian Age*, Athlone Press, 1987.

Spada 1868: Giuseppe Spada, *Storia della Rivoluzione di Roma*, 3 vols, Firenze, 1868.

Stanmore 1906: Lord Stanmore, *Sidney Herbert Lord Herbert of Lea: A Memoir*, 2 vols, John Murray, 1906.

Strachey 1918: Lytton Strachey, *Eminent Victorians*, Chatto & Windus, 1918.

Thackeray 1986: W.M. Thackeray, *The History of Pendennis*, Harmondsworth, Middx: Penguin, 1986.

Thorpe 1972: Michael Thorpe (ed.), *Clough: the Critical Heritage*, New York: Barnes and Noble, 1972.

Trawick 1964: Buckner B. Trawick (ed.), *Selected Prose Works of Arthur Hugh Clough*, Alabama: Univ. of Alabama Press, 1964.

Trevelyan 1919: G.M. Trevelyan, *Garibaldi's Defence of the Roman Republic*, Longman, Green & Co., 1919.

Trevelyan 1923: G.M. Trevelyan, *Manin and the Venetian Revolution of 1848*, Longman, Green & Co., 1923.

Varriano 1991: John Varriano, *Rome: A Literary Companion*, John Murray, 1991.

Veyriras 1964: Paul Veyriras, *Arthur Hugh Clough*, Paris: Didier, 1964.

Williams 1840: Isaac Williams, *Tract 80: On Reserve in Communicating Religious Knowledge* in *Tracts for the Times*. J.G. & F. Rivington, 1840.

Woodward 1957: Frances Woodward, *The Doctor's Disciples*, OUP, 1957.

Sources of poetry cited

Byron: Jerome J. McGann (ed.), *The Oxford Authors: Byron*, OUP, 1986, or from Jerome J. McGann (ed.), *Byron: The Complete Poetical Works*, OUP, 1986.

Donne: Herbert J.C. Grierson (ed.), *Donne: Poetical Works*, OUP 1971; rpt 1979.

Gray: Roger Lonsdale (ed.), *Gray and Collins: Poetical Works*, OUP, 1977.

Marlowe: J.B. Steane (ed.), *Christopher Marlowe: The Complete Plays*, Harmondsworth, Middx: Penguin, 1969; rpt 1982.

Matthew Arnold: Miriam Allott (ed.), *Arnold: The Complete Poems*, 2nd edn, London and New York: Longman, 1979.

Milton: Alastair Fowler (ed.), *Paradise Lost*, Longman, 1968; rpt 1971; other poems from Gordon Campbell (ed.), *John Milton: The Complete Poems*, London and New York: Dent, Dutton, 1980.

Shakespeare: the Arden edition.

Tennyson: T. Herbert Warren (ed.), *Tennyson: Poems and Plays*, OUP 1971; rpt 1986.

Wordsworth: John O. Hayden (ed.), *Poems*, 2 vols, Harmondsworth, Middx: Penguin, 1977; rpt 1982.

Translations from classical sources

Aristotle, *Ethics* (trans. J.A.K. Thomson), Harmondsworth, Middx: Penguin, 1955; rpt 1986.

Horace, *The Complete Odes and Epodes* (trans. W.G. Shepherd), Harmondsworth, Middx: Penguin, 1983.

Horace, *Satires and Epistles* (trans. Niall Rudd), Harmondsworth, Middx: Penguin, 1979.

Suetonius, *Lives of the Caesars* (trans. J.C. Rolfe), Cambridge, Mass. and London: Heinemann, 1935.

Thucydides, *The Peloponnesian War* (trans. Rex Warner), Harmondsworth, Middx: Penguin, 1954; rpt 1961.

Virgil, *The Aeneid* (trans. David West), Harmondsworth, Middx: Penguin, 1990.

All quotations from the Bible (unless otherwise stated) are from the Authorised Version.

Select Bibliography

1. Prose Writings

A selection of C.'s prose writings can be found in Mrs Clough (ed.), *Poems and Prose Remains of Arthur Hugh Clough*, (Macmillan, 1869), the prose portion of which was reprinted as *Prose Remains of Arthur Hugh Clough* in 1888. This has been supplemented by Buckner B. Trawick (ed.), *Selected Prose Works of Arthur Hugh Clough* (Alabama: Univ. of Alabama Press, 1964), which contains fuller versions of some of the articles in *Prose Remains* as well as a number of unpublished items such as undergraduate essays and lectures. Greenberger (1974) contains some interesting additional material. Also of interest is C.'s revision of Dryden's translation of Plutarch's *Lives*, 3 vols (London and Toronto: J.M. Dent and Sons, 1925).

2. Biography

(a) *Biographical materials*
The essential account of C.'s life is the 'Memoir' in 1869 *Poems and Prose Remains*. Useful information can also be found in: C.E. Norton, 'Arthur Hugh Clough' in *Atlantic Monthly* 9, No 54 (April 1862): 462–9; F.T. Palgrave, 'Memoir' in *Poems of Arthur Hugh Clough* (Cambridge and London: Macmillan, 1862); Wilfrid Ward, *William George Ward and the Oxford Movement* (London: Macmillan, 1889), esp. ch. 6; Blanche Athena Clough, *A Memoir of Anne Jemima Clough* (London and New York: Edward Arnold, 1897); and Thomas Arnold, 'Arthur Hugh Clough: A Sketch' in *The Nineteenth Century* XLIII (January–June 1898). The *Prose Remains* contains a number of C.'s letters, but a much fuller selection is given in F.L. Mulhauser (ed.), *The*

Correspondence of Arthur Hugh Clough, 2 vols (OUP, 1957); also of interest in this respect are H.F. Lowry (ed.), *The Letters of Matthew Arnold to A.H. Clough* (OUP, 1932) and James Bertram (ed.), *New Zealand Letters of Thomas Arnold the Younger, 1847–51* (OUP, 1966). More recently, Anthony Kenny has published *The Oxford Diaries of Arthur Hugh Clough* (OUP, 1990), a selection from the journal that C. kept during his years at the university.

(b) *Biographical studies*

The most useful of the twentieth-century biographies of C. is Katharine Chorley, *Arthur Hugh Clough: The Uncommitted Mind* (OUP, 1962). Most of the book-length studies of C.'s poetry also contain a significant element of biography; see, in particular, Veyriras (1964) and Biswas (OUP, 1972: full details below, p. 287). C.'s intellectual development is studied in E.B. Greenberger, *Arthur Hugh Clough: The Growth of a Poet's Mind* (Cambridge, Mass.: Harvard UP, 1970); the influence of Dr Arnold upon this development is examined in Chapter 3 of Frances Woodward's *The Doctor's Disciples* (OUP, 1957). C.'s religious difficulties have always been a particular focus of interest; on this subject see Veyriras (1964), Kenny (1988), and Patrick Scott, 'A.H. Clough: A Case Study in Victorian Doubt' in Derek Baker (ed.), *Schism, Heresy and Religious Protest* (CUP, 1972).

3. General Critical Studies

Nineteenth-century opinion on C.'s poetry is well documented in Michael Thorpe (ed.), *Clough: The Critical Heritage* (New York: Barnes & Noble, 1972). Of particular interest are: the exchange of letters between C. and his friend J.C. Shairp on an early version of *Amours de Voyage*; the exchange of letters between C. and Emerson on the published version of the poem; and the pieces by David Masson, Walter Bagehot, J.A. Symonds, and R.H. Hutton. Hutton's 'Memoir' of Walter Bagehot in Bagehot's *Literary Studies*, 3 vols (London: Longman, 1895) contains some stimulating remarks on C.'s characteristic habits of thought.

The modern critical monographs on C., which began to appear in the early 1960s around the centenary of the poet's death, are listed (and briefly described) below:

1. Isobel Armstrong, *Arthur Hugh Clough* (London: Longman, 1962): A brief but lucid introduction to the essential features of Clough's work.
2. Walter Houghton, *The Poetry of Clough: An Essay in Revaluation* (New Haven and London: Yale UP, 1963): Houghton rejects the

biographical emphasis of previous criticism and attempts to focus on the poetry itself, devoting chapters to each of the major narrative poems.

3. Paul Veyriras, *Arthur Hugh Clough* (Paris: Didier, 1964): By far the most comprehensive and informative general critical and biographical survey of C.'s life and work, with a wealth of detail on the poet's intellectual background.

4. Michael Timko, *Innocent Victorian* (Ohio: Ohio UP, 1966): A study which suggests that C.'s poetic technique is essentially a satirical one, with the 'innocent' hero in C.'s narrative poems exposing the artificiality and corruption of the society around him.

5. Wendell V. Harris, *Arthur Hugh Clough* (New York: Twayne Publishers Inc., 1970): One of the best modern discussions of C.'s work; sees the poetry as a kind of spiritual biography, detailing C.'s gradual abandonment of the search for a 'revelation' which would free him from debilitating spiritual uncertainty.

6. R.K. Biswas, *Arthur Hugh Clough: Towards a Reconsideration* (OUP, 1972): A thorough, biographically-based survey which does however tend to reinforce the myth of C.'s failure, and is dated somewhat by its Leavisite critical jargon.

There has been no book-length study devoted exclusively to C. since Biswas. Anthony Kenny's *God and Two Poets* (Sidgwick & Jackson, 1988) is a parallel study of C. and Hopkins which (as its title suggests) concentrates on their religious poetry. Both Isobel Armstrong's *Victorian Poetry* (Routledge & Kegan Paul, 1993) and John Maynard's *Victorian Discourses on Religion and Sexuality* (CUP, 1993) contain extensive and wide-ranging discussions of C.'s work. Mention should also be made of Patrick Scott's *The Early Editions of Arthur Hugh Clough* (New York and London: Garland, 1977), the definitive study of C.'s tortuous publication history.

4. Studies of individual poems

(a) *Amours de Voyage*

This poem has (not surprisingly) received most of the critical attention devoted to C. John D. Jump's article in *English* 9 (Summer 1953) is still of interest, but the most influential brief study of the poem is John Goode's 'Amours de Voyage: The Aqueous Poem' in Isobel Armstrong (ed.), *The Major Victorian Poets: Reconsiderations* (London: Routledge & Kegan Paul, 1969). Goode departs from the practice of previous critics by isolating the poem from its immediate intellectual context and reading it as a radical and experimental work, drawing particular attention to the way in which it undermines and eventually abandons its own key metaphors. The influence of Goode's work can be seen in recent studies such as W. David Shaw's chapter on C. and Borrow, entitled 'The Burden of Role-Playing', in his *Victorians and Mystery* (Ithaca and London: Cornell UP, 1990), and in E. Warwick Slinn's study of 'Fact and the Factitious in *Amours de Voyage*' in *The Discourse of Self in Victorian Poetry* (Macmillan, 1991), both of which continue to emphasise the poem's open and exploratory character. Slinn's chapter is particularly noteworthy for its focus on one of the most problematic areas in the poem, namely the nature and function of the Elegiacs. Taking a slightly different approach, Patricia M. Ball undertakes a comparison between *Amours* and Arnold's 'Marguerite' lyrics in *The Heart's Events* (Athlone Press, 1976). Dorothy Mermin analyses the poem's relation to the dramatic monologue tradition in *The Audience in the Poem* (New Brunswick, NJ: Rutgers UP, 1983). Finally, Patrick Scott's 'Introduction' to his edition of *Amours de Voyage* (St Lucia: Univ. of Queensland Press, 1974) provides a good deal of information on the process of the poem's composition, and the effect of the changes made to the poem by C.

(b) *Dipsychus and The Spirit*

In spite of Walter Houghton's claim that *Dipsychus* was C.'s masterpiece (a claim revived in Maynard (1993)), the poem has received scant critical attention in recent years; the most extensive and thorough discussion is probably Kenny (1988: chs 10–13). The treatment of the poem's text in the 1951 Oxford edition of C.'s poems edited by Lowry, Mulhauser and Norrington is subject to a scathing attack by Richard M. Gollin in *Modern Philology* 60 (1962): 120–7. Clyde de L. Ryals, 'An interpretation of Clough's Dipsychus' in *Victorian Poetry* 1 (1963): 182–8 challenges the notion that the poem is a record of C.'s disillusionment, and instead argues for a reading of it as a satire on some of C.'s own youthful attitudes and the Romantic metaphysics which inspired them. Paul Dean and Jacqueline Moore's article ' "To own the positive and present": Clough's Historical Dilemma' in *Durham University Journal* n.s. 45 (1983): 59–62 provides a reading of *Dipsychus* and *Amours* which emphasises the underlying presence of 'the Eden-myth' in both. The chapter on C. in Armstrong (1993) also has some brief but thought-provoking remarks on the poem.

(c) *Other poems*

Articles on C.'s less well-known poems are even rarer. *Adam and Eve* is examined in Paul Dean and Jacqueline Johnson: ' "Paradise Come Back": Clough in search of Eden' in *Durham University Journal* n.s. 38 (1977): 249–53, and (at greater length) in R.A. Forsyth's 'Clough's *Adam and Eve* – a debating Tract for the Times' in *Durham University Journal* n.s. 53 (1992): 59–78. Both articles stress the importance of the motif of the Fall in C.'s thought and poetry. Forsyth also discusses

Epi-Strauss-ium in his 'Herbert, Clough, and their Church-Windows', *Victorian Poetry* 7, No. 1 (Spring 1969). M.K. Louis compares C.'s *Easter Day* and Swinburne's *Before a Crucifix* in *Victorian Newsletter* 72 (Fall 1987): 1–5; and W. David Shaw discusses 'Hymnos ahymnos', a favourite poem with nineteenth-century reviewers, as an instance of the 'agnostic imagination' in *The Lucid Veil* (The Athlone Press, 1987).